Creativity and Innovation

in Content Area Teaching

Creativity and Innovation in Content Area Teaching

Edited by

Maureen McLaughlin

and

MaryEllen Vogt

Copyright Acknowledgments

Every effort has been made to contact copyright holders for permission to reproduce borrowed material where necessary. We apologize for any oversights and would be happy to rectify them in future printings.

All student work used with permission.

Screen from "Modern Presidency" website used with permission of Michael Hutchinson, Lincoln High School, Vincennes, Indiana.

Christopher-Gordon Publishers, Inc.
1502 Providence Highway, Suite 12
Norwood, MA 02062
(800) 934-8322

Printed in the United States of America

10 9 8 7 6 5 4 3 2 1   05 04 03 02 01 00

Library of Congress Catalog Card Number: 99-076806
ISBN: 1-929024-13-4

Dedication

For my sister, Judy Burke Gress

MM

For Keith, for his unwavering support

MEV

Contents

Introduction

Creativity and Innovation in Content Area Teaching is designed as a re-source, a compendium of ideas, to facilitate teaching and learning in a constructivist classroom culture. It is predicated on Elliot Eisner's (1985) belief that

> Teaching can be done as badly as anything else. It can be wooden, mechanical, mindless, and wholly unimaginative. But when it is sensitive, intelligent, and creative—those qualities that confer upon it the status of an art—it should not be regarded, as it so often is by some, as an expression of unfathomable talent or luck but as an example of humans exercising the highest levels of their intelligence.
> (p. 77)

As the title indicates, the book presents teaching ideas that incorporate both creative and innovative thinking. According to *The Literacy Dictionary* (Harris & Hodges, 1995) creative thinking is "thought processes characterized by unique powers of problem identification, hypothesis formation, and solution evaluation" (p. 47). Divergent thinking, often viewed as a synonym for creative thinking, is defined as "the process of elaborating on ideas in order to generate new ideas or alternative interpretations of given information" (p. 62). *Innovative* refers to those ideas that are nontraditional and suggest a new perspective. In this volume creative and innovative teaching ideas are characterized by inventive, reflective thinking; meaningful, multifaceted contexts; and active learning.

Creativity and Innovation in Content Area Teaching is divided into four sections. Part I provides an introduction to content area teaching and learning and serves as a foundation for the rest of the volume. Chapter 1 discusses the tensions many teachers feel about implementing creative teaching ideas and offers suggestions for alleviating such tensions in the classroom. In chapter

2, a theoretical and historical introduction to content area teaching and learning is presented.

Part II introduces a wide variety of activities, approaches, and methods for integrating creative and innovative teaching ideas into the content areas. Chapter 3 presents a framework for constructivism and offers numerous ideas for using inquiry in the content areas. Chapters 4, 5, and 6 explore the roles of visualization, dramatic play, and music. Chapter 7 focuses on using fiction and nonfiction read-alouds in the content areas, while chapter 8 describes ways to use poetry as a creative content resource. Chapter 9 is entirely devoted to innovative teaching practices in mathematics, and chapter 10 delineates ways to use the Internet in content area teaching.

In Part III, we take a closer look at several innovative approaches that include actual classroom lessons with examples of student performances. Chapter 11 examines the RAFT, a creative approach to writing about content information, and chapter 12 discusses strategies to create lifelong learners. Chapter 13 describes an inquiry-based approach to researching and chapter 14 focuses on literacy, content, and curriculum.

Part IV provides ideas to facilitate the use of creative teaching ideas in everyday classroom situations. Chapter 15 presents innovative assessments for the content areas including performances, portfolios, and profiles. Chapter 16 provides a teaching and learning context for students needing modifications, including those who are English language learners and struggling readers. The chapter concludes with specific suggestions for how teachers can implement the creative and innovative ideas in this book with all students.

As always, there are many people to thank for helping to make this book a reality. We are grateful to Rich Vacca for his encouragement when we first shared the idea for this book with him. We both offer special thanks to our undergraduate and graduate content area students for their enthusiasm and willingness to become creative teachers. Finally, we extend our gratitude to all of the chapter authors for their invaluable contributions.

References

Eisner, E. W. (1985). *The educational imagination: On the design and evaluation of school programs* (2nd ed.). New York: Macmillan.

Harris, T. L., & Hodges, R. E. (1995). *The literacy dictionary*. Newark, DE: International Reading Association.

Part I

Framework for Teaching and Learning: An Innovative Perspective

Chapter 1

Beginning the
Conversation

Maureen McLaughlin
MaryEllen Vogt

As teachers, we all share the responsibility for preparing students to deal with an increasingly complex world. We help them to connect the present with the past and the abstract with the concrete. We create effective contexts for learning and teach tremendous amounts of information in a variety of ways in numerous content areas.

Clearly, teaching is a complex task, filled with unique professional challenges. If you are a preservice or inservice teacher who is challenged by covering extensive content, integrating the language arts, generating critical thinking, utilizing technology, and infusing creativity, all while trying to meet students' needs, this book will be a valuable resource for you. All of the authors of this text are teachers; together, we have nearly 500 years of teaching experience! It is our hope that as you explore the innovative ideas we share, you will find that we have written from a teacher's perspective to our colleagues in the field. We've all been there, we share your commitment to preparing students to succeed, and we fully understand the realities of today's classrooms.

One thing we've learned while teaching elementary, middle school, high school, and undergraduate and graduate students is that we must keep abreast of current approaches to teaching and learning. We therefore engage in professional development and regularly read our professional journals. We discover terrific ideas for improving teaching effectiveness and learn about many creative ways to motivate students. However, we have also learned that once we discover these innovative ideas, there are challenges associated with putting them into practice. The everyday realities of teaching can create tensions that mitigate successful implementation of new approaches, methods, and techniques.

Tensions Related to Implementing Creative and Innovative Ideas

In order for effective and innovative content area teaching to occur, the tensions related to implementation of creative ideas must be acknowledged and overcome. From our experience, the tensions teachers may encounter when they try to implement innovative content teaching and learning activities include the following.

Time

Most teachers agree that there is not enough time in a day to do all they need to do. Educators need time for planning, scheduling, and teaching, yet because students bring their own diverse academic, linguistic, and cultural needs to content learning, schedules are often difficult to maintain. While teachers may feel pressed to "finish the book," students may have varying degrees of background knowledge and experience that affect the pace of instruction. An additional challenge found in many middle and secondary schools is the limited time that teachers have to interact with their students. Periods of 45–50 minutes a day are not uncommon for content area classes. This may be insufficient time to develop key content concepts, and it therefore creates tension when there is so much information to be taught and learned.

Another time factor is the need for continuing professional development that includes reading content area journals, attending seminars, interacting with colleagues, and taking graduate classes. Keeping current takes commitment and time.

We recognize this tension and encourage you, as you read each of the chapters in this book, to think about how you might adjust your teaching schedule to accommodate the time for planning and implementing the various activities. You may find that the time you're currently spending preparing and "delivering" content, through means such as lectures, worksheets, and study guides, is actually more than is required by the innovative approaches described in these chapters. In many cases, with the activities suggested here, the students are involved in researching and exploring content topics. Your role changes because you don't have to be the primary source of all or most information. Your time may be spent in helping students to access the information, whether from the Internet or from your school resource center. Class time may be utilized with students working in groups preparing presentations, creating projects, or in other ways applying what they're learning. The concern about time will always be there for teachers; how you choose to utilize the time you have is something you may wish to think about as you read this book.

Content Standards

National and state content standards have been developed in virtually every area of the curriculum, and most state assessments are based upon them. These standards delineate how students should be able to use content knowledge at various grade levels. The tension results from the pressure that teachers feel to cover the content necessary for students to perform at acceptable levels on "high stakes" state assessments. This tension is exacerbated when students lack the requisite background information and skills to successfully learn and apply content concepts.

What may lessen the tension about the role of standards is the understanding that creativity and innovation in content area teaching is standards based. We suggest that as you read this text, you begin to relate the various activities to your own district or school standards. In doing so, you'll see that you don't "lose the content" by implementing innovative approaches. Rather, you support and enhance it. If you're a preservice teacher, think about the content areas you are learning to teach and how specific topics can be taught utilizing these approaches. We're convinced that once you use them, you'll see that you will never sacrifice content for creativity. Instead, you will uncover what is really important in your curriculum.

Texts and Other Resources

Many school districts throughout the country provide teachers with outdated content texts and supplemental materials. Problems associated with this tension include inaccurate information, uninteresting text formats, few opportunities for student interaction, absence of critical thinking activities, and lack of strategy integration. In response, some content teachers rely on outmoded methods of presenting content such as introducing terms in isolation, lecturing, and asking questions of a literal nature. As a result, students and teachers may be unmotivated, which impacts not only the amount of learning that takes place but the quality of the experience for everyone involved.

If this is a tension that you can relate to, get ready to explore information other than that provided in an outdated textbook. Many of the activities described here suggest or could incorporate Internet searches and other creative resources. Clearly, students must be taught how to read textbooks, but we should never feel limited by using textbooks. Appropriate theme-related literature can also add significantly to students' understandings of people, events, and time periods. Informational text from magazines, newspapers, and catalogs can readily and inexpensively supplement the incredible amount of information available on the Internet and in the library.

Perceived Lack of Creativity

Some content teachers believe that only "creative people" can teach creatively, and that elementary teachers are by nature more creative than secondary teachers. These people may avoid innovative approaches because of a perceived lack of talent and as a result they rely on more traditional teaching methodologies. Because they are uncomfortable with taking creative risks in the classroom, they fail to realize their own potential to be successful. However, when creative teaching ideas are modeled using actual classroom examples, teachers seem more willing to take the risk.

If you identify with this tension, we recommend that you share this book with a teacher friend and that you explore these ideas together. Although it may be true that many elementary teachers choose their grade levels because they love *teaching,* whereas many secondary teachers choose their grade levels because they love their *content area*, it certainly doesn't mean that elementary teachers have a genetic disposition for creative teaching! We encourage you to work through these activities with grade level team members or with a colleague with whom you share content or teaching responsibilities. In reality, that's how many of these ideas came about— as collaborations between colleagues.

Dissonance Between Innovation and Reality

Another tension often experienced by preservice and inservice educators who regularly participate in professional development is the contrast between what they're learning and what they're seeing practiced. Often they are learning about new and interesting content area techniques, yet when they go into the field they are seeing more traditional teaching methods. Without the opportunity to share trials and successes with colleagues, teachers may try a new approach but never fully integrate it into daily teaching.

In part, the recommendation given for the previous tension—implementing these activities with another teacher who is doing the same—holds true here. Having the opportunity to observe colleagues who have successfully implemented a new idea validates teachers' efforts and encourages them to continue working with the concept.

If it is difficult to find other teachers who choose to teach content subjects in creative and innovative ways, don't be discouraged. While some teachers enthusiastically endorse new and creative approaches, others remain in a fixed position—teaching the way they've always taught. So, we recommend that *you* become the trailblazer if you're surrounded by those for whom content teaching means only lectures, outlines, tests, and study guides. You and your students will be the winners!

Student Diversity

One common and totally legitimate concern of content teachers at all levels is meeting students' individual needs. Factors such as background knowledge and experience, language proficiency, learning styles, reading abilities, and culture all impact students' access to content. Classroom realities include large class sizes, increasing numbers of English language learners, inappropriate materials for students' reading needs, unmotivated students, and teachers who may feel unprepared to deal with these challenges.

We believe that creative and innovative content teaching ideas can bridge differences and help both teacher and students to coalesce into a learning community. Research supports teaching that incorporates creative, generative, strategy-based approaches for all students, including English language learners and students with special needs. If we all can adopt the belief that "thinking" exists regardless of reading or language ability, then we can see that for many students, "other ways of knowing" may include drama, music, technology, hands-on manipulation, art, poetry, and physical movement. Incorporating these into content teaching provides the opportunity for students with special needs and abilities to contribute, and in many ways it levels the learning playing field for everyone.

Classroom Organization and Management

Sometimes teachers resist creative and innovative content teaching ideas because they believe that keeping students in their seats and using more traditional methods is easier to manage. The tension here involves the concern about freeing students and teachers from trusted routines.

This tension also has to do with how a teacher perceives his or her role as "manager." If maintaining a tight hold on everyone's behavior is a priority, then it is sometimes difficult to venture out and try new ideas. However, when teachers release some of the responsibility for learning to students, classroom management issues change, as does the role of the teacher. Once everyone becomes accustomed to more flexible classroom organization— including group configurations, daily schedules, the locus of control, and the ownership of teaching and learning—management becomes more of a shared responsibility.

Keeping an open mind and being versatile with classroom organization enhances students' experiences in content area learning. You will read more about this in the individual chapters, and as you do, think about how you might organize your own classroom so that management issues are not paramount. Also, think about how you might organize the groups of students who will work together, plan for a system of accountability for the students (such as daily group progress checks), and determine the degree to which you must provide control or oversight for each activity. Thinking through these issues carefully before you implement the innovative approaches will help to ensure success for everyone concerned.

Assessment and Evaluation

Traditionally, tests and quizzes have been the most frequently used means of assessing student content knowledge. Chapter tests, unit tests, problem sets, vocabulary quizzes, written essays, and reports are familiar means of assessing student knowledge of content material, and they have been in use for decades. These methods of assessment have been relatively quick to grade, the "correct answers" have been easy to determine, and teachers, administrators, parents, and students have all understood what the grades have meant.

This feeling is entirely normal because when integrating creative and innovative teaching ideas, dynamic measures such as observation, oral discourse, strategy use, informal writing, and projects are necessary to document student progress. In this area the tensions arise when assessment is viewed as separate from instruction, when the role of informal assessments is not understood, when the measures used do not accommodate students' strength modalities, and when criteria for student performance are not provided. As creative teaching ideas are integrated, assessment becomes a natural part of everyday teaching and learning. In such contexts, informal and formal assessments combine to offer a fuller, more meaningful picture of students' abilities. Another valuable benefit is that students can become more engaged in self-assessment, reflecting on their roles as active learners as well as their levels of understanding.

Trust in Students

On occasion, we hear colleagues express concerns about their students' ability to work independently, their students' motivation or apathy, and the need to constantly be "on them" to make sure that work is completed, homework is done, and students are prepared. Some teachers believe that work will be successfully completed only when the teacher has total control and students are allowed little freedom within the classroom context. In these more traditional, teacher-centered classrooms, the daily routine varies little. Both students and teacher know what to expect and what the outcomes will be.

Clearly, the tension here arises when we are reluctant to let students "go," when we feel that we need to be "in charge," and basically when we lack trust in our students' ability to self-direct, self-motivate, and follow a task through to completion, independent of the teacher's constant oversight. If you're feeling this way, you're not alone. All of us have experienced these frustrations, and we appreciate the dilemma you face each time you enter the classroom. We also believe that classroom contexts can and should change.

We have found that one of the most positive effects of innovative content teaching is that students, regardless of age or ability, surprise us with their clever, creative, humorous, and often unexpected responses to innovative teaching approaches. We find these responses in content classrooms where students are researching, creating, performing, experimenting, and stretching themselves in ways that they have not experienced before.

We have discovered that this type of teaching *is* different. In many of the activities described in this volume, the teacher's role has changed from the traditional purveyor of information to one who provides resources and guidelines, who encourages, monitors, assesses, models, and assists when requested. Trusting the students requires patience and confidence that they can work through many of their own problems. As they begin to dazzle you and themselves with what they've accomplished, your trust in their abilities and in their natural curiosity about how the world works will develop beyond your expectations. Reaching this point makes the apprehension, frustration, and missteps along the way well worth it. The tension dissipates as the students clearly demonstrate for you and each other their deep understanding of content.

Concluding Thoughts

As you read this book, we hope that you will cover it with your own jottings—with your ideas, questions, insights, and experiences. We want this book to be a resource for your teaching: Something you read, reread, and *use* again and again. We hope it will energize your teaching and your students—that the ideas included here will serve as a springboard for all the other innovative, creative methods and approaches out there—and that you'll use these to develop creative teaching ideas of your own.

Chapter 2

Taking the Mystery Out
of Content Area Literacy

Richard T. Vacca

Meet Olaudah Equiano, an African slave, who lived in the 1700s. Equiano kept a diary that eventually was published as a book called *The Interesting Narrative of the Life of Olaudah Equiano, or Gustavus Vassa, the African: Written by Himself,* first published in London in 1789, and later abridged and edited by Paul Edwards (1967). Equiano was kidnapped from his West African tribe as a child and sold into bondage to a ship's captain. His diary is a fascinating account of his life and times: how he educated himself and how he eventually purchased his freedom.

In his diary Equiano tells about the mysterious process that his master engaged in whenever he read books on long voyages across the seas. Although he didn't know how to read, Equiano was in awe of the relationship that his master had with books. What was this thing that his master called reading? He longed to be able to read books the way his master did. So when he was alone in his captain's cabin, he would pick up a book, open it, and begin *talking* to it. Then he would put his ears near the pages of the book in the hope that the book would *talk* to him. But the book remained silent. Equiano felt helpless in the presence of the silent text. Reading remained a mystery to him until he learned to read and write.

Much to his credit, Equiano was on the right track when he picked up a book and started talking to it in the hope that it would talk back to him. Writers and readers engage in communication, but the talk is not usually the kind of loose, expressive discourse that might take place between two friends.

The language of school-related texts is more formal than everyday discourse because the ideas that academic texts communicate often are complex and demanding.

One way to think about reading is that it involves a dialogue between the author of the text and the reader. Authors use language to communicate their ideas to someone else. Readers use *cognitive* and *metacognitive strategies* to engage their minds in the dialogue so that they can understand, respond to, and perhaps even question and challenge the author's ideas. Equiano intuitively recognized that reading is a process of communicating with a text and its author. However, he didn't know how to go about the process. He didn't have the strategies needed to understand and respond to what he was reading until he learned how to make books "talk" to him.

The process of reading is as mysterious for many students in today's schools as it was for Olaudah Equiano. Students of various abilities experience Equiano's helplessness when confronted with academic tasks that require reading. Often they struggle to make sense of the process. Teachers routinely indicate that more and more of their students do not, cannot, or will not read text assignments. The more they urge their students to learn with texts, the more the students resist by reading just enough to answer the assigned questions or by circumventing reading altogether. Teachers want to know why today's student struggles with texts and what they can do, short of abandoning reading as a way of learning, to help students use literacy processes to learn.

Students who struggle with texts, regardless of ability level, often get lost in a maze of words as they sit down with a book or scroll through an electronic page on a computer screen. The book they are reading, or the computer screen they are staring at, doesn't "talk" to them in ways that permit them to think deeply about the ideas encountered in text. As a result, reading seems like a great mystery to them. How can teachers take some of the mystery out of learning with academic texts? How can they help students to become *content literate*? How can they make connections between the *content* they teach and the *language processes* that students need in order to learn with texts?

Helping Students To Become Content Literate

National surveys of reading performance, such as the National Assessment of Educational Progress (NAEP), suggest that the majority of students in grades 4, 8, and 12 are able to read for literal understanding. The NAEP in Reading, for example, supports what many content teachers already know about their students: Young adolescents (around 60%) are capable of reading at a *basic* level of performance—reading for main ideas and details—

but fewer than 5% of the students surveyed in grades 4, 8, and 12 perform at an *advanced* level, where they are required to interpret, extend, and elaborate the meaning of literary and informational texts (Campbell, Donahue, Reese, & Phillips, 1996). The NAEP in Reading data suggest that today's students can use reading to "do school"—to satisfy assignments that require literal information to answer questions. In this respect, they can "get by" as readers.

Getting by, however, isn't enough. Literacy expectations, and the demands placed on students to use literacy to learn, have accelerated in this century and are likely to increase dramatically in the coming decades. Yet the dilemma facing most students who struggle with texts is that few effectively learn how to use reading to construct meaning beyond acquiring bits and pieces of information.

Low-achieving students are often genuine in their resistance to reading. They are easy to identify in a content area classroom. For them, the process of reading is labored, superficial, and often self-defeating. Teachers who have worked with low-achieving students are no strangers to resistant learners. All too often the low achiever is overage, underprepared, and weighed down with emotional baggage. These individuals score low on intelligence and achievement tests and are tracked in basic classes for most of their academic lives. Struggling readers can often be found "hiding out" in content classrooms. They have developed a complex set of coping strategies to avoid reading or being held accountable for reading. These coping behaviors run the gamut from avoiding eye contact with the teacher to disrupting lessons, forgetting to bring books or assignments to class, and seeking help from friends (Brozo, 1992).

Low-achieving students aren't the only ones who struggle with reading, however. Average and above-average students who are on a fast track to go to college might also experience difficulty in text learning situations. Often these students go through the motions of reading and are likely to conceal some of their difficulties with texts. If asked to read aloud in class, they do so fluently—that is to say, with accuracy and speed. Fluent reading, however, isn't always a guarantee that students understand what they are reading, especially if they are reading texts that are conceptually difficult. Although they may have developed the ability to read print smoothly and accurately, average and above-average students who struggle with academic texts usually don't know what to do with texts beyond just saying the words. They appear skillful in the mechanics of reading but aren't *strategic* enough in their ability to handle the conceptual demands inherent in academic texts.

How students achieve as readers reflects such factors as motivation, self-concept, prior knowledge, and the ability to use literacy to learn. For some struggling students, reading is a painful reminder of a system of schooling that has failed them. They wage a continual battle with reading as an academic activity. The failure to learn to read has contributed to these students' disenchantment with and alienation from school. Although students who struggle with academic texts may have developed some reading strategies, the strategies are often inappropriate for the demands inherent in course materials. As a result, their participation in literacy-related activity, such as writing or discussion, is marginal. Getting through reading assignments to answer homework questions is often the only reason to read, if they read at all.

Learned helplessness is an expression often associated with students who struggle with texts in content classrooms. It refers to students' perceptions of themselves as being unable to overcome failure. Unsuccessful readers usually sabotage their efforts to read academic texts by believing that they can't succeed at tasks that require reading. They struggle because they command a limited repertoire of strategies, lacking knowledge of and control over the procedural routines required to engage in meaningful transactions with texts. Rarely do struggling readers consider what their role should be as readers. Rather than take an active role in constructing meaning, they often remain passive and disengaged (Vacca & Padak, 1990).

To be literate in content classrooms, students must learn how to use language processes to explore and construct meaning with texts. The International Reading Association (IRA) and National Council of Teachers of English (NCTE) publication, *Standards for English Language Arts* (1996), underscores the importance of preparing students at all grade levels for the literacy demands of today and tomorrow. When the process of developing national standards began, IRA and NCTE recognized that being literate means being active, critical, and creative users not only of print and spoken language but also of the visual language. The IRA and NCTE standards underscore the importance of language and literacy in use. Students throughout the grades must learn how to use language and literacy clearly, strategically, critically, and creatively. Through language they can make sense of the world, understand, and be understood. When students put language to work for them in content classrooms, it helps them to discover, organize, retrieve, and elaborate on what they are learning.

Demystifying the Process of Learning With Texts

One way that teachers can demystify literacy-related learning in content areas is to *scaffold* instruction so that students become aware of and competent in the use of the strategies required to be successful. Used in construction, scaffolds serve as supports, lifting up workers so that they can achieve something that otherwise would not have been possible. The word *scaffold* is used as a metaphor in teaching and learning to suggest helping students to do what they cannot do alone at first. Instructional scaffolding allows teachers to support struggling readers' efforts to think clearly, critically, and creatively about literary texts while showing them how to use strategies that will, over time, lead to independent learning. Scaffolding reading, writing, and discussion experiences is the key to initiating and sustaining students' dialogue with texts.

Instructional scaffolding simply means giving students a better chance to be successful with texts than if left on their own to use literacy to learn. Teachers provide content literacy scaffolds through the use of well-timed questions, explanations, demonstrations, and activities in well-planned lessons. These scaffolds provide instructional support for students in the application of strategies *at the point of actual use* before, during, and after engaging in a dialogue with text.

Connect Literacy and Learning Through Well-Planned Lessons

Well-planned content literacy lessons help students to understand and to be understood when they engage in reading, writing, and talking to learn. Lesson structure, which is often referred to as the teacher's *instructional framework* (Vacca & Vacca, 1999), involves planning and organizing literacy-related activities before, during, and after text assignments. A well-conceived instructional framework lets students in on the secrets of having the text "talk" to them in meaningful and constructive ways. Putting literacy processes to work in an instructional framework starts well before students pick up a book, turn on the computer, or get out a sheet of paper on which to write. Moreover, these processes continue after students have finished reading or putting words on the paper or the computer screen. An instructional framework makes provisions for literacy-related learning at different points in a lesson.

Before Reading

When faced with having to read an academic text, most students jump into the reading and plow through it as fast as they can just to get it finished. Plowing through what they read without getting conceptually ready to explore ideas is not an effective strategy. It is similar to an athlete who fails to warm up before the game or a musician who doesn't rehearse before going on stage to perform. Before students even begin to take on a text, there are things that they can do that will prepare them for the ideas they will encounter when they begin reading. Preparing students to read will break some of the ineffective habits that they may have developed as readers. Some suggestions follow for helping students to mentally prepare for reading.

Provide instructional support that helps students to analyze the reading task that is ahead of them. Students should ask questions such as the following: What is my primary reason or purpose for reading the text assignment? Should I try to remember details or read for the main ideas only? How much time will I spend on the reading? What do I already know about the topic? What will I need to find out more about?

Help students to generate interest in the reading even if the topic doesn't appeal to them. What students read in school may not be what they would choose to read for recreational purposes. Academic texts are often perceived as boring and uninviting. But the important thing for students to understand—and to keep in mind if they want to be successful in text learning situations—is that they will have to work up some enthusiasm for reading even if the material seems boring. Scaffolding a demonstration shows students how to approach a text assignment with some interest. For example, have them imagine being locked in a telephone booth for 2 hours with a disconnected phone and only a telephone book to read. How would they make the telephone directory interesting? If they take a little time to think about the question, they are bound to generate some creative and interesting ways to read a telephone book. Have the students share their responses. Then make the connection to the text that they will be reading in class and have students brainstorm (invent) ways to make the text interesting.

Scaffold prereading experiences that engage students in thinking about ideas before they are encountered in text. Brainstorm, raise questions, make predictions, study pictures and graphics, survey titles and subtitles. Do whatever needs to be done to help students make connections between what they know already and what they will be reading about. Engagement with the text is more likely to occur if students have opportunities to think about what they will be reading before they actually begin reading. For example, making predictions about the material will help students to actively focus on the ideas encountered during reading. Were their predictions accurate? Did they have to modify them once they started reading? Or did they abandon them altogether in favor of new ideas?

During Reading

Reading is all about making sense. The more skillful students become at using thinking strategies, the more likely they will make sense by comprehending and interpreting what they read. While reading, it is important that students keep their minds active as they engage in a dialogue with an author. A successful reader monitors and keeps track of whether the author is making sense by asking: What is the author trying to say here? What does the author mean? So what? What is the significance of the author's message? Does this make sense with what the author told us before? Does the author explain this clearly? These queries are designed to help students "question the author" and to understand that text material needs to be challenged— "taken on" as one might challenge a friend in a debate or conversation (Beck, McKeown, Hamilton, & Kucan, 1997).

In order to provide students with instructional support to guide their thinking while reading, consider some suggestions for this phase of the instructional framework.

Help students to decide what's important and what's not important while reading. Some ideas are more important than others in informational text. One of the things a reader can do while reading is tune into the main ideas of an author's message. A strategic reader knows how to tell the difference between main ideas and supporting ideas.

Show students how to look for organization in everything they read. Authors have nothing to gain and much to lose if they present their ideas aimlessly. A good writer organizes ideas so that a reader will not have to struggle to grasp what the writer is trying to say. As students read, provide activities such as *graphic organizers* to guide them in their search for the different patterns of organization, such as *cause and effect, comparison-contrast, problem-solution, sequence,* and *main idea-detail.*

Model for students how to ask questions while reading to construct meaning and to better understand the author's intent. Successful readers act upon the author's message. They raise questions or challenge what the author is saying if what they are reading doesn't make sense to them. Beck et al. (1997) recommend the instructional strategy Questioning the Author (QtA) to guide students to think more deeply about segments of a text while reading. QtA places value on the quality and depth of students' interactions with the text and their responses to the author's intended meaning. QtA shows students how to read a text closely, as if the author were there to be challenged and questioned.

After Reading

When students engage in a dialogue with an author, the ideas that they encounter before and during reading may need to be responded to and extended after reading. This phase of the instructional framework is an opportunity for students to "go public" with what they have learned from reading. It is a time to share their best thinking about the author's message, either in discussion with other students, writing in response to what they have read, or some other means of expression that gets at the meaning of the author's message. What is the significance of what students have read? Do they agree or disagree with the author? How does the author's message make them feel? Did the author's message help to solve a problem or to look at an issue or event from a different perspective?

Reading begins to make sense to students when they recognize that learning with texts is not a solitary act. Reading is social. A student learns not only in the company of an author but also in the company of other students and teachers. How teachers connect content learning to language processes contributes greatly to students' dialogue with text.

Connect Reading With Talking to Learn

The instructional framework is a blueprint for classroom interaction. When teachers put a well-planned lesson into action, talk permeates the classroom. It is the primary means by which teachers and students communicate, yet teachers often underestimate the powerful role that talk plays in text learning and content acquisition. Rubin (1990) compares classroom talk to the parable about fish in water: Just as fish are the least likely creatures to ever become aware of water, teachers and students hardly recognize the power of talk as a medium for learning. Talk can be a springboard into reading, and reading can be the basis for talk.

The predominant type of talk in content area classrooms usually revolves around question-and-answer exchanges known as *recitations,* in which students take turns answering questions with "bits and pieces" of information (Vacca & Vacca, 1999). Recitations represent a formal type of classroom communication that restricts spontaneous, exploratory talk among students. The social and psychological context for learning during recitation is dominated by teacher-talk, with little opportunity for students to explore and clarify ideas, think critically and creatively, and reflect on what they are learning. Because they are formal and directed to large groups, recitations tend to silence student voices and limit response to one- or two-word answers.

Teachers who make talk visible in their classrooms recognize the limitations of recitation and seek alternative forms of classroom discussion. They recognize that students need opportunities to talk spontaneously and to respond personally and critically to ideas they are encountering in a text. Rather than rely on question-and-answer exchanges that limit student talk, teachers engage students in more informal, collaborative classroom talk. Seminar-like discussions and small-group collaborative interactions allow students to question and plan; express doubt, difficulty, and confusion; and experiment with new language as they connect content learning to literacy. There are numerous ways to encourage talking to learn. Consider, for example, how *Socratic seminars* and *idea circles* help students to explore ideas and construct meaning.

Teaching Idea: Socratic Seminars
Content Areas: All
Levels: Middle School, High School

The Socratic seminar is an after-reading discussion strategy. The instructional goal of a Socratic seminar is to revolve discussion around students' talk as a medium for constructing knowledge (Tanner & Cassados, 1998). Socratic seminars are named as a tribute to Socrates, the ancient Greek philosopher who believed that people learned more effectively through self-discovery than through being told the "correct" answer or interpretation. The teacher's role in what has been called the *Socratic method* is to guide learners to discovery through the artful use of questions. Socratic seminars, therefore, are designed around "core questions" that lead to thoughtful discussions in which students engage in reasoning, predicting, projecting, and imagining.

A Socratic seminar can vary in its format and delivery, depending on the purpose for discussion. Tanner and Cassados (1998) provide general guidelines for facilitating the seminar utilizing an "inner circle/outer circle" framework.

Guidelines for the teacher:

- Analyze the content of the text selection to be discussed. Familiarize yourself with the major concepts, insights, vocabulary, text cues, and features to which you want students to pay attention.
- Prepare a set of discussion questions that raise issues and that probe, apply, and synthesize information. Also prepare metacognitive questions for use during the debriefing session, such as, "Did we learn a useful strategy? What was confusing in this reading? What was useful? What did you learn about_____from reading?" (e.g., math: " What did you learn about doing math from this reading?")
- Arrange the room for a seminar by creating an inner circle (for the discussants) and an outer circle (for the note takers). Within the inner circle designate one seat as the "hot seat." When a student wants to speak, he or she sits in the hot seat. (You may consider phasing out the hot seat once students become accustomed to talking within the inner circle.)
- Set 15 to 30 minutes for discussion and begin with a core question.
- End the discussion with a summary statement or invite students from the inner or outer circle to summarize the discussion.
- Conduct a 5- to10-minute debriefing session to improve the quality of the discussion. Focus on the process underlying the seminar. Invite students to make suggestions for improving the seminar format. Ask the types of metacognitive questions suggested above.

- Serve as the discussion leader by helping students to reconstruct the author's meaning and to construct their own meaning. Start the discussion with a question that raises an issue.

Guidelines for the students:
- Focus on the content of the text selection.
- Listen to one another.
- Outer-circle students take notes on the discussion.
- Inner-circle students speak clearly to one another.

Another format for the Socratic seminar is simply to arrange the room in a circle in which everyone in the class participates in the discussion. The seminar involves the whole class in talk. Idea circles, in contrast, involve students working collaboratively in small groups to learn concepts around a central topic or concept.

Teaching Idea: Idea Circles
Content Areas: All
Levels: Intermediate, Middle, High School

Idea circles are a spin-off of *literature circles*, a popular discussion strategy used in literature-based reading programs. Literature circles bring readers together to discuss trade books based on students' personal response to what they have read. Idea circles, as proposed by Guthrie and McCann (1996), bring students together in peer-led group discussions to explore concepts fueled by multiple texts. Whereas the aim of literature circles is to foster literary interpretation (through narrative texts), idea circles engage students in concept learning through informational books and other text resources, such as Internet documents, CD-ROMs, magazine articles, and reference materials.

Idea circles facilitate small-group inquiry by helping students to explore ideas, the relationship between ideas, and explanations around a central topic or concept. When students collaborate in small groups, individual expertise is distributed among the members and is likely to result in a wider search for information, the pooling of ideas, and deeper thinking about the topic. Through the enactment of idea circles, students develop text learning strategies that include searching, gathering, comprehending, interpreting, and integrating concepts.

Guidelines for teachers:
- Select a central topic for inquiry and discussion. The topic should be interesting, explanatory, and expansive. Choose a concept for group inquiry that has multiple categories of information associated

with it. For example, if a class is engaged in the exploration of the concept *animal adaptation*, then idea circles might be organized around subareas of habitat, feeding, breeding, and survival skills (Guthrie & McCann, 1996). The conceptual topic should have enough depth to warrant extended inquiry and conversations within the idea circles.

- Collect relevant trade books and text resources at various levels of difficulty.
- Form heterogeneous groups (three to six members) and designate a group leader.
- Make sure that students understand the guidelines for interaction (below).
- Share the results of each idea circle's inquiry through group presentations, which may take the form of poster board displays, panel discussions, mock conference presentations, and the like.

Guidelines for students:
- Listen to each other during group discussions.
- Let everyone have a turn contributing to the discussion and development of the topic.
- Speak one at a time.
- Give your best effort.

The use of discussion strategies like the Socratic seminar and idea circles results in a response-centered classroom that values and fosters the student's personal reaction to the ideas encountered in texts. As students engage with texts, they construct meanings that are influenced by their own knowledge, values, and life experiences. When they share their understandings of a text within a class discussion, their own personal responses are often extended and enriched. This is in stark contrast to classrooms dominated by teacher-talk, in which students come to class

> expecting the teacher to do all the talking and fill 'em up each day with information, directions, and assignments; and then they pretty much expected and accepted the job of working silently and alone filling up the forty-two minute class period [with classroom activities] that demand little original thought. (Krogness, 1997, pp. 28–29)

Connect Reading With Writing to Learn

Writing, like talking, demystifies learning with texts in a response-centered classroom. Informal, spontaneous writing is best suited for exploration and discovery. When students "think on paper" to express thoughts, feelings, and opinions, they are more likely to respond to and explore the ideas encountered in a text. Vacca and Linek (1992), however, note that informal writing often is absent in content area classrooms, especially in situations where teachers have not been exposed to the theory and practice of writing as an instrument of learning, reflection, and discovery. As a result, students do not experience the kind of "internal talk" or "thinking aloud on paper" that allows them to make connections between what they know already and the texts that they are studying. When students respond to a text by thinking on paper, they have more to reflect upon and work with in class discussions than when this step is totally bypassed.

Students write more and think more when they engage in *low-stakes* writing assignments (Elbow, 1997). Low-stakes writing tasks allow students to use writing to interact personally with ideas and information without the pressure of producing polished, finished products. Teachers assign writing not to get students to produce excellent pieces of writing but to get them to explore ways of making sense of text material. Figure 2-1 illustrates some differences between low-stakes and high-stakes writing assignments.

Figure 2-1. Low-Stakes Versus High-Stakes Writing Assignments	
Writing Assignments	
Low-Stakes	**High-Stakes**
Unfinished	Finished
Nonthreatening	
Nongraded	Graded
Journals	Reports
Writing to Learn Activities	Essays

According to Elbow (1997), high-stakes writing assignments also produce learning, but they are more "loaded" because teachers judge the writing carefully for soundness of content and clarity of presentation. A research paper or a persuasive essay, for example, often represents high-stakes writing in which students work through steps and stages to compose a finished product. Low-stakes writing, on the other hand, is often pre-draft or first-draft writing. It usually is messy, tentative, and unfinished in the sense that the writing does not merit the teacher's careful scrutiny (Gere, 1985). Low-stakes writing is more concerned with students' exploration of ideas than clarity of presentation. More often than not, it prompts students to tap into their storehouse of memories—their prior knowledge—in order to connect what they know to what they are studying.

Because writing promotes different types of learning, students need many occasions to connect reading to writing in content area classrooms. Depending on the instructional objectives of the teacher, students might engage in various low-stakes writing assignments to think about and interact with ideas and information being studied. Consider the following suggestions.

Create low-stakes writing activities that move students beyond recall of information. When writing focuses on information recall, it plays a restricted and narrow role in students' thinking about course material. Numerous possibilities exist for informal writing activities. Consider, for example, *quickwrites* (in which students write freely and quickly for a short period of time in response to a question) or *point of view* prompts, in which students write from different perspectives or stances (e.g., "You are about to be interviewed as if you are a river turtle living in a river community along the west coast of Florida. After reading the text, respond to these questions: As a young river turtle, what is your typical day like? How does your typical day differ from when you were a young turtle?").

Use journal writing to support personal interactions with texts. Entries in academic journals or learning logs represent low-stakes writing assignments that allow students to use expressive language to interact personally with ideas and information encountered in course material, class lectures, and discussions. Journals may be used regularly to create a visible, permanent record of what students are thinking and learning throughout the school year. They can be used at the beginning, middle, or end of class lessons to generate ideas, write down predictions about topics to be studied, record thoughts and feelings in response to what students are reading, or explore concerns as students respond to questions such as the following: What did I like or dislike about class today? What did I understand about today's class work? What is unclear or confusing about the ideas presented in today's class? (Vacca & Vacca, 1999).

Use imaginative writing to encourage students to play with ideas and think creatively about the subjects being studied. Students need opportunities to interact with ideas and information by engaging in imaginative types of writing. Students can write imaginatively by creating *scenarios, dialogues, unsent letters, fictitious interviews*, and *poems* (Vacca & Vacca, 1999). Poems in particular provide a creative form for showing learning. Young (1997) explains that writing poems allows students to generate new and fresh perspectives on the subject under study. For example, teachers have been experimenting with the use of *biopoems* as a writing-to-learn tool. Biopoems allow students to put large amounts of material into precise language within the context of a poetic form (Gere, 1985). Other poetic patterns such as a *diamante* (a poem in the shape of a diamond) can be used to have students play with ideas they are studying. In addition to writing poems with preset patterns, teachers often encourage students to write poetically without imposing a structure for them to follow. (For more information about poetry, see chapter 8.)

Low-stakes writing assignments should be read but not necessarily graded by teachers for content, organization, or mechanics. Teachers should not expend energy on students' errors but should attend to the role that writing plays in helping students to become more knowledgeable and conversant with the texts being studied.

Concluding Thoughts

Showing students how to use language processes that make use of reading, writing, and talking to learn in the content classroom doesn't require specialized training. Nor does the development of text learning strategies diminish the teacher's role as a subject matter specialist. The term *content literacy* underscores the ability to use language processes to learn subject matter in a given discipline. To the extent that texts are an integral part of disciplinary learning, content teachers have a role to play in students' development as readers, writers, and oral communicators. On a practical, day-to-day basis, teachers need to reflect on the strategies that students need to be successful in academic subjects. What does it mean to read, write, and engage in discussion effectively like a scientist, a literary critic, a historian, a mathematician, an auto mechanic, a health care provider, or a business professional? How is reading a literary text different from reading an informational text or, for that matter, from reading a teen magazine in popular culture or a job-related technical manual? Questions such as these recognize that learning through literacy is situational; and the way to take the mystery out of learning with texts is to help students to develop literacy-related strategies in the context in which the strategies are used to learn.

References

Beck, I. L., McKeown, M. G., Hamilton, R. L., & Kucan, L. (1997). *Question the author: An approach for enhancing student engagement with text.* Newark, DE: International Reading Association.

Brozo, W. G. (1992). Hiding out in secondary content classrooms: Coping strategies of unsuccessful readers. *Journal of Reading, 35,* 324–328.

Campbell, J., Donahue, P., Reese, C., Phillips, G. (1996). *NAEP 1994 reading report card for the nation and the states.* Washington, D.C.: U.S.

Department of Education, Office of Educational Research and Improvement.

Edwards, P. (1967). *Equiano's travels: The interesting narrative of the life of Olaudah Equiano or Gustavus Vassa, the African.* New York: Praeger.

Elbow, P. (1997). High stakes and low stakes in assigning and responding to writing. In M. Sorcinelli & P. Elbow (Eds.), *Writing to learn: Strategies for assigning and responding to writing across the disciplines* (pp. 5–13). San Francisco: Jossey-Bass.

Gere, A. (Ed.). (1985). *Roots in sawdust: Writing to learn across the curriculum.* Urbana, IL: National Council of Teachers of English.

Guthrie, T., & McCann, A. D. (1996). Idea circles: Peer collaborations for conceptual learning. In L. B. Gambrell & J. F. Almasi (Eds.), *Lively discussions: Fostering engaged reading* (pp. 87–105). Newark, DE: International Reading Association.

International Reading Association and National Council of Teachers of English. (1996). *Standards for the English Language Arts.* Newark, DE: Author.

Krogness, M. (1997). Changing voices: Working with middle schoolers. *The Ohio Reading Teacher, 32* (1), 28–31.

Rubin, D. L. (1990). Introduction: Ways of thinking about talking and learning. In S. Hynds & D. L. Rubin (Eds.), *Perspectives on talk and learning* (pp. 1–17). Urbana, IL: National Council of Teachers of English.

Tanner, M. L., & Cassados, L. (1998). Promoting and studying discussions in math class. *Journal of Adolescent and Adult Literacy, 41* (5), 342–350.

Vacca, R., & Linek, W. (1992). Writing to learn. In J. Irwin & M. Doyle (Eds.), *Reading/writing connections: Learning from research* (pp. 145–159). Newark, DE: International Reading Association.

Vacca, R., & Padak, N. (1990). Who's at risk in reading? *Journal of Reading, 33,* 486–489.

Vacca, R., & Vacca, J. (1999). *Content area reading: Literacy and learning across the curriculum* (6th ed.). New York: Addison Wesley Longman.

Young, A. (1997). Mentoring, modeling, monitoring, motivating: Response to students' ungraded writing as academic conversation. In M. Sorcinelli & P. Elbow (Eds.), *Writing to learn: Strategies for assigning and responding to writing across the disciplines* (pp. 5–13). San Francisco: Jossey-Bass.

Part II

Engaging Students' Thinking

Chapter 3

Inquiry:
The Key to Critical and
Creative Thinking in
the Content Areas

Maureen McLaughlin

Although inquiry-based learning can be traced back to Socrates, its most recent emergence is linked to the constructivist movement. Brooks and Brooks (1993) define *constructivism* as a theory of knowledge and learning. From a constructivist perspective, learning is understood as "a self-regulated process of resolving inner cognitive conflicts that often become apparent through concrete experience, collaborative discourse, and reflection" (p.vii). Principles that guide the teacher's role in constructivism include the following: posing relevant problems, structuring learning around primary concepts, seeking and valuing students' ideas, adapting curriculum to address such ideas, and assessing student learning in context.

According to Short and Burke (1996), constructivism frees students from fact-driven curricula and encourages them to focus on larger ideas; allows students to reach unique conclusions and reformulate ideas; encourages students to see the world as a complex place with multiple perspectives; and emphasizes that students are responsible for their own learning and should attempt to connect the information they learn to the world around them through inquiry.

Constructivism is manifested in classrooms that are characterized by student-generated ideas, self-selection, creativity, interaction, critical thinking, and personal construction of meaning. In such contexts, authentic content area tasks assimilate real-world experiences, provide a purpose for learning, and encourage students to take ownership of learning (Hiebert, 1994; McLaughlin & Kennedy, 1993; Newmann & Wehlage, 1993). The paradigm shift to student-centered learning and the infusion of the constructivist view have naturally led to innovative and creative practices in content area instruction.

These inquiry-based creative and innovative teaching ideas are the focus of this chapter. Having reviewed the theoretical underpinnings of the constructivist culture, including inquiry-based learning, the chapter next presents viable content area activities that promote inquiry in a variety of contexts. Finally, it provides technological resources that support inquiry in these contexts.

Teaching Ideas That Promote Inquiry

This section of the chapter focuses on a variety of ways to integrate inquiry into content area teaching and learning. These techniques, illustrate the critical and creative thinking processes naturally embedded in inquiry-based experiences.

Teaching Idea: Problem-Based Learning
Content Areas: All
Levels: Intermediate, Middle, High School

> Problem-Based Learning is an instructional method that uses a real world problem as the context for an in-depth investigation of core content. The problems that students tackle are ill-structured; they include just enough information to suggest how students should proceed with an investigation, but never enough information to enable students to solve the problem without further inquiry. (Checkley, 1997, p. 3)

Problem-Based Learning is generally characterized by four stages: engaging students, inquiry and investigation, solution products, and debriefing. These stages are linked by each level building a foundation for the next (Stepien & Gallagher, 1997). Students become better problem solvers through problem-based learning because they refine their reasoning abilities, collaboration skills, and persistence as they engage in self-directed searches for solutions (Checkley, 1997).

The following scenario offers an example of Problem-Based Learning.

Ask students to imagine that the classroom is actually their home. After a knock is heard on the door, students begin to respond to it. Before they open the door, the students begin brainstorming about what awaits them when the door is opened. Students may ask questions of the visitors before opening the door. After the questions are raised and answered, the students open the door.

After the visitors have entered, students develop a conversation with them. As the scenario progresses, students learn that the visitors are runaway slaves who were destined for a stop on the Underground Railroad when they noticed lawmen near that house. To avoid apprehension, they journeyed on in the darkness to the students' door.

Once all the information is revealed, the students realize that they must confront the situation and find a solution to this problem. The matter is, of course, complicated by the illegality of hiding runaway slaves. This leads to a number of fact-finding activities, including library and Internet research, personal interviews with members of the police force and legal profession, reading a journal kept by a runaway slave and newspaper articles from the 19th century, and roundtable discussions about particular facts involved in the decision making. The entire process is inquiry-based and continues until the students come to a consensus on whether to hide the visitors in their home.

When engaging in Problem-Based Learning, students' critical and creative thinking are situated in life experiences. Students take an active role, raise questions, apply content area knowledge, use multiple sources, work cooperatively with others and engage in decision making, all skills they will use well beyond their school years.

Teaching Idea: Ripped from the Headlines:
Real Life Investigations
Content Areas: All
Levels: Intermediate, Middle, High School

When using Ripped from the Headlines: Real-Life Investigations (McLaughlin, 1998), teachers or students select an intriguing story from an actual newspaper as the basis for inquiry. The goal is for students to use multiple research sources to gain and report information that will be used in the dramatized resolution of the case. Students brainstorm the types of information they need to know to make informed decisions and decide which research sources they will use. This is similar to Problem-Based Learning, but in Ripped from the Headlines, the stories are always current, the basic information about the problem comes directly from a published newspaper article, and all of the information in the article is released to the students at the commencement of the investigation.

These long-term investigations are usually cross-curricular in nature. An application of this strategy was developed by Debi Stinner and her colleagues at the Bangor Middle School in Bangor, Pennsylvania. It focuses on integrating physics, history, and reading/language arts.

In this multiple-phase, cross-curricular unit, students follow the events of an actual bus and train crash from its occurrence to its closure in the judicial system. The unit lasts for approximately 4 weeks. The students' ultimate task is to decide who is to blame for the accident. Students research to locate information about the accident through newspapers and the Internet. They carefully examine this information and participate in discussions with guest speakers, such as a defense attorney and a district attorney. Students also view the film *Twelve Angry Men*. As time progresses, the students develop courtroom evidence, such as aerial scale drawings of the accident scene and calculations concerning momentum, stopping distance, speed, and force of impact.

The students then decide who they think caused the accident. They have determined that there are a variety of possibilities, including the following: the bus driver, for not realizing that the back of the bus was over the tracks; the train engineer, for speeding; the bus company, for improperly training substitute bus drivers; the highway department, for widening the highway and not checking the timing on the trip switch; the town council, for insisting the highway be widened on the side toward the tracks.

Next, the students participate in a mock trial. Prior to starting the unit, students have studied the judicial system, the roles it encompasses, and appropriate courtroom procedures. Students perform all roles, including judge, jurors, prosecuting and defense attorneys, witnesses, and bailiff. Over the next several days, members of the court do a variety of things, including the following:

- Witnesses prepare their statements by researching their role and the comments they made in the newspaper articles.
- Lawyers prepare their cases, including interviewing the witnesses.
- Lawyers are provided with the National Transportation Safety Board report of the accident.
- The judge reviews the rules of the courtroom.
- The jurors review literature about types of evidence.

The actual trial then takes place. After the verdict has been determined, members of the court reflect on the roles they played. For example, the judge might ponder how he or she impacted the outcome of the trial and discuss whether he or she agrees with the verdict. Members of the jury might document why they felt the defendant was guilty or innocent. The lawyers might describe the bases of their cases and what they would do differently if the trial could be held again.

Ripped from the Headlines: Real-Life Investigations enhances students' learning in a number of ways. First, it requires students to interact with the newspaper, a primary information source for our society. While students may have already been reading the newspapers for sports, comics, advertisements, or advice columns, this activity helps them to connect to actual news stories and to raise their own questions. Students become attuned to the print medium and often continue reading the news after the project is complete, frequently suggesting topics for future investigations. In addition, the integrated nature of Ripped from the Headlines helps students to see connections between and among subject areas. Furthermore, students interact not only with classmates and teachers but also with community members whose professions are linked to the topic of investigation. Finally, dramatizing the event accommodates individual learning styles and offers students an alternative way to demonstrate what they have learned. (For more information about dramatization, see chapter 5.)

Teaching Idea: First-Person Experiences
Content Areas: All
Levels: Intermediate, Middle, High School

In First-Person Experiences, the student takes on the identity of a person who played an active role in the event that he or she has chosen to investigate. This motivates the student, which in turn directly impacts his or her learning.

First-Person Experiences are based on four student-directed decisions. First, students decide what content-related topic they would like to investigate. Second, they determine which person in the event they would like to become in order to report their investigation. Third, they choose the format through which they will share their investigation. Fourth, they select the information sources and inquiry techniques they will use to conduct their investigation. Examples of topics and perspectives students have selected include the following:

- Isaac Newton, mathematician and scientist, on the discovery of gravity
- Robert Hooke, biologist, on the discovery of the cell
- A young girl on the *Mayflower,* on her journey to a new world
- A crew member from one of Columbus's ships, the first journey from Europe
- A Cherokee Indian, on the Trail of Tears
- A friend of John Wilkes Booth, on Lincoln's assassination
- A young girl growing up in Spain, on cultural experiences
- A young Taino, on Columbus's interactions with members of the Taino tribe
- A soldier in the Vietnam War, on betrayal
- A Confederate soldier, on fighting in the Civil War

Student-selected formats have included diaries, personal narratives, videotapes, advertising campaigns, dramatizations, parchment documents, alphabet books, messages in bottles, correspondences, children's books, inventions, projects, travel brochures, songs, journals, poetry, newspaper articles, radio scripts, interviews, and computer software. Student information sources have included books, articles, newspapers, public documents, videotapes, television programs, personal interviews, correspondence, field trips, CD-ROMs, and the Internet. Research techniques have included interviews, surveys, library and computer research, experiments, letters of inquiry, and e-mail.

In the following excerpts from first-person experiences, students have selected famous people in history, biology, and mathematics as topics for their investigations. Joan Ricker takes the perspective of a young Cherokee boy on the Trail of Tears:

> After waiting many days where the soldiers had placed us, the people of my village were led in long lines, Many of my people have no shoes or blankets, When we leave my village, I look back many times until I can see our mountain home no more. My family walks along with heavy hearts. Many, many days we walk. Cold is all around us. Snow and rain fall from the sky. Many of my people die. The wise old people of my village die from the hurt in their heads and bones from this endless journey. We do not stop to give them a Cherokee burial. The dead are covered next to the trail that we still walk.

Yvonne Stoffey takes on the identity of Robert Hooke, the biologist who discovered the cell, through a diary that Hooke maintained throughout his life with the woman he loved:

> September 1665
>
> Dearest Grace,
>
> This is perhaps the greatest day in my entire scientific career! I was casually looking through an instrument called a microscope. I was examining various objects and trying to figure out how the microscope can be helpful in applications to different aspects of sciences. I took a piece of cork and placed it under the scope. Alas! There were many small compartments. After studying them closer, I concluded they were pores. I also believe that they are passages to carry liquids for the plant's growth, and I am trying to locate the valves that must obviously be present.
>
> I continued my investigation and examined materials from the mineral, vegetable, and animal kingdoms. I realized that they all consisted of the same tiny "cells"! This is the term my fellow researchers and I have decided to label these small compartments. The cells have various shapes and sizes. I drew diagrams of my discovery. My

work will now be published in a book called *Micrographia*.

I miss you and wish you could be here to share these exciting times!

Robert

Shawn Seidel takes on the identity of a mathematician living in Newton's time through an excerpt from *Isaac Newton: Greatest Mathematician.*

> It was amazing to me that the son of a farmer would not only attend the likes of Trinity College at Cambridge, but also eventually succeed Isaac Barrow as Lucasian professor. Newton spent eighteen years teaching there and it was there that he developed the calculus material that eventually found its way into his great work, *Principia*, which was published in 1687. Soon after its publication, I was fortunate enough to obtain a copy and proceeded to read it numerous times. I, being a fellow scholar, could barely follow Newton's notation and techniques and could not contemplate how such thoughts got into Newton's head. Newton's work excited me in such a way that I began studying all sorts of mathematical concepts in my spare time.
>
> In 1692, Newton suffered from an illness that lasted nearly two years. After he recovered, Newton shifted his attention to chemistry, alchemy, and theology. It was after this that I had the great pleasure to be involved in a search for the greatest mathematician of all time . . .

Student reactions to the First-Person Experiences have been highly enthusiastic. Comments have included the following:

> "The first-person accounts were explicitly written and stunningly factual."
>
> "This type of investigation brings the topics to life."
>
> "Taking on the identity of a famous biologist and reporting in a diary format helped me to become much more familiar with Hooke and see things from his point of view."
>
> "It gave me a much different perspective to investigate the Civil War as a Confederate soldier. I felt as if I were right there."
>
> "The First-Person Experience encouraged me to be factual and creative at the same time."
>
> "It really required me to think in depth about my topic."
>
> "It offered amazing variety and unlimited creativity."
>
> "It was useful and interesting. It stirred my imagination and helped

me adopt the mindset of the person, time, place, and event."

"This technique touched me. I felt I was the person in the report. I felt what he felt and how he lived through the entire experience."

First-Person Experiences help students to make better connections to the people and events they are researching. This type of activity promotes inquiry through student choice: Students self-select the target of their research as well as the sources and the format they will use.

Teaching Idea: Student-Authored Alphabet Books
Content Areas: All
Levels: Intermediate, Middle, High School

Alphabet books are currently enjoying a renaissance in children's literature. Books that were once characterized by "A is for apple, B is for boy" have recently emerged as themed volumes filled with in-depth research designed to inform students of all ages. *Amazon Alphabet, A is for Asia, The Desert Alphabet, The Ocean Alphabet*, and *The Dinosaur Alphabet* are examples of such published works.

Students from elementary school through high school create alphabet books to share information they have chosen to investigate. The format also affords opportunities for students to illustrate their entries. They learn early in the experience that although everyone may not be a gifted artist, everyone can be creative. The result is books that are informative and visually appealing. Titles of alphabet books that students have created include the following: *Bullfighting From A to Z, French Essentials: An Alphabetical Visit to the Zoo, The ABC Book of American Presidents, The ABCs of American Art, The ABCs of Biology, The ABCs of Dinosaurs, The ABCs of Endangered Animals, The ABCs of the French Language, The ABCs of Geometry, The ABCs of Greek Culture, The ABC Book of Health and Fitness, The ABC Book of Time, The ABC History of Science, The Computer ABC Book, The Native American Alphabet Book, The ABCs of Math, The ABCs of Mathematical Computation, The ABCs of Noise Pollution, The Science Alphabet Book, The Space Science Alphabet Book*, and *The Pioneer Alphabet Book* (see Figure 3-1).

Figure 3-1. Student-Created Alphabet Books

Creating alphabet books requires students to investigate 26 aspects of a self-selected topic. The books also challenge students to develop illustrations that complement each item discussed in the text. This activity incorporates student choice, research, writing, and creativity.

Teaching Idea: Student-Authored Picture Books
Content Areas: All
Levels: Intermediate, Middle, High School

While picture books were once enjoyed only by very young children, they are now widely used at all levels of education to stimulate students' engagement with the learning process (for information on using picture books in the content areas, see chapter 7). Students often choose to create picture books to report their research. The books are then shared with classmates to stimulate their interest in the book's topic. They may also become part of the classroom library or be shared with younger learners.

Creating a picture book presents a number of challenges to the students. These include selecting a content-related topic for the book and researching it; conveying the essential elements of their research topic in a 32-page narrative; developing illustrations to support the text; and writing a story that is creative and motivational yet logical and informative. Students also choose the book style that best complements their story. Shape books, accordion books, pop-up books, television scrolls, and computer-animated books are among the styles most frequently selected. Finally, the book must incorporate appropriate conventions of writing. A rubric explaining each of these elements is shared with the students before the research project begins (for more information on rubrics, see chapter 15).

In their writing, students have addressed topics from outer space to Egyptian mummies. Some titles of books they have created include the following: *John and Wayne's Excellent Outer Space Adventure, Geometry Is All Around Us, Man on the Moon, The Medieval Castle, The Seven Wonders of the World*, and *The Mummy Walks at Night* (see Figure 3-2).

Figure 3-2. Student-Created Picture Books

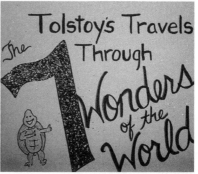

Teaching Idea: The Rest of the Story
Content Areas: All
Levels: Intermediate, Middle, High School

Most of us can clearly recall particular facts we learned in science or social studies, such as a list of inventors and their inventions or explorers and their discoveries. An example of this is Alexander Graham Bell. Most of us know his name as the person who created the telephone. But what was the rest of the story? Did you know that Bell was very dedicated to helping the deaf and was a mentor to Helen Keller? Did you know that he was the cofounder of *National Geographic*? Did you know that he filed his patent for the telephone just hours before another man filed a similar patent and that a lawsuit contesting ownership of the patent ensued? These are the types of information that are revealed when students choose to research and report The Rest of the Story.

The Rest of the Story is an inquiry-based investigation that encourages the researcher to go beyond the basic facts generally known about a person, a discovery, an invention, or an event in content area study (McLaughlin, 1998). Students use numerous resources to locate the information, including the Internet. Technology also plays a role in the way that students choose to format their investigations to share them with the class; they often elect to design a homepage or create software. Audiotapes or videotapes are other popular formatting selections. When using videotapes, students may report their research as a news story or choose to dramatize the results of their investigation (for more information about drama in the content areas, see chapter 5).

Teaching Idea: Investigative Journals
Content Areas: All
Levels: Intermediate, Middle, High School

Content area students keep Investigative Journals to record ideas they are interested in investigating in the future. The journals are also used to record ideas about ongoing research. To prompt the students to think about such inquiry, encourage them to begin their journal entries with the phrase "I wonder . . . " Once ideas are recorded, students' "wonderings" can serve as the basis for Written Conversations or peer discussions. This activity promotes inquiry, reflection, and critical thinking.

Teaching Idea: Written Conversations
Content Areas: All
Levels: Intermediate, Middle, High School

Written Conversations offer an effective format for students to share their wonderings with peers. In this process, a student selects an idea from the "I wonder" section of his or her Investigative Journal and shares it in a Written Conversation with another class member. That student then reacts to the original idea, raises questions, and the correspondence continues. This process not only promotes student interaction but also encourages reflection. Because it is a Written Conversation, it can occur while others in the class are working on different aspects of inquiry without disturbing the rest of the class. The completed conversation then becomes the basis of further inquiry for the student who originated the dialogue and can be kept in either the student's Investigative Journal or course portfolio.

Teaching Idea: Press Conference
Content Areas: All
Levels: Intermediate, Middle, High School

The Press Conference is an inquiry-based activity that promotes oral communication. Students peruse newspapers, magazines, or the Internet to find articles of interest to themselves and their audience. After reading an article, focusing on its essential points, raising questions, and reflecting on personal insights, the student presents an informal summary of the article to a group of classmates or to the entire class. Members of the audience then raise questions that can lead to "wonderings" for their Investigative Journals.

Teaching Idea: Inquiring Minds (Gallery Walk)
Content Areas: All
Levels: Intermediate, Middle, High School

Inquiring Minds is an inquiry-based, small-group research activity based on students' interests. When using Inquiring Minds, students select content-related topics they would like to investigate and form small groups based on their choices. The small groups brainstorm three to five questions about their topic that they would like to be able to answer through their research. This sets a purpose and offers direction to their investigation. Group members list their topic and the questions on a piece of chart paper. Each group in the class uses a different colored marker to record this information.

After all the groups have completed their questions, the charts are posted around the room. Each group then engages in a gallery walk, moving together from paper to paper reviewing the topics and the questions that each of the other groups is researching. Each group in the class then adds any questions its members may have to the posted lists.

Next, the chart paper about each topic is returned to the group that created it. Each paper now contains the original topic and questions as well as queries that have been added by other research groups. The use of the different colored markers allows the students to see how many groups made inquiries about their topics and also allows them to contact a particular group if any of the questions are unclear. This strategy leads the original group to broaden the scope of its research and creates great interest among class members when all the research is reported.

Teaching Idea: Cross-Age Experiences
Content Areas: All
Levels: Intermediate, Middle, High School

Cross-Age Experiences typically involve a novice working for a specified period of time with a person considered to be more experienced. This relationship is highly applicable in education when practitioners model their expertise for novice learners (McLaughlin, 1995). Vygotsky (in Forman & Cazden, 1994) supports the idea of cross-age experiences and notes their particular importance in school settings, where they offer alternatives to traditional adult-child interactions. Examples of some common cross-age experiences are described in Figure 3-3..

"The Year of the . . ." is an investigative cross-age project developed by Joan Crotty at Milne Grove School in Lockport, Illinois. The primary goal is to model how to learn. It is based on the belief that if students can learn how to investigate one topic, they can use those strategies to learn about other things. The following example describes the roles that first graders and sixth, seventh, and eighth graders played in a cross-age, inquiry-based experience.

Each school year Joan focuses on a theme animal that she and her first grade will study for the entire year. Over the summer, she begins collecting posters, seeks information from the Internet, and chooses a stuffed animal to serve as a mascot. She also informs colleagues, friends, and family about this year's animal so they can be on the lookout for resources to support the students' learning. Each study has been enriched by their support.

When students arrive in August, the classroom has an environment that encourages thinking about the selected animal. The "K-W-L" strategy (Ogle, 1986) serves as the foundation for student inquiry: Students begin by listing what they *know* and what they *want* to know. Several times during the year, they update what they have *learned*. Each year they find many ways to gather and use the animal information. Each student maintains a "read, write, and share folder" throughout the project.

For example, 1998 was "the Year of the Gorilla." The first-grade students had a special partnership with the sixth-, seventh-, and eighth-grade EXCEL students. These students were participants in the school's gifted and talented program, which Michele Zeko, another teacher, coordinated. The older students researched and designed learning centers about gorilla facts for the first graders. In one center, they measured each first grader's arm span, height, weight, and footprint on paper. Then they mounted this information next to the same data from a male gorilla at the St. Louis Zoo. In December the first graders and their EXCEL pals went on a field trip to the Lincoln Park Zoo. The EXCEL students took the primate tour and then served as personal tour guides for the first-grade students, sharing information on a very meaningful one-to-one basis. Gorilla communication was the focus during the second semester. EXCEL students designed new learning centers, and the first-grade students learned some of their vocabulary words using the manual alphabet. In March they visited the gorilla collection at the Brookfield Zoo. The zookeeper confirmed much of what the students had learned about gorillas in class, and the students felt well prepared to discuss "Dear Miss Gorilla Manners," the informational format posted at the zoo. In April the EXCEL students rewrote the story "Princess Gorilla and the New Kind of Water" into a play for the first graders, made the costumes and scenery, and helped with blocking the stage so students would know where to stand during the play.

The feedback from the EXCEL students and the cooperating teachers encourages the continuation of this cross-age project in future years. Parents have also been supportive. One father drew a freehand pencil drawing of a gorilla for the class. He also noted how his son's drawings of gorillas changed as the student learned more about them throughout the year. In May a graduate student at Northern Illinois University who had learned about the project from one of the parents offered to give a presentation about gorillas to the class. Joan previewed the graduate student's notes and challenged her to ask the students questions about gorillas instead of doing her presentation. The students answered all of her questions correctly, except one about the male's head formation. She was truly awestruck by the children's knowledge. In June, students took their gorilla folders home. Each folder showed how the child's knowledge of the animal had grown throughout the year.

Figure 3-3. Ideas for Content Area Cross-Age Experiences

E-Pals	Students use e-mail to become acquainted and to engage in inquiry about particular topics, such as the solar system or geometry in everyday life.
PALS	Partners Always Learning Something is a successful cross-age program that involves primary and upper grade students communicating through journals on a weekly basis. The students' communications address a wide variety of issues including favorite books, the community, and plant growth processes.
U Buddies	University students engage in cross-age experiences with middle school or high school students to discuss various works of literature, scientific procedures, historical occurrences, or current events. Discussion groups, e-mail, and journal writing are featured in this program.

"The Year of the . . ." is just one example of many successful cross-age experiences. These activities involve inquiry at multiple levels and provide valuable learning experiences for students and teachers. Benefits include the following: Younger students have the older students to model various experiences, older students are challenged to convey accurate information in appropriate and motivational ways, and teachers have the opportunity to creatively interact with peers and students. The resulting relationships are positive and the learning experiences are meaningful and memorable.

Teaching Idea: T-Shirt Reports
Content Areas: All
Levels: Intermediate, Middle, High School

In her fourth-grade class at J. M. Hill School in East Stroudsburg, Pennsylvania, Dolores Anders creates multiple cross-curricular connections through the students' investigations of the 50 states. To begin, the students used library and computer sources to research the state of their choice. Their focuses included topics such as how and when the state came into being, population make-up, types of industry, economy, geography, special attractions, and climate. The students decided which information was relevant to their state and important enough to be included in their reports, which they prepared on word processors or computers.

The reports began in social studies class and extended across the curriculum. In art class, the students turned the physical outline of their state into a caricature, depicting something the state is known for or associated with on the front of a T-shirt. On the back of the T-shirt, the students placed the state's abbreviation, state symbol, flag, and other facts (see Figure 3-4). In math class, the students used measurements to design their caricature to scale, accommodating it to the size of the T-shirt. In addition, some of the information included in the reports required an understanding of place value, ranking, averages, fractions, and computation. In science class, the students discussed course-related facts they had discovered through their research.

The students integrated technology by using computer encyclopedias and atlases as well as the Internet during the research phase. They also wrote letters and e-mails to communicate with the state tourism departments. The students engaged in public speaking as they shared what they had learned about the states they had chosen. The T-shirts were later worn by members of the school chorus as they sang "Fifty, Nifty United States" at the annual spring concert.

Figure 3-4. T-Shirt Reports

Teaching Idea: Six Thinking Hats
Content Areas: All
Levels: Intermediate, Middle, High School

Six Thinking Hats is an approach that promotes critical and creative thinking through discussion (DeBono, 1985). The thinking hats represent six different ways of viewing a topic: The white hat views the information from an objective point of view, the red hat from an emotional perspective, the black hat from a critical point of view, the yellow hat from a positive point of view, the green hat from a creative perspective, and the blue hat from the perspective of monitoring and summarizing what the other hats have done. According to DeBono, putting on a particular color of hat focuses the students' thinking, and switching hats allows students to view the situation from alternative perspectives.

Although each of the colored hats has a particular meaning, the strategy is easily adapted to "hats" that allow students to take on the perspectives of different people in a given situation. For example, when studying about Christopher Columbus, instead of following the suggested hat roles, one person could take on the identity of Columbus, and others could be Queen Isabella, a member of Columbus's crew, a young Taino from the island where Columbus first landed, King Ferdinand, and the ship's navigator. This technique provides a stimulating format for students to think about a topic from diverse perspectives and then engage in a discussion or dramatization.

Teaching Idea: Debate
Content Areas: All
Levels: Intermediate, Middle, High School

When structuring a debate, students select the issue and prepare pro and con arguments to support their thinking. In math class, they may choose to debate the applicability of a particular formula or mathematical concept; in science, they may debate the use of the scientific method or the results of an experiment; in history, they may debate political issues or whether to fund a particular exploration; in literature class, they may debate who deserves the title of greatest American author. Whatever the topic, students have owner-ship of the debate process from the outset. They select the topic, establish debating teams, raise issues, and conduct the actual debate. The teacher serves as a moderator.

Debates can be conducted between two people or between two teams. This technique can be used as an alternative format to discuss a day's topic or as a more long-term project in which students engage in in-depth re-search. Whichever time frame is selected, debate offers students an op-portunity to focus their thinking, develop persuasive argumentative skills, reflect on the ideas presented, and interact with peers.

Teaching Idea: Concept-Oriented Reading Instruction (CORI)
Content Areas: All
Levels: Intermediate, Middle, High School

Concept-Oriented Reading Instruction (CORI) integrates a content area with purposeful reading. In this process, students investigate areas within a curriculum by posing their own questions, thereby generating their own internal reasons for reading (Guthrie et al, 1996). CORI is "embedded in a reading/language arts–science program, which emphasizes real-world sci-ence observations, student self-direction, strategy instruction, collaborative learning, self-expression, and coherence of literacy experiences" (p. 307).

After generating their own questions, students use trade books and teacher-supplied information packets to develop a presentation for the class. This approach allows students the pleasure of learning for its own sake, in which they immerse themselves in literacy tasks and cultivate a frequent use of reading strategies (Guthrie, Alao, & Rinehart, 1997).

Seven themes permeate this technique: real-world observation, concep-tual theory, strategy instruction, self-directed learning, collaboration, self-expression, and coherence (Guthrie et al., 1997). Examples of steps in each stage of student activity include the following: observe and personalize (ex-amine artifacts, conduct experiments, formulate questions); search and re-trieve (use library, link photographs to observations, skim for information);

comprehend and integrate (paraphrase, use imagery, determine cause and effect); and communicate to others (make videotapes, write in journals, create dioramas, write poetry, author books).

CORI promotes inquiry-based learning and fosters student motivation at multiple levels. While the original research focused on science, the concept is applicable throughout the content areas.

Teaching Idea: Using the Internet
Content Areas: All
Levels: Intermediate, Middle, High School

Technology offers amazing and immediate access to seemingly boundless information. While it is critical for students to be able to access this information, they also must be able to evaluate it and place it in context (Caruso, 1997; Pool, 1997).

Students and teachers frequently use the Internet as a resource for inquiry-based learning. Descriptions of selected Internet sites, categorized by academic discipline, which facilitate this process can be found at the end of this chapter. These are followed by a list of suggested readings for teachers who wish to learn more about using technology in the classroom. (For more information about Internet, see chapter 10).

Concluding Thoughts

Learning experiences that are inquiry-based foster creativity, variety, and innovation. Classrooms become places where ideas are born, valued, and nurtured. Students become problem seekers as well as problem solvers. Inquiry-based experiences, and the resulting critical and creative thinking, serve as the foundation of dynamic teaching and learning. This is, without question, the direct antithesis of the "read the chapter and answer the questions" context in which many students experience content area instruction. Rather, it is the classroom that Vacca and Vacca (1999) describe as "a crucible, a place where the special mix of teacher, student, and text come together to create wonderfully complex human interactions that stir the minds and spirits of learners" (p. 4).

Internet Resources for the Content Areas

Maureen McLaughlin and Christine Shoemaker

The following Internet resources are ones we frequently use in our teaching. Most are categorized by content area, but sites that offer information that extends across disciplines are categorized as multidisciplinary. Each entry includes the site's address and a description of its contents. The annotations are followed by a list of readings intended to enhance teachers' understanding and use of technology.

Multidisciplinary

Title: Virtual Library Museum Page
Site*: http://www.icom.org/vlmp
This site can link you to almost any museum in the world. The descriptions are written in everyday English. You can access the museums by country or name. Each connection offers a history of the museum and detailed descriptions and images of the artifacts. This site could be used to view artwork that represents any time period.

Title: Smithsonian Museums
Site: http://www.si.sgi.com/sgistart.htm
All the resources available through the Smithsonian Museums can be accessed by using this site. It contains information about the museums, including outreach and educational guides. It also provides lesson plans with detailed resource guides covering the topics of art, science, and social studies.

Title: PBS
Site: http://www.pbs.org
PBS offers a multitude of resources and information about a variety of topics including history, technology, art, and science. The articles are written in any easy-to-understand manner, covering a wide variety of topics. Teacher resources are also available.

Title: ArtsEdNet
Site: http://www.artsednet.getty.edu
Supported by the Getty Education Institute for the Arts, this site focuses on different aspects of integrating art and education. It contains lesson plans and curriculum ideas, cultural heritage sites, image galleries, worlds of art, explorations of ancient worlds, and interdisciplinary materials. The browsing-room feature is a showcase of student artwork that focuses on cognition and creation at all grade levels.

Title: Houghton Mifflin Education Place
Site: http://www.eduplace.com
Eduplace offers information about math, social studies, science, and reading/language arts. Teaching centers and bilingual resources are also featured. This is a resource site that presents creative ideas and lessons for teacher use.

Foreign Languages

Title: Foreign Language for Travelers
Site: http://www.travlang.com/languages
This site allows you to learn the basics of more than 70 languages. The user puts in the language spoken and the language to be learned. The user then selects types of words to learn, including basic words, numbers, shopping, dining, travel, or directions.

Title: Center for Advancement of Language Learning
Site: http://www.call.lingnet.org
This site presents foreign language resources that link to instructional materials, references, cultural studies, and authentic sources such as foreign language newspapers. The user clicks on a language, with choices ranging from Afrikaans to Zulu, and then a list of links is displayed.

Math

Title: The Annenberg Math and Science Project
Site: http://www.learner.org
This is an interactive site designed to involve students in learning. It contains an exhibits collection and links to resources about lesson plans. Further, it provides information about subjects such as the abacus, geometry, and integrating math across the curriculum.

Title: Eisenhower National Center for Mathematics and Science Education
Site: http://www.enc.org:80/index.htm
This site displays classroom links, lessons and activities for all age levels, a featured "innovator of the month," and resources for hot topics. Each segment of the site contains puzzles and projects for student interaction.

Title: Census Bureau
Site: http://www.census.gov
This site is maintained by the Census Bureau and contains information on people, the census, geography, a population clock, and facts by county and state. This site also has an American FactFinder feature that allows the user

to search for information about communities, business, or industry. The facts and figures contained in this site provide authentic ways to connect math curriculums with experiences beyond the classroom.

Science

Title: Discovery Channel Online
Site: http://www.discovery.com
Feature stories, news, mind games, and expeditions are some of the features of this site. You are invited to search through a variety of topics such as extreme weather, archeology/fossils, and travel. There is also a live camera feature that displays images taken within a minute of viewing and gives a description of the location being viewed.

Title: NASA's Online Interactive Projects
Site: http://www.quest.arc.nasa.gov/interactive/index.html#archives
This site provides interactive projects that focus on linking the classroom with actual, ongoing scientific investigations. A variety of current online projects allow the user to view notes, ask questions, and obtain background information.

Title: Science Learning Network
Site: http://www.sln.org
This site is an information center designed to provide numerous links to science-related topics. It encourages the user to explore a variety of resources such as science museums and working collaboratively with other science classes.

Title: How Stuff Works
Site: http://www.howstuffworks.com
This site gives engaging, detailed descriptions on how things work. The objects described are divided by categories that include engines, basic technologies, food, body, around the house, and the Internet. Colorful diagrams accompany all descriptions. This site also contains a question of the day that students can view. Students can also submit questions of their own.

Social Studies

Title: The History Channel
Site: http://www.historychannel.com
The History Channel's site contains a variety of information including areas such as "This Day in History" and the "Traveler," with the destination site changing periodically. Under "Great Speeches," you can listen to re-

cordings from a variety of historical and modern figures. Speakers include Martin Luther King, Jr., Colin Powell, and Joseph Stalin. The original recordings are replayed with all the scratches and background noises.

Title: National Geographic Society Home Page
Site: http://www.nationalgeographic.com/index.html
This site contains a plethora of information, including photographs, archives, daily features, travel planning tools, and "info central." It also contains access to the various publications of the National Geographic Society. "Info central" offers information on topics including history, geography, biographies, and phenomena.

Title: The Primary Source Network
Site: http://www.primarysources.msu.edu
This site contains primary source artifacts on a variety of subjects. Its goal is to show how the use of artifacts can help people to understand individuals and society. It has segments including professional development, a gallery of artifacts, and classroom resources. It is an interactive, user-guided module that contains vivid images and articles to explore. Some of its topics include the history of the telephone, images of World War II—the Homefront, and the automobile. The site contains different levels of description so it can be used by a wide variety of grade levels.

Title: Cybrary of the Holocaust
Site: http://www.remember.org
On this site, stories from survivors, photos, poems, an online forum, and teacher guides are available to help create vivid images to connect students to the events of the Holocaust.

Technology: Suggested Readings

Algava, A. (1999). Animated learning. *Educational Leadership, 56* (5), 58–60.

Berman, S., & Tinker, R. (1997). The world's the limit in the virtual high school. *Educational Leadership, 55* (3), 52–54.

Caruso, C. (1997). Before you cite a site. *Educational Leadership, 55* (3), 24–25.

Davis, S. J. H. (1997). How mastering technology can transform math class. *Educational Leadership, 55* (3), 49–51.

Harris, J. (1998). *Design tools for the Internet-supported classroom.* Alexandria, VA: Association for Supervision and Curriculum Development.

Leininger, L., & Rowan, C. (1997). *The kid-friendly web guide.* Palo Alto, CA: Monday Morning Books.

Leu, D. J., & Leu, D. D. (1997). *Teaching the Internet.* Norwood, MA: Christopher-Gordon.

Lewin, L. (1999). "Site-reading" the world wide web. *Educational Leadership, 56* (5), 16–20.

Lonergan, D. (1997). Network science: Bats, birds, and trees. *Educational Leadership, 55* (3), 34–36.

Mohnsen, B. (1997). Stretching bodies and minds through technology. *Educational Leadership, 55* (3), 46–48.

Teicher, T. (1999). An action plan for smart Internet use. *Educational Leadership, 56* (5), 70–74.

Thoman, E. (1999). Skills and strategies for media education. *Educational Leadership, 56* (5), 50–54.

Thomas, L. G., & Knezek, D. G. (1999). National educational technology standards. *Educational Leadership, 56* (5), 27.

References

Brooks, J. G. & Brooks, M. G. (1993). *In search of understanding: The case for constructivist classrooms.* Alexandria, VA: Association for Supervision and Curriculum Development.

Caruso, (1997). Before you cite a site. *Educational Leadership, 55* (3), 24–25.

Checkley, K. (1997). Problem-based learning: The search for solutions to life's messy problems. *ASCD Curriculum Update,* 1–8.

Chin-Lee, C. (1997). *A is for Asia.* New York: Orchard Books.

DeBono, E. (1985). *Six thinking hats.* Boston: Little, Brown.

Forman, E. A., & Cazden, C. B. (1994). Exploring Vygotskian perspectives in education: The cognitive value of peer interaction. In R. B. Ruddell, M.R. Ruddell, & H. Singer, (Eds.), *Theoretical models and processes of reading* (4th ed., pp. 391–413). Newark, DE: International Reading Association.

Gordon, R. (1998). Balancing real-world problems with real world results. *Phi Delta Kappan, 79* (5), 390–393.

Guthrie, J. T., Alao, S., & Rinehart, J. M. (1997). Engagement in reading for young adolescents. *Journal of Adolescent and Adult Literacy, 40,* 438–446.

Guthrie, J. T., VanMeter, P., McCann, A. D., Wigfield, A., Bennett, L., Poundstone, C. C., Rice, M. E., Faibisch, F. M., Hunt, B., & Mitchell, A. M. (1996). Growth of literacy engagement: Changes in motivations and strategies during Concept-Oriented Reading Instruction. *Reading Research Quarterly, 31*, 306–332.

Hiebert, E. H. (1994). In R. B. Ruddell, M. R. Ruddell, & H. Singer, (Eds.), *Theoretical models and processes of reading* (4th ed., pp. 391–413). Newark, DE: International Reading Association.

Jordan, M., & Jordan, T. (1996). *Amazon alphabet*. New York: Kingfisher.

Manzo, A., & Manzo, U. (1990). *Content area reading: A heuristic approach*. Columbus, OH: Merrill.

McLaughlin, M. (1995). *Cross-age literacy: Apprenticeship and self-assessment*. Paper presented at the 40th Annual Convention of the International Reading Association, Anaheim, CA.

McLaughlin, M. (1998). *Creativity and innovation in content area instruction: A pre-convention institute*. 43rd Annual Convention of the International Reading Association, Orlando, FL.

McLaughlin, M., & Kennedy, A. (1993). *A classroom guide to performance assessment*. Princeton, NJ: Houghton Mifflin.

Newman, F. M., & Wehlage, G. G. (1993). Five standards for authentic instruction. *Educational Leadership 50* (7), 8–12.

Ogle, D. (1986). K-W-L: A teaching model that develops active reading of expository text. *The Reading Teacher, 39,* 564–570.

Pallotta, J. (1986). *The ocean alphabet*. Watertown, MA: Charlesbridge.

Pallotta, J. (1991). *The dinosaur alphabet book*. Watertown, MA: Charlesbridge.

Pallotta, J. (1994). *The desert alphabet book*. Watertown, MA: Charlesbridge.

Pool, C. R. (1997). A new digital literacy: A conversation with Paul Gilster. *Educational Leadership, 55* (3), 6–11.

Rasmussen, K. (1997). Using real-life problems to make real-world connections. *Association for Supervision and Curriculum Development Curriculum Update*, 4–5.

Short, K. G., & Burke, C. (1996). Examining our beliefs and practices through inquiry. *Language Arts, 73*, 97–103.

Stepien, B. & Gallagher, S. A. (1993). Problem-based learning: As authentic as it gets. *Educational Leadership, 50* (7), 25–28.

Stepien, B., & Gallagher, S. A. (1997). Infusing critical thinking skills into the problem-based learning process. Paper presented at the Assessment-Instruction Connection: ASCD Conference on Teaching and Learning, Orlando, FL.

Vacca, R. T., & Vacca, J. A. (1999). *Content area reading* (6th ed). New York: Addison Wesley Longman.

Chapter 4

Make It Visual: A Picture Is Worth a Thousand Words

Donna M. Ogle

> The image is the greatest instrument of instruction. What a child gets out of any subject presented to him is simply the images, which he himself forms with regard to it. If nine-tenths of the energy at present directed towards making the child learn certain things were spent seeing to it that the child was forming proper images, the work of the instructor would be indefinitely facilitated.
>
> —John Dewey

John Dewey makes a strong case for visualizing. Many researchers have demonstrated that good readers create visual images while they read. As adults most of us experience the joy of our own visualizations so much that it isn't unusual to hear someone say, "I don't want to see the movie yet. I haven't finished the book!" So why not include drawing and visualizing as a tool to help students learn? Young people love it. Drawing relieves the monotony of the surfeit of words that permeates most classrooms. It taps into the part of the brain that we teachers often overlook. Working with urban students who need to engage more deeply in content materials, we have found that both drawing and illustrating can facilitate more active learning.

This chapter offers a theoretical foundation for using visualization as a component of learning. This is followed by descriptions of several visualization activities. Intermediate, middle school, and high school teachers' applications of the activities are integrated in the text. Finally, examples of large-scale visualization projects are discussed.

The Importance of Visualization

Support for a focus on visualization comes from several sources. First, the current interest in the brain and how it functions has suggested that ideas are stored in both verbal and nonverbal image forms (see Sylwester, 1990). Recall is often easier through images or pictures than through words. Linking verbal and visual images increases students' avenues of storage and retrieval of information. The adage "A picture is worth a thousand words" has been corroborated in many studies. In the area of literacy specifically, Sadoski, Paivio, & Goetz (1991) have developed a dual coding theory of reading, recognizing the importance of both verbal and visual thinking. They explain that "for language to make sense, it is necessary for it to be both semantically and syntactically systematic and to conform to the nonverbal world in some imaginable way" (p. 590). From their work and reviews of other studies, they conclude that "mental imagery appears to be spontaneous, consistent, and natural in reading a variety of text types for students of various ages at the sentence, paragraph and extended text levels" (p. 593).

There is strong reading-research support for the importance of creating visual images during reading. Many years ago Durrell and Catterson (1980) included visual imaging as one of the aspects of reading in the *Durrell Analysis of Reading Difficulty*. They reported that poor readers tend not to create images in their mind when they read and that proficient readers do this imaging automatically. Long, Winograd, and Bridge (1989) found that fifth graders experienced imagery spontaneously and consistently. Gambrell and Bales (1986) conducted a series of studies with young readers and found that training in visualizing while reading enhanced comprehension and the memory of a text. Pressley et al. (1989) also identified visualizing as one of the key strategies characteristic of proficient readers.

We're also aware that many students are not fully engaged in our classrooms, and alternative ways of "hooking" students are always welcome. With increasing numbers of English language learners, we need to find learning strategies that can best facilitate their success. Therefore, more global, visual tools can build a scaffold, offering these students access to content learning.

Setting the Stage

There are several research-based implications for teaching visualization strategies. These include ensuring that students do the following:

- Learn that visualizing is a strategy used by proficient readers and learners

- Experience many opportunities to practice creating their own visual images as they read
- Know more than one way to create images during reading
- Reflect on their own visualizing and compare their ideas and images with others so that self-awareness and evaluation can develop
- Enjoy creating and sharing images as part of learning.

How can we facilitate students' use of visualization? There are several tools that can be used with which students are already quite familiar: graphic organizers, mind mapping, and drawing.

Teaching Idea: Graphic Organizers
Content Areas: All
Levels: Intermediate, Middle, High School

The creation of graphic organizers for thinking is perhaps the most widely used bridge to visualization. Many schools use some variation of graphic organizers to help students organize their thinking. Although these don't convert ideas into visual images, they do provide an alternative to linear text and the traditional outlining of ideas. Several excellent books are available that can guide students to create visual diagrams that show the relationships among ideas in more graphic formats. In his book, *Visual Tools for Thinking,* Hyerle (1996) lays out an all-school design to gradually introduce a set of graphic organizers to help stimulate thinking. His goal is for students to become masters of the basic frames and use them across content areas. For secondary students, *Inductive Towers* (Clarke, Raths, & Gilbert, 1989) is a rich resource that helps students to use both deductive and inductive reasoning. Bellanca (1992) published two volumes of graphic organizers to teach thinking that include many of the excellent visual indicators of thinking, from Venn diagrams to the decision maker's flow chart.

Teaching Idea: Mind Mapping
Content Areas: All
Levels: Intermediate, Middle, High School

In the 1990s applications of visualization were developed that moved beyond words and depiction of linear relationships to the use of logos or images. They stimulate readers to create their own pictures from the ideas in the texts. Buzan's Mind Mapping (Wycoff, 1991) is one example. This strategy provides a way to activate the brain to think visually, using color pictures and symbols. In mind mapping, students are instructed to put a central image on a piece of paper, then create branches out from that concept using key words, symbols, and pictures to add subordinate ideas.

I See What You Mean (Moline, 1997) explores other ways that students can create diagrams, maps, and charts to present information. The author contends that with the increased use of graphic images in our society, students must both be able to read and to represent ideas more fully in visual forms. Teachers have been discovering great potential in helping students to develop charts, diagrams, and maps of ideas. This increased familiarity with visually presented information helps students to focus on similar formats in magazines, in textbooks, and on the Internet.

Teaching Idea: Sketch to Stretch
Content Areas: All
Levels: Intermediate, Middle, High School

Within the field of literacy, Short, Harste, & Burke (1996) have developed Sketch to Stretch, a strategy that integrates visualizing and drawing. In this after-reading strategy, individual students in small-group settings create visual symbols expressing what they believe is the central concept of a piece of text. When all members have created their pictures, each takes a turn showing the others what he or she has chosen to represent. As each picture is shared, the other group members describe verbally what they see and provide their interpretation of the drawing. After the group members share their responses, the reader-artist has an opportunity to respond with a further explanation about why he or she created the particular image and what the drawing means. After all members of each small group share their drawings, one drawing can be selected and presented to the whole class for a final reflection time.

Teaching Idea: Sketch to Stretch Paired Activity
Content Areas: All
Levels: Intermediate, Middle, High School

Once when I visited an English classroom, I immediately noticed the drawings on the bulletin board. Looking more closely, I saw a series of pictures and in the center the poem by S. Cisneros, " My Wicked, Wicked Ways." Peter Cusack, the teacher, explained that the idea to use Sketch to Stretch as a partner activity came to him while teaching S. Cisnero's poem. He knew that the students could identify with the poem, but they weren't doing so. He told the students to read the poem individually and then draw what they thought the poem meant. When the class was ready, partners would share their drawings with each other and see if they understood each other's representation. Each person wrote what he or she saw in the other's drawing and then referred to the poem. After making comparisons, the partners created a joint drawing (see Figure 4-1 for a sample drawing).

Figure 4-1. Students' Sketches of "My Wicked, Wicked Ways"

Peter had made several observations during this adaptation of Sketch to Stretch. First, the students kept returning to the poem as they drew. They realized that one reading was not sufficient to create the rich images they wanted; they needed more of the details in the descriptions and returned to the text frequently. Once each student had created an illustration, it was time to share it with a partner. Peter chose a partner activity rather than small groups because he knew that his students were quite shy about sharing, and he worried that drawing might intimidate them even more. What he found was that the students were eager to see each other's work and were not critical or derisive. He reported that sharing with just one person seemed to help some students overcome their shyness about speaking in class.

The comparison of drawings also stimulated more thinking and reflection. When the students looked at each other's drawings and noted the differences, questions emerged, and again the students referred to the poem. "I'd never had students reread poetry like this before! Many reread the poem seven or eight times. That never happens," Peter reported. The final drawings created by each team also reflected a deeper understanding of the poem than did the originals. In many instances the original and final drawings were complementary. The originals dealt mostly with the appearances of the two characters, the father and the mother. The final joint drawings were more action filled, reflecting the conflict introduced by the lines in the second and third stanzas referring to the other woman. As a result of this activity, Peter knew the students understood the poem at a level much deeper than they had before. It was also clear that the students took real pride in seeing their before-and-after drawings displayed on the board. As a result of this effort, Peter has decided to use variants on this sketching activity with his novel units.

Teaching Idea: Drawing Visualizations
Content Areas: All
Levels: Intermediate, Middle, High School

Eighth graders reading John Steinbeck's *The Red Pony* also benefited from drawing visualizations of this image-filled book. Their teacher, Sally Maro, decided to try to stimulate a more careful reading of this classic work by asking students to draw a picture of what they thought was most important in each chapter. Sally modeled the activity, and then the students tried it and used a small-group format for sharing. After completing the drawings (some were done as homework), the groups at each table shared their artwork. Each student had an opportunity to make one statement about each piece: "I see . . ." or "I think the drawing represents. . . . " After each member shared his or her comments, the illustrator then explained what the drawing meant.

As we reviewed the students' work on the chapter about the mountains, it was clear that some students focused on literal images in the text while others took a more symbolic approach to their drawings (see Figure 4-2). The sense of longing to know what lay beyond and the contrast between the two sets of mountains were more fully represented in some drawings than in others. Seeing students' responses provided an avenue for further discussion. Instead of the discussion being teacher-dominated, the students own drawings provided the focus for shared talk. With the students' personal interest engaged, the teacher used the occasion of sharing the drawings to guide the students to a discussion of the various levels on which *The Red Pony* could be read and imaged. As teachers use drawing more regularly, students begin to understand the value of these activities. Sketching functions in many ways to help students think about their reading. We have also noticed that students learn to anticipate what images they can use to summarize and represent important text content. This creates more active readers because students read with an expectation that they will extend their reading in some way. Just the awareness that they can draw an image during or after reading provides a focus and stimulates part of the brain.

Figure 4-2. Students' *Red Pony* Drawings

These approaches to visualizing include the creation of pictures and the drawing of symbols that cause students to represent ideas in holistic ways that go beyond a reliance on words. They encourage a deeper or different level of visualization than the more linear graphic organizers. Drawing ideas helps students to begin to think of imaging as part of their engagement with a text. Creating an expectation that there will be time to draw stimulates some students to begin creating images both before and while they are reading. This is certainly beneficial and helps some students to approach reading much more actively.

Drawing provides a great opportunity for all class members to activate a different level of thinking about a topic. It also recognizes children with artistic talents who are often not leaders in content area learning. It gives them status and an academic role in the classroom. Finally, drawing helps students to frame pertinent questions because they can see the differences in their drawings very clearly.

Visualization: A Basic Component of Learning

Visualizing is a powerful activity that broadens the way we build our knowledge and understanding. Teachers often use visualizing intuitively as part of their teaching, periodically asking students to form or identify some visual images in their work, but they may not consciously think of the potential of a more systematic introduction and use of images. Actual classroom experiences are included in this section to illustrate the power of a conscious use of visual activation as part of content learning.

These examples, coming at all points in the lessons, suggest that visualization should be thought of as a basic component of learning, not just as a final way to represent new knowledge. While most of the applications reviewed above use drawing and imaging as ways to consolidate learning, teachers have found visualization to be very useful in all parts of their lesson framework. Visualizing can be used before engagement with texts as a knowledge-activation and purpose-setting activity; it can be used while reading and constructing interpretations of content; and it can be used as part of the reflection and consolidation phase of learning. The results are new and exciting variations tailored to student needs and content expectations. The more teachers encourage students to think visually and the more the technique is used by students, the more everyone will reap the benefits of expanded thinking.

The work of these teachers may provide stimulation for you to think about how you can deepen students' engagement with the content while having the fun of illustrating and visualizing. Remember that learners can use visualizing before, during, and after reading content materials. Our minds can function more actively when we use more than one modality of thinking.

Before Reading: Activation of Knowledge

Teaching Idea: K-W-L and Drawing
Content Areas: All
Levels: Intermediate, Middle, High School

I realized the power of visualizing before reading and learning when I was using the K-W-L (Know, Want to know, Learn) (Ogle, 1986) with a large group of second grade children who were not able readers. As I began a discussion of spiders and wrote what students said they knew about spiders, I was concerned that I was doing most of the work and that the 29 children might not have the focus to stay on task. I intuitively decided to encourage them to include in the brainstorming not just verbal descriptions of what they knew about spiders but also drawings of what they knew. I asked each child to take out a piece of paper and draw what a spider looked like and where it lived. The results were remarkable. All at once the children began to think about their knowledge. They looked at each other's drawings, which were quite different. Then they began to ask questions of each other: What does a spider look like? Does it have more than one body section? How big are they? What does a web look like? I'll never forget the web one student drew that looked like a swirling tornado or mass of scrambled spaghetti. It was the neat web that most students drew, but it did stimulate thinking and discussion. Later we found out that some spiders do create masses of tangled threads, and from this we get the term cobweb. This child was not so far off in his drawing as we had assumed!

This and other contrasts in drawings provided the stimulus for the students to engage in a heated discussion, and it set a clear purpose for reading. Rather than activating language about spiders, children were creating fuller images of the arachnid and its home. As a teacher I learned a great deal from this simple addition to my brainstorming activity.

Since then, I have frequently used drawing as a way to activate young students' prior knowledge as part of K-W-L. I have come to appreciate the value of including both verbal and visual prereading activation. When teachers are preparing children to read about concrete topics, this activity will help the students to clarify their real level of knowledge.

Teaching Idea: Visualization in Preview Science Labs
Content Area: Science; adaptable to All
Level: High School; adaptable to Intermediate and Middle School

When I walked into a chemistry lab one day, I saw Larry Perez's high school students at tables of four with large sheets of paper, colored markers, and the lab guide directions before them. Larry had been reflecting on how he might use various strategies in his own teaching of science. He liked the idea of visualization and realized that he is a visual learner himself. Therefore, he decided to use visualization to supplement the program materials and to make the content more comprehensible.

Larry explained that prior to the actual chemistry labs, students create a visual map of what they will be doing in the lab based on reading the manual. He pointed out that the lab manual used in the high school includes directions without a single illustration (see Figure 4-3). He began to realize how little visual support the chemistry lab manual provided and decided to use visualization as a prereading activity. He explained that by having students first read through the steps and then draw the full lab, their lab experiences were more successful (see Figure 4-3).

Figure 4-3. Chemistry Preview Lab Illustrations

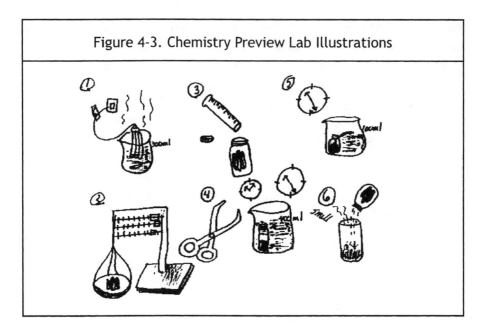

I watched his students work in teams to create drawings of the steps in breaking down cinnamaldehyde on their butcher paper. Periodically, a student would rush to a lab drawer and retrieve a piece of equipment in order to draw it more accurately. It was fascinating to see these students totally engrossed in preparing for their labs, and doing so in a totally new way. Each group represented the lab in a somewhat different way, yet all were reading and rereading, visualizing what they would soon be doing, and anticipating both the process and the chemical changes that would occur through their actions. Creating a visual model of the lab is helping these students to become more active, engaged learners.

During-Reading: Engagement With A Text

Teaching Idea: Sketching and Writing
Content Areas: Humanities
Level: High School; adaptable to Middle School

Charles Kuner, teaching a ninth-grade humanities course to students who were low-level readers and English language learners, combined sketching with writing as a strategy to help students read a challenging text, *Auto-*

biography of Frederick Douglass. After each chapter, the students recorded their reactions on index cards. On one side they drew their central image of the chapter, and on the other side two prompts guided their writing: "What did you think was most important?" (paralleling the drawing) and "How did that make you feel?" With a class of English language learners, the combination of drawing and writing permitted the students to express their ideas through images and then to use that stimulation of thought to create a written elaboration of their drawings.

The levels at which some students identified with the issues in the book were revealing. In response to the description by Douglass of his brutal treatment by the slavemaster, one student wrote. "This is when Frederick decided to stand up and be a man. He wouldn't take Covey's treatment any more." In response to the prompt about feeling, the student continued, "I know how he feels. When I was 4 years old I had to go live with my grandparents—my mom couldn't afford to take care of all of us any more. It hurt a lot—even when she took me back 3 years later. You have to find your own sense of identity and stand up for it."

Teaching Idea: Reading and Drawing
Content Areas: All
Levels: Intermediate, Middle, High School

Students at all levels and in all content areas can draw a logo or an image to represent the key idea in a paragraph of text. This variant on active engagement can be illustrated by using a short newspaper article. One simple way that elementary teachers have devised to keep imaging in students' minds is to have them create bookmarks, with four squares on each one. As they read, the students noted the page number and drew a simple picture of what came to their minds while engaged with that segment of text.

A secondary teacher, Colleen Murray, decided to use the basic mind mapping idea. She first instructed students in the ways they could represent ideas graphically. After some practice, students used logos to represent their reading of a simple news article about a court case in Chicago. Finally, they turned to their textbooks and worked as partners reading paragraph by paragraph and creating visuals of the key ideas together. With lots of discussion the partner teams finally focused on a single image or set of images to represent each paragraph.

Colleen has used this paired reading and drawing activity several times, finding it to be a great way to focus students' attention and deepen their thinking. She has noticed that some students turn to other resources, especially the Internet, to find images for ideas they are studying, and this has certainly enhanced their attention to print and images in texts. Some of her less engaged students are now finding a new role in the class as illustrators and gaining new respect from their classmates. Some are also finding that they want to do their own mapping rather than work in a partnership. She sees this as positive, since it means that the students are adapting to their own preferred styles of learning.

After Reading: Extending Students' Thinking

Teaching Idea: Illustrating Scientific Processes
Content Area: Science
Level: Intermediate

In an ecology class in which half the students were special education inclusion members, Karen Boran decided to have students not only describe the scientific processes being discussed but also draw them. She gave the class the choice of illustrating the process of photosynthesis or respiration (see Figure 4-4). Her guidance was quite clear, and the students responded with more engagement than usual. They seemed to like the challenge of drawing. Each student drew four frames illustrating the process chosen. Beneath the drawings the students wrote the formula or process step they had illustrated. The writing followed the drawing and helped many students to consolidate what they were learning.

Karen has continued to work with drawing with this group and has extended the visual component to the vocabulary cards that students create for key terms. On one side of an index card they write the term and illustrate it. On the other side they write the definition and elaborate on the meaning as they continue learning. After doing unexpectedly well on a chapter test, one of the least enthusiastic students in the class reported that it was "those dumb baseball cards" that did it. Because he had been curious about what his friends had drawn, he spent more time than usual looking at the topic, going through his friends' cards and his own.

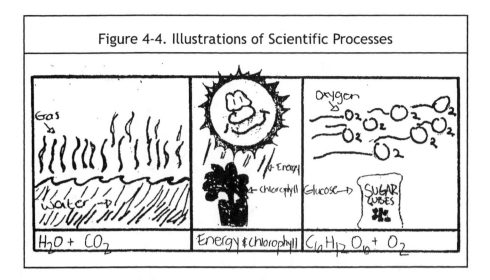

Figure 4-4. Illustrations of Scientific Processes

Teaching Idea: Making Diagrams
Content Area: Science
Level: Intermediate

This is also an intermediate-level activity. A teaching team took seriously the desire to develop the students' ability to read diagrams and charts. Following the examples provided by Moline (1997), the team members decided to incorporate more visual representation in the unit they were doing on insects. Because they were also working with a drama teacher, they decided to see if the students could work in small groups and use their bodies to create specific insects – a dragonfly, a butterfly, and a dung beetle. Once the group members had worked out the use of their own bodies to create the body parts, they formed themselves into the insect. What fun and what confusion, until the four or five students finally came together without totally convulsing. (For more information about drama in content areas, see chapter 5.) After this body space challenge, the teachers asked the students to draw a diagram of their creations. They were encouraged to create diagrams from more than one vantage point—from above and from a side view. As a result of this challenge, the students tended to look more carefully at diagrams and to respect the work that goes into creating good diagrams, the teachers report (see Figure 4-5).

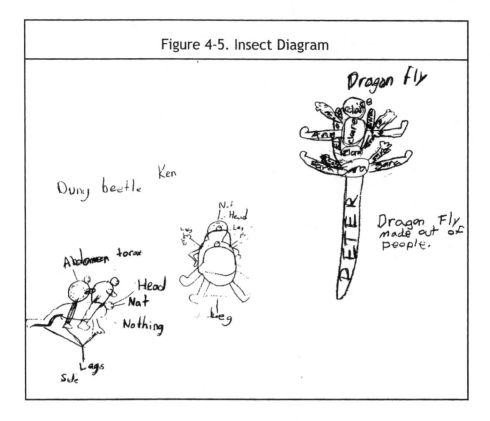

Figure 4-5. Insect Diagram

Teaching Idea: Creating Books
Content Area: Science
Levels: Intermediate, Middle, High School

Another science method is demonstrated by a teacher who showed us small books that his students constructed to illustrate biological processes. He had learned the simple strategy in a writing workshop. Students created the small 12-page books by cutting letter-size paper in half. Each page became the frame to illustrate one part of the process. The teacher found that by using this "summarization" activity, his students seem much more attentive to the content, and they return to the text frequently as they try to create their illustrations of the body processes. Previously he had experienced difficulty motivating students to take any interest in biology, despite its natural connection to their own lives. The simple book project gave them something even more tangible and concrete to work on and create. The students also spent a great deal of time enjoying each other's books, so the benefit of review was practiced without any nudging from the teacher. I too learned much from reading the pictures in the book illustrating the digestive system. This framework is ideal for the study of all parts of the body system. (For more information about student-created books in content areas, see chapter 3.)

Large-Scale Visualization Projects

While visualization is frequently used with individuals and small groups, it is also beneficial when used at the whole-class or whole-school level. The following examples delineate two such large-scale visualization projects.

Teaching Idea: Gallery Images
Content Areas: All
Levels: Middle School

In 1999 the U.S. Postal Service conducted a competition to find the symbols that best represent each decade of the 20th century. From an initial set of ideas respondents selected two to four images that best represent each decade. For the 1960s, as an example, Martin Luther King and the dove are the images used on the commemorative stamps. A middle school social studies teacher has adopted a similar activity as a culmination of the study of this century. Kathleen McKinna asked her students to contribute images that they thought were most illustrative of each decade after they wrote individual research papers. The process began with students thinking of three to five images to express their own identity. The hall space above the lockers then became a gallery of images, with each decade receiving its own section of space. A computer, a cellular telephone, and a rocket represented the 1990s. This process of thinking of illustrative images is an interesting and challenging one.

Teaching Idea: Murals
Content Areas: All
Level: High School

At Steinmetz High School in Chicago, the art teacher and world history teacher teamed up to create a large-scale mural of the history of the world. They designed the space in a long corridor to show world history from prehistory through the 20th century. Each 6-foot panel illustrated a long period of time—the first panels a thousand years each from 3000 B.C. to 1000 A.D. From there the mural proceeds by 100-year intervals up to the present. Planning and creating this mural was an enormous effort on the part of students and teachers. The results are outstanding and engage viewers regularly as they try to connect the visual images with the events they represent.

Although the last two projects are larger in scale, they represent the variety of ways that teachers and students can use visual images to deepen their thinking about whatever content they are studying. Mathematics has always used a symbol system to represent ideas. Other academic areas have not relied as heavily on other than verbal forms of communication, but our society is changing. The predominance of the written word is being augmented with an onslaught of visual images and visual forms of communication. Therefore, the more we can do to help students utilize the innate capacity we have to learn and store information that comes visually, the more we can enhance learning and also prepare students for the 21st centry. Humans have thought in images since our earliest records, cave drawings found in sites around the world. Computer and advertising experts have expanded our awareness of how powerful images are. Using visualization in the content areas reenergizes participants and enhances the teaching and learning process.

Concluding Thoughts

This chapter has provided a background for using visualization in the content areas and has shared several teachers' uses of visualization in various grade levels across the curriculum. From these examples, perhaps you can find some new ways to stimulate students' imagery in your own classrooms. Not all students find visualizing helpful in their learning. However, there are many students who respond very positively to opportunities to conceive ideas in new ways. All students should be able to create images and to combine text with visual representations. These strategies also provide new opportunities for communication. The sharing that is possible when concrete images are placed before groups of students is very worthwhile. New students enter the discussion, and more students have access to the flow of ideas. Visualization activities provide new avenues for learning and the social construction of meaning.

References

Bellanca, J. (1992). *The cooperative Think Tank II: Graphic organizers to teach thinking in the cooperative classroom.* Arlington Heights, IL: IRA Skylight.

Clarke, J., Raths, J., & Gilbert, G. L. (1989). Inductive towers: Letting students see how they think. *Journal of Reading, 30* (2), 86–95.

Durrell, D., & Catterson, J. H. (1980). *Durrell analysis of reading difficulty* (3rd ed.). New York: New York: Psychological Corporation.

Gambrell, L., & Bales, R. (1986). Mental imagery and the comprehension-monitoring performance of fourth- and fifth-grade poor readers. *Reading Research Quarterly, 21* (4), 454–464.

Hyerle, D. (1996). *Visual tools for constructing knowledge.* Alexandria, VA: Association for Supervision and Curriculum Development.

Long, S. A., Winograd, P. N., & Bridge, C. A. (1989). The effects of reader and text characteristics on reports of imagery during and after reading. *Reading Research Quarterly, 24*, 353–372.

Moline, S. (1995). *I see what you mean: Children at work with visual information.* York, ME: Steinhouse.

Murgulies, N. (1991) *Mapping inner space: Learning and teaching mind mapping.* Tucson, AZ: Zephyr Press.

Ogle, D. (1986). K-W-L: A teaching model that develops active reading of expository text. *The Reading Teacher, 39*, 564–570.

Pressley, M., Johnson, C. J., Symons, S., McGodrick, J. A., & Kurita, J. A. (1989) Strategies that improve children's memory and comprehension of text. *Elementary School Journal, 89* (1), 3–32.

Sadowski, M., Paivio, A., & Goetz, E. T. (1991). A critique of schema theory in reading and a dual coding alternative. *Reading Research Quarterly, 26,* 463–484.

Short, K. G., Harste, J. C., & Burke, C. (1996). Sketch to stretch, sketch me a story, interwoven texts and song maps. In *Creating classrooms for authors and inquirers* (pp. 528–535). Portsmouth, NH: Heinemann.

Steinbeck, J. (1945). *The red pony.* New York: Viking Press.

Sylwester, R. (1990). Expanding the range, dividing the task: Educating the human brain in an electronic society. *Educational Leadership, 48* (2), 71–78.

Vaughn, J. L., & Estes, T. H. (1986). *Reading and reasoning beyond the primary grades.* Boston: Allyn & Bacon.

Wycoff, J. (1991). *Mindmapping.* New York: Berkley Books.

Chapter 5

Active Learning:
Dramatic Play in the
Content Areas

MaryEllen Vogt

The school day had begun. The door to the classroom was flung open and in ran 28 students in grades 4–8, ready for another morning of enrichment summer school. Expecting to find their usual chairs and tables, they found an empty room. Not a chair or table was in sight. As the students went to put their sack lunches into their "cubbies," they found strips of masking tape forming a large X over the partitioned boxes, blocking their entry. A large "for rent" sign hung from the front of the boxes, and upon seeing this my students looked at me for answers.

With feigned seriousness, I put a crown on my head and declared myself "Queen of the Classroom." I then directed the students to line up against the wall, handed them each $50 in Monopoly money, and told them that if they wished to put their lunches away, they would have to pay me a $5 tax. Their chairs and tables had a $10 tax attached to each, and without paying the tax they would have to stand or sit on the floor. Their bathroom and drinking fountain privileges were also taxed, as were all pencils, paper, and other supplies.

After many questions, some whining, and considerable consternation, the students took action. One group obediently paid the taxes and stored their lunches, retrieved their tables and chairs, and settled in comfortably for the activities of the day. Another group, however, became active resisters, declaring that they would not pay the taxes. One or two students broke away and began secretly searching for the missing tables and chairs, while other group members kept me, the Queen, occupied in conversation.

In one group of five students, two offered to store the lunches of the other three, thus avoiding $15 in taxes. They paid taxes on two pencils and two sheets of paper, and then broke the pencils and tore the paper to accommodate those without the materials. While another group sat on the floor passively resisting, pooling their money and trying to decide what to do, the last group plotted revolution, and before long they had determined a plan to overthrow the Queendom.

Thus began our day's lesson on the Stamp Act, one in a unit of study about the American Revolution. After our simulation was discontinued and the tables and chairs were restored, the students eagerly compared their actions and decisions to those of the colonists who resisted England's taxation. They discussed their own feelings of frustration, helplessness, and outrage and identified to a degree with the colonists' actions that preceded the Boston Tea Party.

Background

In the above dramatic simulation, students constructed personal understandings about a historic event that occurred more than 2 centuries ago. They were able to make relevant connections between what they experienced and how the colonists may have felt when the king of England imposed the Stamp Act. This type of dramatic play, which encourages students to reflect on the complexities of the world from a personal vantage point, promotes understanding and the construction of knowledge.

Within a constructivist perspective, "teachers invite students to search for understanding, appreciate uncertainty, and inquire responsibly" (Brooks & Brooks, 1993, p. 6). These teaching practices help students to internalize and shape new information, enabling them to make connections between what they know and what they are learning (Keene & Zimmerman, 1998; Wagner & Barnett, 1998). Understandings are further expanded through a process identified as transmediation (Short, Harste, & Burke, 1996; Hoyt, 1992). During this process, students transfer information and knowledge from one communication system to another.

For example, in the preceding dramatic simulation, students transferred and reshaped their learning about taxation from a previously read text chapter. After the simulation, students produced a pamphlet complete with political cartoons advocating that colonists resist the Stamp Act, thus providing transfer to yet another communication system.

It is the purpose of this chapter to encourage drama activities such as the simulation described above in order to facilitate this transfer between communication systems and to promote what Spolin (1986) calls *transformations*. She describes these as environments that arise spontaneously out of thin air. Impossible to capture fully in words, transformations seem to arise out of heightened physical movement and of exchange of this moving energy between players. Change occurs not once but over and over again. Transformations are theater magic and an intrinsic part of most theater games. (p. 4)

The drama activities included here encourage this kind of change in students' thinking, and because they are highly motivating, they promote joyful experiences with reading and learning about content subjects. The term *ludic reading*, from the Latin *ludo*, meaning "I play," has been associated with reading for pleasure, that "which is engaged in for its own sake" (Nell, 1994, p. 42). Generally, this term refers to the avid reader, but I believe it can also be related to pleasurable learning experiences when reading and dramatic play become intertwined. Reading becomes not only purposeful, but also playful. Students work together to find the perfect story to dramatize, the most compelling way to act out an event they have read about, or the subtle personal qualities of a historical or fictional character to personify.

Dramatic responses to reading also can assist students in organizing and clarifying information as well as personalizing it. An instructional context is created that supports literacy engagement when teachers assist students in making connections between content information and learning strategies, such as searching, interpreting, and composing (Guthrie & McCann, 1997). Engagement is further supported through classroom activities like dramatic play that enhance social and cognitive development. This engagement has been effective in fostering the development of community in urban as well as other classrooms (Wagner & Barnett, 1998).

For students who are acquiring English as a second or multiple language, dramatization engages them in play that can help to relieve the self-consciousness often associated with learning another language. Opportunities to revisit newly learned information through rehearsal provide "the many passes through the material, necessary for acquisition to occur" (Richard-Amato, 1988, p. 182). Language acquisition is further facilitated by multiple interactions among students and through engaging in a variety of learning experiences (Echevarria, Vogt, & Short, 2000). New learning is scaffolded through these experiences and content knowledge is facilitated because all language processes are utilized: reading, writing, listening, and speaking (McMaster, 1998; Vygotsky, 1978).

Finally, drama activities enable students to develop strengths and to foster talents (Wagner & Barnett, 1998). Students who are usually shy and reluctant to speak out during content discussions can put aside their own shy personalities and become a historical figure, an inventor, or simply a tree. Because many classroom drama activities in the content areas exist for the dramatization itself, self-esteem can be nurtured and self-confidence developed without the pressure of performing before a critical audience.

Drama Activities for Content Learning

When I began teaching middle school drama a number of years ago, there were very few books or materials available for teachers of elementary, middle, or high school students. What did exist were collections of improvisations and one-act plays to be performed in class. Today, however, there are a number of resources available that include not only readers' theater scripts and original plays (see Marx, 1997), but also drama games and activities that can be used in any classroom and for students of all ages (see Spolin, 1986).

The types of dramatic play activities included in this chapter require no sets, costumes, or scripts other than stories or informational text. Earlier I referred to "dramatic play"; I distinguish this from "performing a play." Dramatic play activities are intended for teachers with little or no training in the theater and for those who may be reluctant to relinquish a large amount of instructional time for play rehearsal and performance. These activities usually involve minimal preparation on the teacher's part other than supplying resources for student research. Unless otherwise noted, the activities included here are most appropriate for students in grades 4–12, although several can be effectively used with children in grades K–3. Activities requiring text may be adapted for different ages and abilities by selecting material with easier reading levels and adjusting the content topics accordingly.

Teaching Idea: Dinner Party (or Tea Party, for younger
**   students)**
Content Areas: Language Arts, Social Studies, Science, Music
Levels: All

The idea for this activity came from a final exam that I had when I was a senior in high school. The class was English Literature and the question was: "Suppose you could have a dinner party for eight British authors or poets that we have studied. Whom would you invite? Why would you select them? What would be the seating order of the guests at your table and why would you place them in that order? What do you think the guests would talk about during dinner? Include specific references to the authors' lives and works in your response." This creative approach to assessing students' knowledge of English literature served me later as a springboard for dramatic play.

The purpose of the Dinner Party is for students to act out the above questions by assuming personas, such as characters in novels or short stories, authors or poets, historical figures, scientists, the artists, politicians, or military leaders. For example, Alexander the Great might be engaged in conversation with Abbie Hoffman, while General George Patton argues the finer points of military strategy with Jane Fonda. Although scripts can be written, improvisation is more interesting and fun, but its success depends on the age of the students and their content knowledge. During each dinner party, specific content must be included, and the characters must respond to each other as realistically and accurately as possible. It is important to stress that knowledge of the figures' lives, accomplishments, flaws, and works must be used to inform the performance.

Young students can have a tea party and include their favorite characters from stories or nursery rhymes. When you model how a character might act at a tea party prior to students deciding on their "guests," they are more likely to understand the purpose of the activity.

Teaching Idea: Frozen Moment (Schultz, 1998)
Content Areas: Language Arts, Social Studies, Science
Levels: All

For this drama play activity, begin by reading a piece of literature connected to content, such as Allen Say's *Grandfather's Journey,* a beautifully written and illustrated picture book about a Chinese immigrant family. After reading the story, distribute to each group (four or five students) a piece of paper that has a three- or four-sentence scene taken from the story. For example, one scene in the book tells of the grandfather's harrowing journey to America aboard ship, while another describes the grandson's later visit to his homeland in China. Each group takes a few minutes to plan a re-creation of the scene in pantomime. However, the scene must be delivered with absolutely no movement, similar to a tableau, and each person in the group must take a role. The roles may be characters, such as the grandfather or the son, or stage props, such as a cherry tree, the ship, or waves. After sufficient time to practice, students create their "frozen moments" while the rest of the class members close their eyes. When ready, class members view the scene and attempt to identify the particular scene that is being portrayed.

After the students have viewed the scene for a few minutes, the teacher joins the performers and touches one of the actors, who then "comes to life." In character, this student describes what he or she is thinking or feeling at that moment. For example, the ship crossing the ocean might say, "I am so tired. I've been to sea now for weeks and I've been tossed about by huge waves and fierce storms. I must stay afloat and save my passengers."

You end the soliloquy by again tapping the student, who then returns to the fixed, still position. Other players in the scene may be tapped until class members have correctly identified the scene that is being performed.

It's important to let several cast members come to life during the re-creation, even if the rest of the students think they can identify the scene. Much of the fun in this activity is watching the "frozen moment" come to life, and this part of the process should not be rushed.

Teaching Idea: Great Performances
Content Areas: All
Levels: Intermediate, Middle, High School

In this activity, students act out significant events either in pantomime or through improvisation, such as Alexander Graham Bell's first use of a telephone, Henry Ford's realization that automation could increase the production of Model Ts, or Neil Armstrong's first steps on the moon. Depending on the content and grade level, students select either an event that is very well known or one that is interesting and important but not as famous. In pairs, students conduct research on their selected topic, learning as much as possible about the specific sequence of events leading up to the "great performance."

With an activity such as this, I have found that it is easier to start students with pantomime, then move to improvisation with speaking, then move on to writing and performing brief scripts. Students, including English language learners, who are shy about speaking in front of peers can effectively and creatively pantomime events and situations. Through pantomime students learn how to communicate with facial expressions, body language and position, and movement.

Teaching Idea: You Are There
Content Areas: Social Studies, Language Arts
Levels: Intermediate, Middle, High School

This activity is based upon the classic television program *You Are There*, hosted by Edward R. Murrow, in which characters involved in actual historical events were interviewed about their involvement and participation in the event. The re-creations were historically accurate, and the historical figures came alive for viewers.

In preparation for You Are There, groups of students conduct research on the event they will be portraying. Once they have completed their research, they select a character who played a crucial role in the event. The students in this research group then write interview questions and responses that an interviewer will use during the dramatic reenactment.

For example, students could interview Sacajawea, the Shoshone guide and interpreter who accompanied Lewis and Clark on their expedition, or they might interview the Wright brothers upon their arrival at Kitty Hawk, North Carolina. Both the interviewer and the interviewee are apprised of all questions and responses prior to the performance.

You may wish to add another dimension to this activity, especially if you are working with older high school students. Audience members can direct unrehearsed questions to the central character. Obviously, all students, including the interviewee, must have a thorough knowledge of the event for this to be a successful dramatic activity.

Teaching Idea: Value Line (Temple, 1998)
Content Areas: All
Levels: All

This activity was originally designed to help students clarify their thinking and beliefs (i.e., their values) about difficult topics. It is also an effective way to involve all students in taking and defending a position based upon how a character in literature or a historical figure would respond to a given question. Value Line requires students to take a stand on a controversial subject. For example, in a Local Government class, high school students studied a piece of pending legislation intended to establish a parent's right to know over a teenager's right to privacy. After reading and discussing the legislation, two students "in character" served as advocates for each position, urging class members to follow and take one of the advocated positions (parents' rights/students' rights). The mock debate between the two opposing positions (the ends of the Value Line) incorporated clear arguments and specific support for the respective viewpoints.

When the advocates were finished arguing their positions, the other students took a position on the spectrum, with one end of the line representing the parents' right to know and the other end of the line representing the students' privacy rights. Before they assumed their places on the line, the students negotiated with those around them in order to determine where they belonged. While doing so, the students were also attempting to persuade other class members to move toward one position or the other. In the end, each class member had to articulate why he or she had chosen a particular spot and how people standing to the left or the right held different perspectives on the topic.

Value Line can become another type of dramatic activity when students assume an identity other than their own. Historical figures or literary characters must take a stand on a line about a topic or event relevant to the characters involved. All students are eventually in character as they take a stand, defend their positions, and try to persuade other characters to move toward one end or the other, just as with the regular value line. For example, in the classic short story "The Lottery" by Shirley Jackson, the ends of the line would represent "yes" or "no" positions in answer to the question "Should the town's annual lottery continue?" Students would assume the role of the townspeople arguing for one position or the other until everyone had taken a stand.

Young students can be involved in this same type of activity using stories, decisions characters must make, and choices. With young students, you can coach with questions such as, "What do you think you would do? What do you think Ramona should do?" Students can begin to see how their own choices might be similar to or different from those of their favorite characters in picture books.

Teaching Idea: Hot Seat
Content Areas: Language Arts, Social Studies, Science
Levels: Intermediate, Middle , High School

This activity provides students with expertise in a particular topic, period of history, character, or event. Unlike You Are There, a re-creation of the event is not enacted; however, people involved in the incident, event, or time period are interviewed about their involvement. Prior to the drama activity, students research the topic or event, learning as much as they can until they feel confident enough to take the hot seat. Class members have the opportunity to put the character on the hot seat, grilling him or her through carefully prepared questions. The person on the hot seat must respond in character but can have coaching from fellow group members if necessary. Those who don't wish to take the hot seat can provide support and coaching from the sidelines while still developing expertise in the content.

Teaching Ideas: Sociodrama (Richard-Amato, 1988)
Content Areas: Language Arts, Social Studies, Science, Health
Levels: Intermediate, Middle, High School

In Sociodrama, students act out solutions to real problems, defining their roles and determining their own solutions and courses of actions. Once a problem is introduced, students choose a role based upon their special interests or perspectives. Prior to the enactment, they read a story or an article related to the conflict in order to provide background and build interest. At the point of climax, the dilemma is discussed, students are selected to play particular roles, and the audience listens as the actors improvise the rest of the story or events in the article, including alternative ways of handling the conflict or dilemma. Class members can offer advice and suggestions, and the drama may be replayed with an alternate solution. Examining a variety of possible solutions is an expected outcome of this activity.

For example, in the intermediate level book *Be Good to Eddie Lee* by V. Fleming (1993), the protagonist is a young girl who lives near Eddie Lee, a boy with Down syndrome. Other neighborhood students tease him and urge her not to play with him, and she is faced with the dilemma of leaving him or being kind. Students could approach this dilemma from varied perspectives, based upon their own experiences.

It's important to coach younger students with questions about the characters they'll play, such as "How old are you?" "What is your relationship to other characters?" "How do you feel about this problem?" The better the students know their characters and their roles, the better their improvisations will be.

Teaching Idea: Meeting of the Minds (Richard-Amato, 1998)
Content Areas: Language Arts, Social Studies
Levels: Intermediate, Middle School, High School

This activity is also patterned after an old television show, *Meeting of the Minds* with Steve Allen. Here students take on the role of characters that have distinctly different viewpoints about a topic. These characters, from literature or history, are interviewed by a "host," another student who directs questions to them with the intent of pitting them against each other in a debate about a particular topic. An interesting variation is an interview between a historical figure and a modern celebrity or expert with considerable knowledge of the same topic.

For example, in a World History class studying the 16th century and Henry VIII, students engaged in a discussion of the role of women. After some additional reading and research, students participated in meeting of the minds. One student played the monarch while another assumed the role of Queen Anne Boleyn, the wife Henry VIII executed in 1536. A third student served as the host of the show, questioning the king and queen about women's rights—but all within the context of England in the early 1500s. Into the conversation came a fourth student assuming the persona of Bella Abzug, who was later joined by students acting the roles of Eleanor Roosevelt and attorney Gloria Allred. Together the women confronted Henry VIII about not only his beliefs but also his methods for eliminating those who fell into his disfavor. The team enacting this meeting of the minds interview and debate researched the role of women during the 1500s, the 1930s, the 1970s, and the 1990s, as well as the contributions of each of the celebrity women, before writing the host's questions.

Teaching Idea: Role-Playing
Content Areas: All Sheltered Instruction Content Areas
  (those designed particularly for English language learners'
  support of content learning)
Levels: All

I am distinguishing Role-Playing from some of the other activities in this chapter because here the teacher is directly involved in the scenarios. For this dramatic play, your role is to model, prompt, or extend the conversation in order to provide target language (L2) practice. Students of mixed abilities and language proficiencies participate together, with some needing more assistance than others. The role-playing activities promote language development while helping to develop confidence in using the new language. The following transcript is from a role-playing episode with a teacher and two English language learners (Richard-Amato, 1988, p. 139). The scene is a grocery store in the produce department. The two students have play money, and have had previous experience counting it.

Teacher: (*playing the role of the clerk*): Strawberries? For you, Pedro? (*She holds up a basket of them.*)

Pedro: aaa . . . Straw . . .

Teacher: Strawberries? Do you want strawberries?

Pedro: . . . Strawberries . . . (*nods his head*)

Teacher (*offering the basket to him*): Do you want to buy the strawberries? Yes? (*points to some play money in the box which serves as a cash register*)

Pedro: Yes . . . buy.

Teacher: One dollar. Give me one dollar. (*Pedro takes some play money from his pocket but looks puzzled.*) One dollar (*points to dollar bill in his hand*).

Pedro: One dollar (*gives teacher the dollar bill*).

Teacher: Thank you (*takes the money and gives him the basket*).

Pedro: Thank you.

Teacher (*turning to next customer*): Do you want some strawberries, Nor?

Nor: I want oranges.

Teacher: Oranges, huh? (*moves to oranges*). I've got juicy ones for you.

Nor: Juicy?

Teacher: Yes, juicy. Lots of sweet juice (*squeezes one to show its softness*).

Nor: Oh, yes. Juice.

Teacher: They cost $1.50 a bag. Do you want a bag?

Nor: Yes, I'll take bag (*gives the teacher the money and takes the oranges*).

Note how the teacher adjusted the input according to each student's language development, with Pedro hearing a repetition of key words and seeing the teacher point to the objects as she referred to them. With practice, students will be able to internalize language structures through these kinds of interactions. Role-playing can therefore provide necessary scaffolded support for students who are acquiring proficiency in English (Echevarria, et al., 2000).

Teaching Idea: Puppetry
Content Areas: All Sheltered Instruction Content Areas (i.e., those
    designed particularly for English language learners'
    support of content learning)
Levels: All

Puppetry and simple storytelling can also be helpful for English language learners while engaging the students in low-risk drama play. You or a student with English proficiency can read a story, a poem, or an article out loud while students physically perform the actions or use puppets to express what is occurring in the text. English language learners should be encouraged to use the target language (L2) as much as possible and to become participating members in the drama activities. Math concepts such as counting, telling time, and measuring can be reinforced through puppetry, as can "news reports" of scientific inventions or historical events. Although the puppets can be quite elaborate, they can also be simply made out of household materials, and all students can be involved in making the puppets, stages, and scenery.

Teaching Ideas: Alternate Endings
Content Areas: All
Levels: All

How many times have you read a newspaper article or seen a newscast and wondered, "What if such-and-such had happened? How would this event have turned out?" Alternate Endings is a great way to involve students of all levels and subject areas in evaluating causal relationships, determining sequence, and predicting how things might have occurred given a different set of circumstances. Although historical events can be dramatized with alternate endings, I also enjoy using the daily newspaper or weekly news magazine for this activity. Alternate Endings is applicable to a variety of content areas because newspaper articles cover so many different topics.

Select a news item that has a dramatic conclusion, one obviously appropriate for school-age students. Make copies of the article but omit the ending. In groups, students read the article, develop a quick improvisation of the events detailed in the article, and create their own ending, which they briefly rehearse and perform for other class members. After all groups have performed their versions of the alternate endings, provide the real ending and discuss how logical (or illogical) some of the manufactured endings were. Be careful to omit the headline if it gives away the ending of the article.

Teaching Idea: Living Newspaper Theater
(Morrison & Chilcoat, 1998)
Content Areas: Social Studies, Government, Economics, Sociology
Levels: Middle School, High School

The Living Newspaper Theater, a government-subsidized presentation of major current issues in a dramatic forum, was born in the 1930s. Its purpose was to educate the citizenry about socioeconomic problems of the times through drama. This same type of structure can be used in middle school or high school social studies, government, economics, and sociology classes today.

First, students working in groups do research on historical topics of interest, with a focus on sociological, economic, and political issues and problems such as child labor laws, the role of women in the workforce, or economic and educational disparity. Students then create a script for a 15 to 20-minute class play involving characters living during that time period. After rehearsal, the groups present their plays for each other in order to involve class members in discussion about the problem and solutions.

The focus of the Living Newspaper Theater is that "authenticity is a guiding principle" (p. 107). Research using text material with different viewpoints and including accurate facts such as dates and real people is integral to the success of the project. The students' scripts should include an explanation of the problem (e.g., child labor in factories at the turn of the century), development of the problem (e.g., the government's role in protecting child laborers), and a solution to the problem (e.g., implementing legislation forbidding child labor despite protests from manufacturers). The Living Newspaper Theater presents the multiple challenges of researching, analyzing, designing, and presenting a dramatization of historical events, experiences, and lives. A desired outcome of this dramatic activity is that students "consider how their insights . . . might inform their current experiences" (p. 114).

Teaching Idea: Truth or Consequences
Content Areas: Language Arts, Social Studies
Levels: Intermediate, Middle, High School

This drama game is an offshoot of Jigsaw, a cooperative learning activity where students become experts about an assigned topic. In Jigsaw, students form heterogeneous "expert groups" as a few members of the cooperative learning groups come together to form a new group. For example, in one classroom's cooperative learning groups, the students are studying dinosaurs. A new group is formed with one or two students from each cooperative learning group. This new group's job is to research a particular topic about dinosaurs, such as types of dinosaurs, possible causes of extinction, or what dinosaurs ate and how they lived. After researching their topics, the expert group members return to their home groups and share what they have learned with their peers.

In Truth or Consequences, based loosely on the television game show of the same name, the expert-group members don't return to their home groups but they prepare questions and answers about the topic they have researched. When they are ready, the teams gather together with one team sitting in front of the class. The class members use the list of prepared questions to quiz the experts. The expert-group members have the option of telling the truth or making up an answer that is incorrect. Class members must then decide whether the answer is correct or incorrect. If the experts stump the class, they receive points; if the class members correctly identify an answer as correct or incorrect, they receive the points. Teams alternate as experts and class members until everyone has participated.

After the game, the expert group members all return to their "home groups" and share the correct and appropriate information with their peers. This is especially important so that the disinformation given during truth and consequences does not become fixed in the students' minds. If you teach younger children, you may wish to closely monitor the nature of the lies that are told and make sure that everyone understands that they are falsehoods.

Teaching Idea: The Rest of the Story (see chapter 3)
Content Areas: All
Levels: All

Paul Harvey, the well-known radio commentator, frequently concludes a segment of his broadcast about a famous person with the line, "And now you've heard the rest of the story." This phrase can also be the punchline for a dramatic reenactment after students research the lives of well-known historical or contemporary people as described in chapter 3. When they have completed their research, they develop a story-script of an unusual event in the person's life and perform it for their peers. The audience is not told the person's name, so they have to use clues from the performance to try to determine who is depicted in the scenario. It's important to help students include enough information so that substantial clues about the person's identify are infused in the dramatization. At the conclusion, class members are asked to identify the person, and then cast members deliver the now-famous Paul Harvey line.

For example, a middle school language arts class studied a variety of American authors, including Wilson Rawls, who wrote *Where the Red Fern Grows*. Rawls grew up in Oklahoma, dropped out of school during the Depression when he was only 13, and published this book (his first) when he was in his mid-40s. The first-person story of Billy Colman, an Ozark farmboy, tells of the relationship between a boy and his coondogs. The story is largely autobiographical.

In fact, during his literature presentations Rawls often talked about his several older sisters with whom he walked each day to school. Before they left each morning, their mother would tie all of them loosely together with a rope, with the youngest child, Wilson, the last in the line. She did this because on the way to school the children had to forge a stream and she wanted them all to cross together to safety. However, after all the girls had made it to the shore, Wilson would still be in the middle of the stream, and his sisters would often tease him and threaten to cut him loose from the rest. Therefore, every morning he tried to behave in ways that wouldn't antagonize his older sisters on their way to school. Students enjoy learning of this humorous event, which can easily be dramatized with the conclusion, "And now you've heard the rest of the story!"

Teaching Idea: Trial of the Century
Content Areas: All
Levels: Middle, High School

This activity works well to help students understand the difficulties that great thinkers encounter when they attempt to convince a skeptical public to implement an idea, an invention, or a concept. Nearly all great thinkers have had to "sell" their ideas to others, whether in the field of science, medicine, political science, or the arts. Along the way, many of them have had to defend their beliefs, their careers, and their livelihoods. The events or work in which these scholars, political minds, or inventors engaged frequently led to their "trials" by inquisitors. Although these were not necessarily held in a courtroom setting, the format lends itself to re-creations with questioning, prosecutors (the detractors), defenders (the supporters), and jurors (those sitting in judgment).

Language arts coordinator Lisa Weidman from Rhinelander, Wisconsin, has shared an example of this activity. She told of a group of high school math students who created a mock trial using scripts. The subject of the trial was Pythagoras, the first "pure" mathematician. Because so little is known about his actual work (no writings of his were ever found), he is represented in history as a man of science but also by some as a preacher of mystic doctrines. Born in 530 B.C., he founded a society that was both a religious community and a scientific school; therefore, it inspired jealousy and mistrust. Pythagoras's Society of Croton was eventually attacked by Cylon, and some historians claim that Pythagoras later committed suicide because of the attack. Today we remember Pythagoras particularly for his famous geometry theorem, which was probably known by the Babylonians 1,000 years earlier but was nonetheless proven by Pythagoras.

The Rhinelander High School geometry students created a trial of Pythagoras in which his beliefs and mathematics were challenged and he was forced to defend both his Society and his theorems. In preparation for the mock trial, the high school students investigated multiple sources of information on Pythagoras. They wrote their script as a trial with prosecutor, judge, and jury. Pythagoras served as his own counsel, defending his theorems as well as his secretive society.

This same type of trial ("trial of the century") could be created with other great minds throughout the centuries. Their critics, detractors, supporters, and benefactors could all have a role in the trial. However, the person's contributions (e.g., geometry theorems) should remain the primary focus for the students rather than the individual (e.g., Pythagoras) per se.

Teaching Idea: A Grave Lesson (Mehta, 1998)
Content Areas: All
Levels: Intermediate, Middle, High School

I learned about this activity from an article in the local newspaper. Science students at Arcadia High School in California created a cemetery with nearly 1,000 headstones on the school grounds. The tombstones were the culmination of 5 weeks of student work. In previous years, the teachers, Janel Coats and Laurel Fretz, had assigned term papers on the scientific accomplishments of the past 500 years. This particular year the teachers proposed that students re-create scientists' lives by making birth certificates, journal entries, newspaper articles, and other memorabilia. The students literally assumed the personas of their respective scientists and reported their accomplishments to peers while in character. Some of the epitaphs on the tombstones were quite humorous: "In loving memory of the nuttiest man who ever lived: George Washington Carver," and "He went out with a bang: Alfred B. Nobel." The photo in the newspaper depicted a large area of ground, covered with tombstones, looking very much like a real cemetery. Teacher Janel Coats, commenting on the project, stated, "A lot of the kids, they're so used to just getting facts and putting them on paper. This really stretches them and stretches their creativity."

Teaching Idea: Snapshots of History (Shurtz, 1998)
Content Areas: Language Arts, Social Studies
Levels: Intermediate, Middle, High School

In the middle 1800s, theatrical tableaus were frequently used to celebrate a striking historical scene such as the signing of the Declaration of Independence. Snapshots of History combines theatrical tableaus and imaginative writing about historical events. Begin by describing how to create a tableau, a scene with groups of people who remain silent and motionless in appropriate postures. Either you or the students select a photograph or painting of a historical event that includes a fairly large group of people. Make copies for all participants.

Begin creating the tableau by adding a few students at a time until about half the class is involved. Then repeat with the other half of the class. Explain that they are now going to make a "talking tableau" by adding dialogue that would lead up to the moment represented in the original picture. Rehearse what the figures might have been talking about prior to the scene being captured in the photo or painting. Upon the cue "Begin," the scene comes alive until you say, "Freeze." At this point, the scene becomes the tableau. Practice the same process with the other half of the class until everyone understands the process.

Now, divide the entire class into three or four groups. Let each group select a historical painting or photograph to depict. Each class member chooses one person in the picture to represent, then writes a first-person narrative from the perspective of that individual. These are shared with other group members, prior to creating their tableaus (For more information about First Person Experiences, see chapter 3). They rehearse both their "frozen" and "talking" tableaus prior to presenting the event for class members.

Your class may be interested in knowing that each year in Laguna Beach, California, great well-known masterpieces of art are depicted as frozen tableaus. "The Pageant of the Masters" is considered to be one of the most popular cultural events of the year.

Concluding Thoughts

Most of the activities described in this chapter have included examples from history, current events, and literature, but, as suggested in A Grave Lesson and Trials of the Century, we can also bring dramatic play into science and math by focusing on famous scientists and mathematicians. A study of their lives yields far more information than does a limited view of their well-known discoveries. For example, Galileo was imprisoned during the Inquisition because of his belief that the sun was at the center of the universe. Archimedes, the Greek mathematician, engineer, and physicist, also discovered the principle of buoyancy. Today, the brilliant physicist and astronomer Stephen Hawkings is a quadraplegic who has overcome more challenges than most of us can imagine as he explores our universe. Jacques Cousteau shared his knowledge of ocean life with those of us who might never see it for ourselves. The vivid tapestries of these lives provide enriching opportunities for students to engage in many forms of dramatic play.

Through dramatization of the lives of people such as these, the world's great explorations and discoveries become meaningful. Dramatic play enables students of all ages to personally experience the thoughts, motives, conflicts, ambitions, and emotions of other people. Through drama, students have the opportunity to view content knowledge not as a series of abstract concepts but as a deeply personal, relevant experience.

References

Brooks, J. G., & Brooks, M. G. (1993). *The case for constructivist classrooms.* Alexandria, VA: Association for Supervision and Curriculum Development.

Echevarria, J., Vogt, M. E., & Short, D. (2000). *Making content comprehensible for English-language learners: The SIOP model.* Needham Heights, MA: Allyn & Bacon.

Fleming, V. (1993). *Be good to Eddie Lee.* New York: Philomel Books.

Guthrie, J. T., & McCann, A. D. (1997). Characteristics of classrooms that promote motivations and strategies for learning. In J. T. Guthrie & A. Wigfield (Eds.), *Reading engagement: Motivating readers through integrated instruction.* Newark, DE: International Reading Association.

Hoyt, L. (1992). Many ways of knowing: Using drama, oral interactions, and the visual arts to enhance reading comprehension. *Reading Teacher, 45* (8), 580–584.

Keene, E., & Zimmerman, S. (1998). *Mosaic of thought: Teaching comprehension in readers workshop.* Portsmouth, NH: Heinemann.

Marx, P. (1997). *Take a quick bow.* Glenview, IL: Good Year Books.

McMaster, J. C. (1998). "Doing" literature: Using drama to build literacy. *Reading Teacher, 51* (7), 574–584.

Mehta, S. (1998, October 31). Project helps students learn a grave lesson. *Los Angeles Times,* p. 1.

Morrison, T. G., & Chilcoat, G. W. (1998). The "Living Newspaper Theatre" in the language arts classroom. *Journal of Adolescent and Adult Literacy, 42* (2), 104–115.

Nell, V. (1994). The insatiable appetite. In E.H. Cramer & M. Castle (Eds.), *Fostering the love of reading: The affective domain in reading education.* Newark, DE: International Reading Association.

Richard-Amato, P. A. (1988). *Making it happen: Interaction in the second language classroom.* New York: Longman.

Say, A. (1993). *Grandfather's journey.* Boston: Houghton Mifflin.

Schultz, A. (1998, May). *Creative reading activities.* Workshop handout, Beach Cities Reading Association, Long Beach, CA.

Short, K., Harste, J., & Burke, C. (1988). *Creating classrooms for authors and inquirers.* Portsmouth, NH: Heinemann.

Shurtz, J. (1998, November). *. . . and YOU are there! Helping your students write about history.* Workshop handout, Drury College Reading Conference, Springfield, MO.

Spolin, V. (1988). *Theater games for the classroom: A teacher's handbook.* Evanston, IL: Northwestern University Press.

Temple, C. (1998). *Reading and writing for critical thinking project workshop handout,* Tallinn, Estonia.

Vygotsky, L. (1978). *Mind in society.* Cambridge, MA: Harvard University Press.

Wagner, B. J., & Barnett, L. A. (1998). *Educational drama and language arts: What research shows.* Portsmouth, NH: Heinemann.

Chapter 6

Music in the
Content Areas

Thomas W. Bean

In Mr. K.'s sophomore World History class, six students are huddled in a circle. Their student desks, normally in neat rows, are now facing each other. They ponder Mr. K.'s handout, which asks them to write a song about the exploration of the Western Hemisphere. Josh, Danny, Brad, Mike, Chris, and Shannon discuss creating a rap based on a Puff Daddy song, "Mo Money, Mo Problems" (Combs, 1997).

Mr. K. has given them a handout with some model verses and tells them that they have the freedom to write in whatever musical genre they choose. As the students brainstorm, some verses start to take shape.

> Come on take a trip on the rocket ship
> The trip won't cost you a dime we're gonna
> Start right here . . . then back it on back
> To the start of America's time.
>
> Got the key . . . got the key . . . to this world's
> Lock explore the globe . . .
> With the good friend the jock.

Each of the groups makes plans to meet over the weekend so they can complete their songs for a Monday performance in class. Students can audiotape the song, videotape it, or perform it live. Other groups are also meeting, brainstorming how they plan to create their musical version of exploration. The bell rings, and time is up.

Mr. K.'s classroom displays countless student projects from the present and past classes. Models of airplanes, castles, and guillotines, as well as other songs, decorate the room. This is a language-rich arena for the study of history. Students take creative risks in this classroom, and they feel a strong sense of voice in their learning. They look forward to being in Mr. K.'s class because he is truly an outstanding educator.

One of the best ways to develop a creative, language-rich classroom is by engaging students in the use of various sign systems to interpret text concepts. This chapter focuses on the use of music, a sign system that captivates students' interest, creativity, and enthusiasm. First I offer a rationale for the use of writing and performing music in content classrooms. Next, I introduce and illustrate the ReWrite music strategy (Bean, 1997) in science, the use of rap music writing in social studies, and additional ways to use music in content classrooms.

You and your students do not have to be musicians to use songwriting in a content classroom. Both ReWrite and rap music have been used effectively in classrooms by teachers and students who share a genuine enthusiasm for creatively reconstructing text ideas and concepts through songs.

Why Use Music in Content Teaching

Very young children naturally use a multitude of sign systems to explore the world around them (Berghoff, 1998). They may use art, music, and drama as natural ways of learning concepts. Unfortunately, as they advance into the middle and secondary grades, the arts take a back seat to more didactic, linear modes of learning that emphasize convergent rather than divergent thinking.

Yet the creativity and problem solving that go into writing a song is highly prized in many careers. For example, in *Educating for the Workplace Through the Arts,* a publication of the Getty Education Institute for the Arts (1996), a number of crucial contributions made by the arts in the classroom and business world are highlighted. In addition to aesthetic contributions, the arts encourage higher order thinking and flexible problem solving. Writing a song about a content area concept requires a tolerance for ambiguity and the ability to work cooperatively with others. Songwriting develops a community of learners in the classroom with a strong feeling of ownership in the song's content. At-risk students and second language learners benefit greatly from this alternative sign system as they explore concepts in science, social studies, and other content areas (Cockburn, 1995). Furthermore, the arts and music help to remove artificial boundaries and discipline subcultures that compartmentalize learning in unproductive ways. Music and songwriting offers yet another way to integrate content area learning (Readence, Bean, & Baldwin, 1998).

In addition, musical intelligence constitutes one of Howard Gardner's seven intelligences (Lazear, 1992). Music can enhance conceptual learning by stimulating the brain. Concentration, memory, and interest thrive when music is made an integral part of the classroom, especially given the often dull, static nature of textbooks.

The language of textbooks can be confining, and music allows students to move beyond linear, informational structures. Adolescents have music as a constant companion, but they are often consumers rather than producers of music. Writing music as a way to explore content area concepts places students in the driver's seat by using the patterns and motifs they know so well from listening to rap, hip-hop, rock, folk, blues, heavy metal, world beat, and the increasingly blurred lines of these musical forms.

Music helps students to make intertextual connections between otherwise obscure content area concepts and the familiar world of songs and lyrics. *Intertextuality* refers to the unique connections that readers make between their current reading and other books, conversations, songs, personal experiences, and memories (Cairney, 1996). When students engage in writing lyrics to explore a concept, they creatively link their world with that of the text. In addition, music helps to develop students' abstract reasoning (Miller & Coen, 1994).

Students' achievement appears to benefit from opportunities to interpret and explore text concepts beyond simply reading and responding through answering questions or writing. Overall, our national assessments show a flat trend in critical thinking. However, on the National Assessment of Educational Progress, students who achieved higher average reading proficiencies had often been asked by their teachers to discuss divergent interpretations of their reading (Campbell, Reese, O'Sullivan, & Dossey, 1996). Music offers a creative form of interpretive performance that easily becomes a forum for critical discussion and increased achievement.

The ReWrite Strategy

About 7 years ago, I began experimenting with the blues as a form for writing about content area concepts. I began listening to the blues and playing blues guitar while growing up in Honolulu. I played rhythm guitar in our high school rock band, the Eldorados, and we played a few blues tunes. By the time I went to college at the University of Hawaii at Manoa, I was listening to blues, writing some songs, playing in a duo at a small Waikiki bar, and sitting in with various groups. The ReWrite strategy described in this section grew out of my passion for the blues, but the steps apply to any style of music, including folk and pop. You can adapt the strategy to fit the musical interests of your students.

When the International Reading Association created *Reading Online*, an electronic journal, the possibility of sharing songs, video clips, links, and other resources became a reality. I wrote a short article demonstrating the ReWrite strategy with fifth graders (Bean, 1997) and later incorporated ReWrite into our content text with a high school science example (Readence et al., 1998). In the next section I offer a high school biology illustration of ReWrite. I am indebted to biology teacher Kyle Kaaa and his students for this particular ReWrite song.

ReWrite involves students in writing musical verses at the prereading and postreading stages of a content lesson (Bean, 1997). To begin, the teacher activates students' background knowledge by engaging them in activities such as an Anticipation-Reaction Guide or a think-pair-share. Then the teacher writes a few verses of the song, deliberately including a few points of misinformation. The students listen to the song verses about the topic that are incorrect or show minimal understanding. For example, fifth graders may think bats are awful, disease-carrying creatures. Following a concentrated study of bats, they "rewrite" a song with verses that reflect this new, more enlightened understanding (Bean, 1997). Some teachers bypass the first part of this and simply go from some guide material to having students write their own song about the concept they are studying. Depending on time constraints, either approach works well, because the main focus is on students creating original verses about a topic.

You can use familiar songs, instrumental music, Karaoke tapes, or a tape that a music teacher makes as an instrumental framework for a song. I tend to use blues songs written in a 12-bar Chicago blues run in the key of E (e.g. Bean, 1997; Readence, et al., 1998). Songs by blues artists like Jimmy Read and John Hammond fit this style and are readily available in compact discs and cassette tapes.

Try not to get too hung up on the background music. Students generally have musical preferences that work fine, and the lyrics are more important than the background music. Although I love the blues, students' musical tastes often lean more toward the mainstream pop that they and their peers hear on the radio.

Teaching Idea: The ReWrite Strategy
Content Areas: Biology; adaptable to All
Levels: High School; adaptable to All

The ReWrite strategy usually takes 2 to 3 days to complete, depending on the time periods you teach in at your school and whether or not you include additional guide material as part of the lesson. For example, I often use a combination of a blues song with misconceptions in the verses along with an Anticipation-Reaction Guide containing accurate and inaccurate statements for students to evaluate and debate.

Day 1

You should start by completing a task analysis of the key concepts that you want students to acquire in a lesson. The example that follows involves high school biology students, spanning various levels of achievement, learning about bacteria. They began with a study guide that defined the key terminology accompanying the reading assignment on the characteristics of monerans in their text, *Biology* (Miller & Levine, 1993).

Introduction to Monerans

Directions: Read the section in chapter 17 assigned to your group. Below is a list of words for your section. Write the definition of the word on your paper. Then use the words to create a verse describing the key characteristics of monerans. Your verse should contain about eight lines, each having five or six syllables. At the end of the period, hand in your definitions and a paper containing your group's verse.

> Group 1. Identifying Monerans (p. 363)
>> bacilli-
>> cocci-
>> spirilla-
> Group 2. Growth and Reproduction (p. 367)
>> binary fission-
>> conjugation-
>> endospore-
> Group 3. Respiration (p. 365)
>> obligate aerobe-
>> obligate anaerobe-
>> facultative anaerobe-
> Group 4. How Monerans Obtain Energy (p. 365)
>> photorophic autotroph-
>> chemotrophic autotroph-
>> phototrophic heterotroph-
>> chemotrophic heterotroph-
> Group 5. Importance of Monerans in the Environment (pp. 369–370)
>> saprophyte-
>> nitrogen fixation-
>> symbiosis-

Based on their text reading and study guide focusing on these key vocabulary definitions, students composed the following song, which they performed during the next class.

Day 2

Bacteria Blues

1. They're *prokaryotic*, they live everywhere
    From the Arctic snow to your mouth and hair
    The *Kingdom Monera* contains bacteria
    And some cause disease but some make us cheese

CHORUS: I got the low down bacteria blues
         And I'm feeling so unhealthy
         I just don't know what to do

2. There are three basic shapes one is *bacilli*
    They are rod shaped the second is *cocci*
    They are spherical third is *spirilla*
    These are spiral shaped
    These are the three shapes

3. *Binary fission* what the heck is that?
    Produces two cells they live in my cat
    Conjugation is a form of reproduction
    Endospores will form bacteria to function

4. *Obligate aerobes* require oxygen
    Obligate anaerobes live without oxygen
    Facultative anaerobes is a bacterium
    That can live with oxygen and can live without it

5. Some are *saprophytes* they break down organisms
    That were once living
    Nitrogen fixation is what some may do
    And *symbiosis* is a relationship between two species

6. *Phototrophic autotrophs* take the sun's energy
    To make its food unlike you and me
    Chemotrophic autotrophs and *heterotrophs* too
    Have ways to obtain energy they need

Combining songs and other guide material like the Anticipation-Reaction Guide or study guide helps students to approach a topic from a number of angles. Moreover, the music dimension piques students' interest. They enjoy seeing the verses that other students in the class create for a song. Integrating songwriting and biology concepts can improve students' engagement and concept learning (Miller & Coen, 1994). In this particular classroom, there were a number of students who would routinely become disengaged, especially in the nonlab portion of the class, but they all demonstrated a high level of involvement in the ReWrite strategy. ReWrite is especially useful in the sciences, where the technical vocabulary load and the abstract concepts can seem daunting to many students. The cooperative songwriting process helps students' relational learning (Glynn, 1994) through the construction of new verses that reflect an expansion of their prior knowledge. Moreover, students can modify misconceptions about a topic (Hynd, McNish, Qian, Keith, & Lay, 1994). The ReWrite song becomes a powerful mnemonic device for long-term memory of foundational information in science and other content areas.

While ReWrite is a fairly structured approach to using music in the content areas, you may want to let students take the lead in creating from scratch their view of concepts they are studying. The following example from 10th-grade world history shows a more open-ended approach to using music in concept learning.

Teaching Idea: Rap Song Writing
Content Area: World History; adaptable to All
Level: High School; adaptable to All

Adolescents have an affinity for rap and hip-hop. It's an accessible form of music that lends itself to creative exploration. In Mr. K.'s high school World History class, rap is one of many musical and artistic forms that sophomore students use to explore concepts. In the example that follows, Josh, Danny, Brad, Mike, Chris, and Shannon collaborated to create a song about the exploration of the Western Hemisphere. Shannon describes their classroom and her view of songwriting in this context.

> Every seat is taken up in our classroom. There are lots of kids. We just turn the desks if we're going to do group work. His whole classroom is decorated with kids' projects—like airplanes, drawings, all sorts of things from before and now. Little castles that people have made and little guillotines, and a big guillotine that actually worked when he first got it. They used to slice big watermelon with it. It's huge and it barely fit in the doors so they had to put a different blade

on it. He cut a pencil in half for us. The blade's not sharp enough to do much else. Some of the displays are from years ago. Some of it is brand new. He keeps in touch with a lot of his students and he tells us about it. Some of them are already teaching.

Mr. K. introduced the rap song as one of many musical options students could adopt to reflect their study of the exploration of the Western Hemisphere. Shannon continues:

> We could do it alone or we could form groups. We could sing it, make a music video, sing it on tape, or we could sing it in front of the whole class. You could do whatever you wanted with it. You could do any type of song to any type of music. Whatever background music we wanted. . . . We got the Puff Daddy single because it has the instrumental version, so it was easy to sing to. It's rap. People in the class did all sorts of things. We had people just singing, people rapping, hip-hop, punk. We had one group use their own band, and they sang to their own band song. You know, made a videotape of it and everything. It's a punk band.

The process of small-group rap song writing spanned classroom time and collaboration outside the classroom to produce an audiotape of their lyrics. Shannon concludes:

> We did most of the writing at school. And we met on the Saturday before we made the tape. He didn't give us much group time during class. He played each one for the whole class so everybody got to hear everybody else's.

Josh, Danny, Brad, Mike, Chris, and Shannon finished writing their lyrics and audiotaped their rap performance at Shannon's house using a simple microphone and cassette tape recorder.

Exploration of the Western Hemisphere

Come on take a trip on the rocket ship
The trip won't cost you a dime
We're gonna start right here . . . then back it on back
To the start of America's time

Got the key . . . got the key . . . to this world's lock
Explore the globe with the good friend the jock

People looked to the East for a better life
Wanted sugar and spice to make the food taste nice
They heard Marco Polo's tale about China's riches
They were ready to sail

Jocko Jocko make it real clear
Who discovered America what was the year
In 1492 Isabella told Chris what he could do
Chris thought his way was best
Tried to reach East Indies sailing West
They said stop it Chris you'll run aground
He sailed on and on 'cause the world was round
Now some folks thought the world was flat
And when you get to the edge that's the end of that

Christopher Columbus was a man with a plan
Didn't find any spices but found a new land

San Salvador . . . Cuba . . . San Domingo are parts of the new world
That you should know
Everyone agreed that Columbus was bold
He excited everybody with the promise of gold

Now listen to the Jock as I keep on wailing
Tell you all about those who kept on sailing
The search for riches had begun
People sailed to the new world one by one

Old Balboa was more than terrific
Discovered an ocean the mighty Pacific
Magellan was a tough man pound for pound
Sailed around the world and proved it was round

Cortez sailed to Mexico had the Spanish flag as we all know
The Spanish conqueror conquistador
Took Aztec gold but wanted more

You can assign points for group performances like this one or use a
rubric with a description of what constitutes a high-, medium-, or low-point
creation. Mr. K. uses a simple point system to grade these projects. Shannon and her group members viewed music as a fun way to consider other-

wise static concepts in history. In Mr. K.'s classroom, music serves as one of many artistic routes to concept learning.

Although Mr. K. has been teaching for a number of years, any teacher can start the process of using music in the content areas by trying out ReWrite or the more open-ended lyric writing of Mr. K.'s approach. Starting with an occasional foray into music will form the foundation for more risk taking as you and your students get comfortable writing and performing original lyrics. "In the classroom, the teacher is the role model for creative risk taking" (Cockburn, 1995, p. 58).

ReWrite has been successful in the secondary, middle, and intermediate levels in content learning. The section that follows considers other ways that music can be used at the middle school level. Lisa Stevens, a middle school reading and learning strategist and doctoral student, shares her experience.

Other Applications of Music in the Content Areas

Teaching Idea: Music and Sustained Silent Reading
Content Areas: All
Levels: Intermediate, Middle, High School

A number of classrooms use music as a relaxing backdrop to create a calm, soothing atmosphere for reading. Lisa Stevens has researched the positive effects of classical music on mood, attention, and relaxation. At a department chair's meeting, Lisa promoted the idea of using classical music as a backdrop to sustained silent reading (SSR):

> I suggested piping Mozart throughout the entire school during SSR
> time, and the department chairs and our principal were in favor of it.
> It has proved to be widely effective at unifying the school during this
> time. We have had to make a few volume and selection adjustments,
> but it's proving to be very worthwhile.

How do middle school students view the combination of Mozart and SSR? Sixth-grader Kristen said, "It's pretty whacko. It's okay to read to." Referring to the volume dynamics of classical music, Kristen noted, "Sometimes it goes with the book, and sometimes not."

Based on feedback from teachers and students, Kristen's middle school tried playing some mellow guitar CDs by Christopher Parkening to accompany SSR. You may want to experiment and involve students in the process of selecting music that is conducive to SSR. Mozart or soft jazz offer good starting points.

In Kristen's middle school, music sets the stage for the onset of SSR, and as the music ends it foreshadows the transition to other classroom activities. This obvious transition into and out of SSR has made it nearly impossible for teachers who are not interested in doing SSR to ignore it.

Teaching Ideas: Song Retellings and Freewrites
Content Areas: All
Levels: Intermediate, Middle, High School

Students are frequently called upon to write summaries or book reports about the novels they read. You can substitute writing a song to retell a story (Finke & Edwards, 1997). Students can share their song retellings with the class with a live performance, a music video, or an audiotape. A song is more likely than a typical book report or summary to have intrinsic value to its creators (Cockburn, 1995).

You may want to get started in using music in your classroom by modeling simple, familiar folk tunes or campfire songs. Movie and television soundtracks also offer a familiar format. In English, students can free-write a story or journal entry to go along with some instrumental music (Scott, 1996). The music can then be replayed while students share their writing.

You may want to involve the music department or music teachers and their students in the development of instrumentals that can serve as SSR and free-writing background music. In addition, inviting musicians into content area classrooms to discuss the various mathematical and scientific dimensions of their art helps to dispel some of the myths surrounding musicians. Like most people, musicians are multifaceted, but the nonmusical dimensions of their lives often remain hidden and result in misconceptions and stereotypes.

Concluding Thoughts

In a marvelous interview, jazz guitarist Pat Metheny said this about music (Small, 1997):

> It reminds us of where we were before and where we are going after. It is a mysterious vapor that somehow slips in the cracks between this plane of existence and some other one. . . . It is something universal that goes beyond language and beyond race, country, or nationality. We recognize it as something we all have in common. More and more, I see that it is the same thing you find wherever there is love, intensity, energy, or human potential. (p. 48)

Take the risk to infuse your content area classroom with some student-created musical compositions. Music is one of the many multiple sign systems you can use to energize students' learning. Along with poetry, drama, and visualization, music offers a way to revitalize content teaching and learning.

Additional Resources

The Internet contains a vast array of music resources for teachers. A complete listing of six major music Web sites can be found in *The Teachers' Complete Guide to the Internet* (Heide & Stilborne, 1996). For example, they list: http://www.music.indiana.edu/misc./music_resources.html as a "vast (60 pages) resource of Gopher, telnet, FTP, and www sites, all related to music" (p. 262).

An elementary example of the ReWrite strategy described in this chapter can be found at: http://www.readingonline.org/literacy/bats/index.html.

In addition, you can search for good instrumental CDs using the software applications available in Tower Records and other music stores. Occasionally reading music magazines available in commercial bookstores and libraries is another good way to get acquainted with various forms of music.

Finally, your students can assist in searching for good background music to use with ReWrite or rap. Over time, you will develop a great collection of songs while becoming comfortable with music as a vehicle for learning in the content areas.

References

Bean, T. W. (1997). ReWrite: A music strategy for exploring content area concepts.. In International Reading Association, *Reading Online* [Online]. Available: http://www.readingonline.org/literacy/bats/index.html

Berghoff, B. (1998). Multiple sign systems and reading. *The Reading Teacher, 51*, 520–523.

Cairney, T. H. (1996). Pathways to meaning making: Fostering intertextuality in the classroom. In L. B. Gambrell & J. F. Almasi (Eds.), *Lively discussions: Fostering engaged reading* (pp. 170–180). Newark, DE: International Reading Association.

Campbell, J. R., Reese, C. M., O'Sullivan, C., & Dossey, J. A. (1996). *NAEP 1994 trends in academic progress*. Washington, DC: U.S. Department of Education, Office of Educational Research and Improvement.

Cockburn, V. (1995). The uses of folk music and songwriting in the classroom. In M. R. Goldberg & A. Phillips (Eds.), *Art as education*. Cambridge, MA: Harvard Educational Review.

Combs, S. P. (1997). *The notorious B. I. G.: Mo money, mo problems*. New York: Bad Boy Records.

Finke, J., & Edwards, B. (1997). Teacher education students' insights from intergenerational literature circles. *Journal of Teacher Education, 48*, 367–378.

Getty Education Institute for the Arts. (1996). *Educating for the workplace through the arts*. Los Angeles, CA: Author.

Glynn, S. M. (1994). *Teaching science with analogies: A strategy for teachers and textbook authors* (Reading Research Report No. 15). Athens, GA: National Reading Research Center.

Heide, A., & Stilborne, L. (1996). *The teachers' complete guide to the Internet*. Toronto, Ontario, Canada: Trifolium Books.

Hynd, C. R., McNish, M. M., Qian, G., Keith, M., & Lay, K. (1994). *Learning counterintuitive physics concepts: The effects of text and educational environment* (Reading Research Report No. 16). Athens, GA: National Reading Research Center.

Lazear, D. G. (1992). *Teaching for multiple intelligences*. Bloomington, IN: Phi Delta Kappa Educational Foundation.

Miller, A., & Coen, D. (1994). The case for music in the schools. *Phi Delta Kappan, 75,* 459–461.

Miller, K. R., & Levine, J. (1993). *Biology*. Englewood Cliffs, NJ: Prentice-Hall.

Readence, J. E., Bean, T. W., & Baldwin, R. S. (1998). *Content area literacy: An integrated approach* (6th ed.). Dubuque, IA: Kendall/Hunt.

Scott, L. G. (1996). Writing to music. *The Reading Teacher, 50,* 173–174.

Small, M. L. (1997). Face to face: Pat Metheny reveals a new side of his guitar artistry. *Acoustic Guitar, 7* (10), 38–48.

Chapter 7

Read-Alouds in the Content Areas: Resources to Promote Critical and Creative Thinking

Maureen McLaughlin
Jesse C. Moore
Fred Fedorko
Aileen Kennedy

The sophomores were listening intently as their teacher introduced the topic of the Japanese American Internment during their unit of study on World War II. Rather than giving a traditional lecture, she chose to activate students' prior knowledge through semantic mapping and discussion. She followed these with two read-alouds. The first was *So Far From the Sea* by Eve Bunting (1998), a picture book that provided the students with a view of one of the internment camps and its long-range effects on a Japanese American family. Next she read aloud several brief passages from the best-selling novel *Snow Falling on Cedars* by David Guterson. The portions she read vividly described the impact the Internment had on an adolescent relationship, portraying situations with which the students could easily identify. As the class ended, everyone was engaged with the topic. For homework, students would use the bookmark technique while reading about the Japanese American Internment in their text.

Read-alouds, as used by this high school teacher, are enjoying a new popularity in middle and high school settings. They invite the learner in, stimulate the imagination, and connect new information to personal experiences. The colorful illustrations of the text found in picture books, the engaging style of writing used to present information in magazine articles, and the skilled artistry with words used by authors of trade books all contribute to the read-aloud's amazing ability to capture students' interest.

This chapter is designed to act as a resource for using read-alouds in the content areas. It begins by presenting a rationale and describing a variety of ways in which read-alouds of trade books and informational articles enhance teaching and learning. This is followed by detailed descriptions of classroom applications. Finally, the chapter provides an extensive annotated bibliography of content-related picture books and a comprehensive directory of informational read-aloud sources.

The Rationale for Read-Alouds

The rationale for using trade books and informational articles as read-alouds in the content areas is multifaceted. However, the most compelling reason for their use is the ever-increasing need teachers have to supplement traditional textbooks with information from other sources. What teachers need are sources that are high quality, up to date, readily available, and cost effective. Content area read-alouds incorporate all of these characteristics.

Further, content-related read-alouds can provide motivation, engage prior knowledge, furnish background information, introduce key concepts, incorporate a variety of genres like biography and poetry, encourage students to view topics from different perspectives, and be used to teach strategies. They also stimulate visualization, pique curiosity, and promote inquiry.

How Trade Books Can Enhance Critical and Creative Thinking

Researchers advocate integrating authentic literature in the instructional process for numerous reasons, including the following:

- Literature allows students to expand their knowledge base (Freeman & Person, 1998).
- The single focus of trade books allows topics to be explored in more depth than most textbooks (Moss, 1991).
- Students are able to develop a richer understanding of a topic than they can when using only textbooks (Savage, 1998).
- Critical thinking is enhanced (Levstik, 1990).
- Students' learning is more connected to their changing world (Greenlaw, 1992) than when learning is limited to textbooks.

Trade books also address a wide variety of content area topics (Greenlaw, 1992; Moss, 1991). This diversity is evident in the following examples, which are designed to use trade books as read-alouds in intermediate, middle school, high school, or university settings.

Teaching Ideas: Trade Books to Enhance Critical and Creative Thinking
Content Areas: All
Levels: Intermediate, Middle and High School

- When teaching science, sharing a selection from Eric Carle's *Flora and Tiger* will not only offer informative ideas but also help students to understand how Carle's interest in science developed during his childhood.
- When rainforests are being studied, reading Jane Yolen's *Welcome to the Green House* will offer students background information greatly enhanced by the book's vivid illustrations.
- If mathematics is the topic, reading Jon Scieszka's *Math Curse*, a humorous classic, will help to alleviate math anxiety for students of all ages.
- When teaching about African American contributions to our society, reading Rosemary Bray's *Martin Luther King* will present the contributions of one man, and Faith Ringgold's *Dinner at Aunt Connie's House* will reveal the contributions of numerous women.
- If the Holocaust is the topic, reading Ruud Van Der Vol and Rian Verhoweren's *Anne Frank: Beyond the Diary* will offer students a succinct understanding of her life, while selections from *I Never Saw Another Butterfly* will offer the perspectives of numerous children who were held in Nazi concentration camps.
- When teaching about the continents of Africa and Asia, sharing the alphabet books *Ashanti to Zulu* by Margaret Musgrove and *A Is for Asia* by Cynthia Chin-Lee will offer students a broad range of information.
- If immigration is the topic, sharing Amy Hest's *When Jesse Came Across the Sea*, and Mary Beruns Knight's *Who Belongs Here?* helps students to understand that there have been a wide variety of immigrant experiences.
- Informative children's books such as *Here Is the Arctic Winter* by Madeleine Dumphy can also be paired with humorous volumes such as *Antarctic Antics* by Judy Sierra to motivate students.
- When teaching about Columbus, reading *In 1492* by Jean Marzollo, *Encounter* by Jane Yolen, and selections from *The Tainos* by Francine Jacobs offers students ideas from both narrative and informational text.

Using trade book read-alouds in the content areas adds a creative dimension to teaching and learning. The trade books may be picture books, young adult novels, or best-sellers. Although the novels are too extensive to list, we've included annotations of our other favorite trade books in a bibliography at the end of this chapter.

How Informational Articles Can Promote Critical and Creative Thinking

In addition to trade books, informational articles from magazines, newspapers and the Internet are valuable sources of content-related read-alouds. These resources are readily available and up to date. Also, since they are major sources of printed text in the adult world, their use in schools makes reading a real-life experience. Informational articles are rich alternatives to traditional textbooks because they are generally well written. The author's voice and point of view are usually quite obvious, which makes them readable and interesting. The high quality of pictures and graphics that accompany these selections add to the information they present and heighten their appeal to students.

Besides providing meaningful read-alouds, the articles in these sources can be very useful tools for educators in a variety of other ways. For example, they can help teachers to stay current with the latest discoveries and theories in their discipline as well as expand the depth of their knowledge of a specific topic. Also, articles usually make connections among the various subjects in the school curriculum, which teachers can draw upon when they need to explain and illustrate how their subject is relevant and applicable in real-world situations. (For a list of magazines to use as resources, see the bibliography at the end of this chapter. For more information about the Internet as a content area resource, see "Internet Sites" in chapter 3, and also chapter 10.)

Although there are potentially several criteria for selecting content-related informational read-alouds, articles that are short, contain vivid illustrations, and promote inquiry are especially useful. Brief, pertinent informational read-alouds can be integrated seamlessly into the flow of a content lesson. They can be used throughout a class session to illustrate a point, to stimulate a discussion, or for many other reasons. The range of purposes and possibilities is delineated in the following examples.

**Teaching Ideas: Informational Articles to Promote Critical and
                  Creative Thinking**
Content Areas: All
Levels: Intermediate, Middle, High School

- **To present the most recent information on a topic**
  Example: Excerpts from "The Search for the Seafloor's Secrets" (Keith, 1998) can be used to examine the Earth's strata and its relationship to the history of climate change to determine what dangers lie ahead.
- **To stimulate interest in a topic**
  Example: Excerpts from "What Time Is It?" (Collins, 1998) can be used to explain how daylight saving time came into being.
- **To answer students' questions**
  Example: "How the Institution Got Its Start" (Anderson, 1998) is a brief article that is very effective for read-aloud purposes, especially since most listeners are surprised to learn that the Smithsonian Institute is named for a European.
- **To initiate discussions**
  Example: An excerpt from "Bang! Went the doors of every bank in America" (1997) can be used to introduce the effect of the Great Depression upon American life in the 1930s. This article intermingles humor and information about the Depression, as it recounts the experience of a man who was caught committing a bank robbery as a "run" on the bank was occurring.
- **To pose dilemmas**
  Example: Excerpts from *The Elegant Universe* (Greene, 1999) reveal that physicists are faced with a dilemma. It has long been accepted that modern physics rests on two foundational pillars. Einstein's theory of general relativity has provided a framework for understanding the universe on the largest of scales (stars and galaxies), while quantum mechanics has provided a framework for understanding the universe on the smallest of scales (molecules, atoms, and subatomic particles). Research confirms the accuracy of each theory but leads to a disturbing conclusion: They are mutually incompatible.
- **To stimulate debates on differing points of view**
  Example: A special panel offers a variety of views on teen culture and violence in "Moving Beyond the Blame Game" (1999).
- **To clarify misconceptions or confusing issues**
  Example: Sharon Begley's (1994) "Why Does Traffic Jam?" reports that scientists suspect that treating traffic as sound waves traveling through the air might reveal how mysterious bottlenecks arise and then dissipate.
- **To connect the theoretical to the real world**

Example: The field of astrophysics is by its very nature one of the most theoretical disciplines. Helping students to understand the concept of a black hole is facilitated by reading a portion of "Death by Black Hole" (Tyson, 1995).

Example: In "Discovering the Odds" (Ross, 1999), the author relates Blaise Pascal's 17th-century probability theory to the revelation that every food, activity, or event in which we participate today involves risk to some extent.

- **To provide vicarious experiences**

Example: An excerpt from Greg Child's (1999) "Hitting the Wall" can be used to invite the reader to experience the ultimate in technical climbing: the 5,300-foot blank wall of Canada's Great Sail Peak.

Example: "Perils in Wonderland" (Widstrand, 1998) offers a clear, vivid description of an experience in the Pantanal flood plain in Brazil, an ecologist's dream destination.

- **To pose questions for investigations**

Example: Reading Chet Raymo's (1999) "Peering Through the Hubble Telescope to Our Distant Past" updates the listener on the most distant object ever observed in the universe: a galaxy 13 billion light years from Earth.

- **To entertain**

Example: In his column entitled "The Final Exam," Dave Barry (1997) offers a humorous perspective on the possibility of national testing.

- **To promote self-understanding**

Example: John Leland's (1999) "The Secret Life of Teens" uses the voices of a generation to describe the lives of teens who feel they are overwhelmed with pressures.

- **To make interdisciplinary connections**

Example: "The Battle Was Lost in a Zone of Silence" (1998) integrates the science of acoustics and history by reporting on the effect of acoustic shadows on major Civil War battles.

Classroom Close-ups: Integrating Read-Alouds and Strategy Instruction

Because of their power to motivate and engage students, read-alouds fit easily and naturally into lessons designed by teachers who want to challenge and extend their students' thinking. In many of today's content area classrooms, the traditional practices of "assign and tell" have been replaced with more student-centered activities (Vacca & Vacca, 1999). Activation and creation of prior knowledge, purpose setting, and motivation occur at the start of such content lessons. A wide array of appropriate, innovative teaching strategies is incorporated into the lessons to focus and guide student thinking during reading. After reading, students extend and apply their learning through creative writing, projects, or other performances (see chapter 2).

The following examples illustrate that content-related read-alouds can also be integrated with strategy use. The scenarios situate the read-alouds in classrooms at the intermediate, middle, or high school levels.

Teaching Idea: Trade Book Read-Aloud and the Venn Diagram
Content Area: Social Studies
Level: Intermediate

Cathy Healy teaches fourth grade in a medium-size suburban school district. There are 24 children in the class, 2 of whom have special needs. In social studies, the class is about to begin a unit on families and lifestyles. Prior to reading the chapter in the textbook, Ms. Healy uses a semantic map and asks the children to brainstorm words that come to mind when they hear the word *homeless*. After she writes the words on the chalkboard, she and the class discuss some of the words to activate and build prior knowledge. Next, Ms. Healy shows the title and cover of a trade book and discusses what the children see in the picture. The class makes several predictions. The teacher then reads aloud the trade book, *Mr. Bow Tie* by Karen Barbour. She stops occasionally for the children to confirm or disconfirm their predictions, to modify them, or to make new ones. When the book is completed, it is discussed, and new words are added to the semantic map on the chalkboard.

Following this activity, Ms. Healy distributes copies of another trade book, *Fly Away Home* by Eve Bunting. The children may read the book independently, with a partner, or in a group led by her. She chooses two students to be part of her group, but others may also join. When the book is completed, Ms. Healy places a poster showing a large Venn diagram (Figure 7-1) on the wall. The students will use the Venn diagram to compare and contrast *Fly Away Home* with *Mr. Bow Tie*. She divides the class into groups of four and gives each group a packet of sticky notes. Each group is directed to use the sticky notes to write one statement about what is unique about each book and one statement about how the books are the same. The students then place their sticky notes in the appropriate section of the Venn diagram. When all sticky notes are in place, Ms. Healy asks for volunteers to read some of the statements, and a discussion follows.

These activities have prepared these fourth graders to read the textbook chapter on families and lifestyles, especially the section about the homeless, a topic that Ms. Healy thought would be unfamiliar to her class. Ms. Healy was able to use authentic literature to prepare her students to read the more difficult expository material in the textbook.

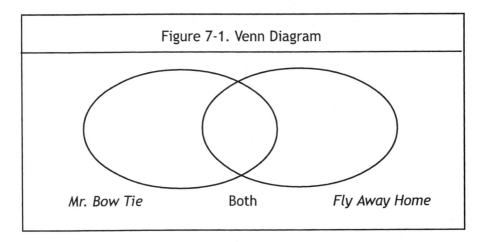

Figure 7-1. Venn Diagram

Mr. Bow Tie   Both   *Fly Away Home*

Teaching Idea: Trade Book Read-Aloud and the RAFT
Content Areas: Music and Literature
Level: Intermediate

Adrienne Yeong teaches 23 fourth graders in a small suburban community. She and the music teacher, Scott Voght, are exploring ways to integrate music and literature. Because Mr. Voght has been introducing his students to the great classical composers and since Ms. Yeong has the book *Beethoven Lives Upstairs* by Barbara Nichol, the following plan is devised. In music class Mr. Voght will introduce the students to Beethoven and play his compositions, and he will also display a large poster with Beethoven's likeness in the music room.

Meanwhile, Ms. Yeong has decided to use *Beethoven Lives Upstairs* as a read-aloud. She points out to her class that the book is a combination of fiction, history, and music. She then tells her students that the format the author used to write the book is an exchange of letters between a young boy and his uncle concerning a strange composer who lives upstairs in a room rented from the boy's mother. The boy poses many questions (the fiction), and the uncle provides the answers (the history). During this read-aloud, Ms. Yeong asks the students to pose their own questions and to predict the uncle's answers to the young boy.

After reading the book, Ms. Yeong explains the RAFT (Role, Audience, Format, Topic) technique to the students, using *Beethoven Lived Upstairs* as a model (Figure 7-2). She notes that RAFT is an excellent way to connect reading and writing, and that it offers students several opportunities for self-selection. (For more information about RAFT, see chapter 11).

Figure 7-2. The RAFT Technique

R = role   An aunt, uncle, or other adult

A = audience   Students in a lower grade

F = format   A series of letters

T - topic   A famous person being studied

Patterned after *Beethoven Lives Upstairs*

Ms. Yeong then divides her class into groups of four. Books, informational articles, and computer software about famous musicians are placed on the classroom reference table. The students are directed to choose a role, audience, format, and topic for a story their group will create. The materials placed on the classroom reference table are available for this task. Students then use the writing process to develop their stories.

Teaching Idea: Trade Book Read-Aloud and Reciprocal Questioning
Content Area: Math
Level: Middle School

Jose Alvarez teaches sixth-grade math in a large middle school in a large suburban school district. He wants to challenge a group of his five top students, so he decides to use a picture book to have these students deal with very large numbers and a special kind of numerical relationship called *factorials*. The book he has chosen is *Anno's Mysterious Multiplying Jar* by Masaichiro and Mitsumasa Anno.

First Mr. Alvarez has the group read the book silently, just for enjoyment. Then he holds a brief discussion and answers any questions, as long as his answers don't reveal what he wants the students to discover on their own. During the read-aloud Mr. Alvarez asks the students to estimate the number of items on each page. The answers are compared and modified when necessary. On subsequent readings, Mr. Alvarez directs his students to use calculators to compute the numbers on each page and to again compare answers and modify them if necessary. He then uses Reciprocal Questioning, also known as ReQuest (Manzo, 1969), to review the author's afterword on factorials. In this strategy teachers model effective questioning techniques, which students, in turn, use as models to create their own questions. Having teachers and students take turns asking and answering questions promotes comprehension.

As an extension activity, Mr. Alvarez asks his students to work in two teams to write their own book, following a similar pattern. When completed, the books will be exchanged and each team will try to solve the problem that the other team presents.

Teaching Idea: World War II Picture Book Museum
Content Area: Social Studies
Level: Middle School

Stephanie Romano created a Picture Book Museum to provide more World War II background information for students who were already reading *Number the Stars* by Lois Lowry in their language arts and/or social studies curriculum. The Picture Book Museum is designed to integrate trade books, read-alouds, social studies and multiple types of student response. In this activity, students read and react to two World War II–related picture books. Students first respond aesthetically to express their feelings and personal connections with the text and illustrations. Next, they respond from an efferent stance to relate what they learned from the text (Rosenblatt, 1994). Finally, students make evaluative comments about the picture books and the project itself.

Student goals for this project include increasing their knowledge of World War II; realizing that there are multiple points of view that affect the perspective of the individual story; understanding the domino effect of the war— that not just soldiers die, but women, children, the elderly, and animals also become victims.

To engage students' thinking, the teacher uses the book *Hiroshima No Pika* as a read-aloud for the whole class. During the read-aloud, the teacher stops periodically to discuss the different feelings that the text and illustrations provoke.

The response sheet (Figure 7-3) is explained to the students on the overhead projector and completed as a whole-class activity. This is followed by a discussion about how people act when they are in a museum. Later, when students are independently reading books from the museum, they share their reflections in small groups. Then students volunteer to share what they've learned with the whole class.

Figure 7-3. Picture Book Museum Response Sheet

Name_____ Date_____

Book Title_____

Author_____

1. In a few sentences, describe what you were thinking about as you read and how it made you feel. Were you able to make any personal connections to this story?

2. Describe two different pictures in the story.

3. Explain what you learned from this book.

4. Rate this book from 1 (low) to 10 (high): _____ . Tell why you rated it as you did.

To guide students' thinking, the teacher focuses their attention on the World War II memorable dates timeline that they created in previous classes. This is followed by a one-minute oral synopsis of each of the 11 books that are featured in the museum (see bibliography on page 117). The Picture Book Museum is then created by arranging the books at various points around the room. World War II music is played while this is occurring.

Next, in pairs, students choose which two books they want to read. After reading their selections, students complete the response sheets for those two books. Teacher observation, student response sheets, and participation in discussion are among the informal assessments used in this project. Students also reflect on what they have learned by recording their ideas on the evaluation sheet (Figure 7-4).

Figure 7-4. Picture Book Museum Evaluation Form

1. What rating do you give the Picture Book Museum?
    Circle your response and justify your choice.

    Excellent   Good   Fair   Poor

2. What did you like about the Picture Book Museum? What
    suggestions do you have to improve it?

3. Do you think that next year's students should experience the
    museum? Explain your response.

4. Do you think that students should experience the museum
    before they read *Number the Stars,* while reading it, or after
    they have finished reading it? Offer reasons to support your
    answer.

5. There is more than one way to view conflicts. Describe a
    point of view on World War II that you had been unaware of
    prior to reading one of the books from the Picture Book
    Museum.

World War II Picture Book Museum

Bunting, E. (1998). *So far from the sea*. (C. Soentpiet, Illus.). New York: Clarion Books.

Bunting, E. (1993). *Terrible things: An allegory of the Holocaust* (S. Gammell, Illus.). Philadelphia: Jewish Publication Society.

Coerr, E. (1993). *Sadako* (E. Young, Illus.). New York: Putnam.

Houston, G. (1992). *But no candy* (L. Bloom, Illus.). New York: Philomel Books.

Innocenti, R. (1985). *Rose Blanche*. Mankato, MN: Creative Education.

Lowry, L. (1989). *Number the stars*. New York: Yearling & Dell.

Maruki, T. (1980). *Hiroshima no pika*. New York: Lothrop, Lee, & Shepard Books.

Morimoto, J. (1987). *My Hiroshima*. New York: Viking.

Sim, D. (1997). *In my pocket* (G. Fitzgerald, Illus.). San Diego: Harcourt Brace.

Tsuchiya, Y. (1988). *Faithful elephants* (T. Lewin, Illus.). Boston: Houghton Mifflin.

Uchida, Y. (1993). *The bracelet* (J. Yardley, Illus.). New York: Philomel Books.

Wild, M. (1991). *Let the celebrations begin!* (J. Vivas, Illus.). New York: Orchard Books.

Teaching Idea: Nonfiction Excerpt and Anticipation-Reaction Guide
Content Area: Mathematics
Level: High School

Tom Burke, the chairperson of a high school mathematics department, believes that students should be exposed to the interesting stories behind the lives of famous mathematicians and the practicality of their work. Prior to having the students read the story of the life of Michael Faraday, he has them complete the first part of the Extended Anticipation Guide (Figure 7-5). Then he leads a brief discussion about why students did or did not agree with the statements. The Extended Anticipation Guide is an effective strategy for getting students to focus on any preconceived notions they might have before making predictions about what they will read. With these internalized purposes, the students tend to pay closer attention to the story. After having them write a brief personal response, Mr. Burke asks the students to share their reflections with a partner.

Figure 7-5. Extended Anticipation Guide

Directions:
Before listening to the story of Michael Faraday, put a check next to the statements with which you agree. As you listen, indicate if your predictions are confirmed. After the story is finished, write a brief paragraph describing what you perceive to be the most important idea.

Agree		**Confirmed**
_____	Magnetism, electricity, and gravity are all variations of the same force.	_____
_____	Two hundred years ago, scientists were considered to be philosophers.	_____
_____	Two hundred years ago, there was no distinction between science and religion.	_____
_____	In order to become a scientist 200 years ago, you had to spend many years studying in a university.	_____
_____	The word *electric* comes from the Greek word for "amber," which is fossilized tree sap.	_____

Source: Guillen, M. (1995). A class act: Michael Faraday and the law of electro-magnetic induction. In *Five equations that changed the world: The power and poetry of mathematics.* New York: Hyperion.

Teaching Idea: Novel Excerpt and Semantic Map
Content Area: Physics
Level: High School

In a high school physics class, Michael Gress begins a study of weather by asking his students to brainstorm in small groups all of the ideas which come to mind when they think about the phrase *weather report*. Among the common associations that the groups make are: *rain, storm, thunder, lightning, rained-out picnics, calm, fair, sunny, chance of precipitation, inaccurate, humidity, blizzard, sleet, snow, hail, cumulus clouds, partly cloudy, temperature, thermometer, barometer, Fahrenheit, Celsius, isobars, windchill factor, tornado, hurricane, sunrise, sunset, Doppler radar, long-range forecast, cold front, warm front, rarely right, wind speed, high pressure, low pressure, map of the United States, small-craft warning, small-stream flooding, 11 o'clock news report, umbrella,* and *rain coat.*

Mr. Gress then directs each group to create a semantic map or outline to classify their brainstormed associations. An abbreviated example looks like Figure 7-6.

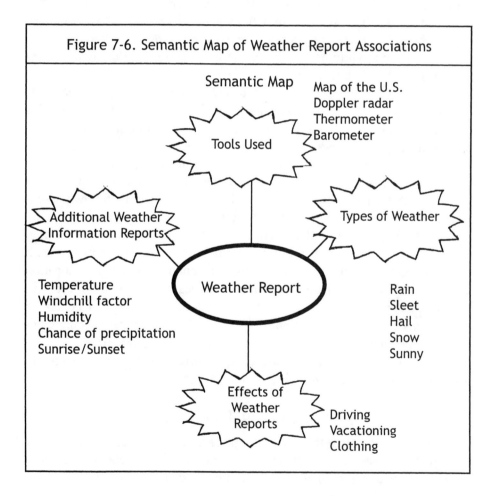

Figure 7-6. Semantic Map of Weather Report Associations

The groups then briefly share their semantic maps with the class, explaining any unclear associations and noting similarities and differences among the groups. This sharing enables the teacher to determine what the class does and does not know about weather forecasting, and at the same time it helps to build a common background knowledge in the students.

Focusing his attention on the "accuracy of weather reports" associations, Mr. Gress asks the class to cite some personal examples of when the weather report was wrong and it had a negative effect on their plans. After several examples have been given, the class speculates on the reasons that they believe the weather report is often wrong even though the meteorologists have many scientific tools, such as those identified during the brainstorming activity. Their ideas are jotted on an overhead transparency. Mr. Gress then asks the class what they think scientists could do to enable perfectly accurate weather prediction. He asks the students to keep their responses in mind while he concludes the class by reading a passage from Michael Crichton's best-selling novel, *Jurassic Park*.

Early in the novel the main characters are flying to an isolated island off of Costa Rica where John Hammond (a very wealthy man) has created a theme park housing a variety of genetically cloned dinosaurs. Among the group of people on the airplane is an unconventional mathematician, Ian Malcolm, who believes that the attempt to create and control completely wild prehistoric beasts is doomed from the start. Dr. Malcolm bases his prediction of failure on the relatively new "chaos theory," of which his fellow passengers know nothing. In trying to help the others to understand this concept, he uses the analogy of the "butterfly effect. A butterfly flaps its wings in Peking, and weather in New York is different." He describes how the weather is such a complex system that even when atmospheric conditions in a given location are identical on two separate occasions, the weather that is produced will never be exactly the same. Malcolm points out that the computer-generated predictions of modern meteorologists can never be completely accurate because of the innumerable factors at work in any weather system.

For homework the students will write a journal entry on the effect of Dr. Malcolm's information on their faith in weather reports.

Concluding Thoughts

Read-alouds may be the perfect content area instructional resource. They are up to date, accessible, cost effective, and easily integrated into all content areas. In addition, they promote critical and creative thinking and enhance the learning experience.

As citizens of a new millennium, our students need to be highly motivated, engaged learners who enjoy quality, meaningful instruction. Using read-alouds as a resource in the content areas facilitates this process.

Content-Related Bibliography

Trade Books

This list of content area picture books focuses on our favorite titles. Each entry includes the bibliographic information, content areas in which the book has been effective, and a content connection. In addition to using these books, you should browse through libraries and bookstores regularly to discover new titles to integrate into your teaching.

Book: Adoff, Arnold. (1982). *All the colors of the race*. New York: Beech Tree Books.
Content Area: Social Studies (History)
Connection: Discrimination

Book: Aliki. (1993). *My visit to the aquarium*. New York: HarperCollins.
Content Area: Science
Connection: Marine life and the environment

Book: Anno, Masaichiro, & Anno, Mitsumasa. (1999). (Reprint Edition). *Anno's Mysterious Multiplying Jar*. NY: Penguin.
Content Area: Math
Connection: Factorials

Book: Ashabranner, Brent. (1988). *Always to remember: The story of the Vietnam Veterans Memorial*. New York: Scholastic.
Content Area: Social Studies (History)
Connection: Vietnam War

Book: Barbour, Karen. (1991). *Mr. Bow Tie*. Orlando, FL: Harcourt Brace Jovanovich.
Content Area: Social Studies (Cultures)
Connection: Homelessness

Book: Bartoletti, Susan Campbell. (1996). *Growing up in coal country*. Boston: Houghton Mifflin.
Content Area: Social Studies (History)
Connection: Mining-town life

Book: Bray, Rosemary L. (1995). *Martin Luther King*. New York: Green Willow Books.
Content Area: English, Social Studies (History)
Connection: Martin Luther King, human rights

Book: Bruchac, Joseph. (1994). *A boy called Slow*. New York:
  Philomel Books.
Content Area: Social Studies (History)
Connection: Sitting Bull, Native Americans

Book: Bunting, Eve. (1988). *How many days to America?* New York:
  Clarion Books.
Content Area: Social Studies (History)
Connection: Immigration, Thanksgiving

Book: Bunting, Eve. (1990). *The wall*. New York: Clarion Books.
Content Area: Social Studies (History)
Connection: Vietnam War Memorial

Book: Bunting, Eve. (1991). *Fly away home*. New York: Clarion Books.
Content Area: Social Studies (Cultures)
Connection: Homelessness, family

Book: Bunting, Eve. (1994). *Smoky nights*. New York: Harcourt Brace.
Content Area: Psychology, Social Studies
Connection: Los Angeles riots, racism

Book: Bunting, Eve. (1996). *The blue and the gray*. New York:
  Scholastic Press.
Content Area: Social Studies (History)
Connection: Racism, Civil War

Book: Burns, Marilyn. (1994). *The greedy triangle*. New York: Scholastic.
Content Area: Math (Geometry)
Connection: Shapes

Book: Carle, Eric. (1987). *The tiny seed*. New York: Scholastic.
Content Area: Science
Connection: Plant life

Book: Carle, Eric. (1997). *Flora and tiger*. New York: Philomel Books.
Content Areas: Art, Science, Social Studies
Connection: Carle's childhood and interest in nature

Book: Cherry, Lynne. (1990). *The great kapok tree.* Orlando, FL: Harcourt Brace Jovanovich.
Content Area: Science
Connection: Environment, life cycles

Book: Cherry, Lynne. (1992). *A river ran wild.* Orlando: Harcourt Brace Jovanovich.
Content Areas: Science, Social Studies (History).
Connection: History of Nashua River, environment

Book: Chin-Lee, Cynthia. (1997). *A is for Asia.* New York: Orchard Books.
Content Area: Social Studies (History)
Connection: Asia

Book: Clement, Rod. (1995). *Counting on Frank.* Boston: Houghton Mifflin.
Content Area: Mathematics
Connection: Counting, size comparison, mathematical facts

Book: Coles, Robert. (1995). *The story of Ruby Bridges.* New York: Scholastic.
Content Area: Social Studies (History)
Connection: Civil rights, desegregation

Book: Dumphy, Madeleine. (1993). *Here is the Arctic winter.* New York: Hyperion Books.
Content Area: Science, Social Studies (Geography)
Connection: Animals of the Arctic

Book: Freedman, Russel. (1991). *The Wright brothers.* New York: Holiday House.
Content Area: Social Studies (History)
Connection: Development of the first airplane

Book: French, Vivian. (1998). *Whale journey.* New York: Zero to Ten Limited.
Content Area: Science
Connection: Migration of whales

Book: Fritz, Jean. (1973). *And then what happened, Paul Revere?* New York: Coward-McCann.
Content Area: Social Studies (History)
Connection: Paul Revere

Book: Fritz, Jean. (1989). *George Washington's breakfast.* Boston: Houghton Mifflin.
Content Area: Social Studies (History)
Connection: George Washington

Book: Fritz, Jean. (1992). *George Washington's mother.* New York: Grosset & Dunlap.
Content Area: Social Studies (History)
Connection: George Washington

Book: Gauch, Patricia L. (1975). *Thunder at Gettysburg.* New York: Putnam.
Content Area: Social Studies (History)
Connection: Civil War

Book: Giblin, James C. (1992). *George Washington: A picture book biography.* New York: Scholastic.
Content Area: Social Studies (History)
Connection: George Washington

Book: Giganti, Paul, Jr. (1992). *Each orange had 8 slices.* New York: Greenwillow Books.
Content Area: Math
Connection: Counting

Book: Gilliland, Judith H. (1993). *River.* New York: Clarion Books.
Content Area: Science, Social Studies (History)
Connection: Amazon River

Book: Gray, Libba M. (1993). *Dear Willie Rudd.* New York: Simon & Schuster.
Content Area: Social Studies (History)
Connection: Racism, Civil rights

Book: Grutman, Jewel H. (1994). *The ledgerbook of Thomas Blue Eagle.* Charlottesville: Thomasson-Grant.
Content Area: Social Studies (History)
Connection: Plains Indians

Book: Hamilton, Virginia. (1993). *Many thousand gone: African Americans from slavery to freedom.* New York: Knopf.
Content Area: Social Studies (History)
Connection: Slavery in America

Book: Hamilton, Virginia. (1985). *The people could fly*. New York: Knopf.
Content Area: Social Studies (History)
Connection: African American folktales

Book: Haskins, Jim. (1995). *The day Fort Sumter was fired on*. New York: Scholastic.
Content Area: Social Studies (History)
Connection: Civil War

Book: Hathorn, Libby. (1994). *Way home*. New York: Crown.
Content Area: Social Studies (Cultures, History)
Connection: Homelessness

Book: Hest, Amy. (1997). *When Jessie came across the sea*. Cambridge, MA: Candlewick Press.
Content Area: Social Studies (History)
Connection: Immigration

Book: Jacobs, Francine. (1992). *The Tainos*. New York: Putnam's.
Content Area: Social Studies (Geography, History)
Connection: Christopher Columbus

Book: Jordan, Marin, & Jordan, Tanis. (1996). *Amazon alphabet*. New York: Kingfisher.
Content Area: Science, Social Studies (Geography)
Connection: Rain forest

Book: Kitchen, Bert. (1994). *When hunger calls*. Cambridge, MA: Candlewick Press.
Content Area: Science
Connection: Animal predators

Book: Knight, Mary Burns. (1993). *Who belongs here?* Gardiner, ME: Tilbury House.
Content Area: Social Studies (History)
Connection: Immigration, Cambodia, racism

Book: Kurelek, William. (1973). *A prairie boy's winter*. Boston: Houghton Mifflin.
Content Area: Social Studies (History)
Connection: Prairie life in the 1930s

Book: Lakin, Patricia. (1994). *Don't forget*. New York: Tambourine Books.
Content Area: Social Studies (History)
Connection: Survivors

Book: Leedy, Loreen. (1994). *Fraction action*. New York: Holiday House.
Content Area: Math
Connection: Fractions

Book: Leigh, Nila K. (1993). *Learning to swim in Swaziland: A child's-eye view of a southern African country*. New York: Scholastic.
Content Area: Social Studies (Cultures, Geography)
Connection: Life in Swaziland

Book: Leighton, Maxine R. (1992). *An Ellis Island Christmas*. New York: Viking.
Content Area: Social Studies (History)
Connection: Immigration

Book: Levine, Ellen. (1993). *If your name was changed at Ellis Island*. New York: Scholastic.
Content Area: Social Studies (History)
Connection: Immigration

Book: Markle, Sandra. (1991). *Outside and inside you*. New York: Macmillan.
Content Area: Science
Connection: The body

Book: Marzollo, Jean. (1991). *In 1492*. New York: Scholastic.
Content Area: Social Studies (History)
Connection: Christopher Columbus

Book: McGrath, Barbara B. (1994). *The M & M's counting book*. Watertown, MA: Charlesbridge
Content Area: Math
Connection: Counting, addition, subtraction

Book: Merriam, Eve. (1993). *12 ways to get to 11*. New York: Simon & Schuster.
Content Area: Math
Connection: Counting

Book: Mochizuki, Ken. (1993). *Baseball saved us*. New York: Lee & Low.
Content Area: Social Studies (History)
Connection: Japanese American internment, World War II

Book: Murphy, Jim. (1990). *The boys' war*. New York: Clarion Books.
Content Area: Social Studies (History)
Connection: Civil War

Book: Musgrove, Margaret. (1976). *Ashanti to Zulu*. New York: Dial Books.
Content Area: Social Studies (Cultures, Geography, History)
Connection: African tribes

Book: Nichol, Barbara. (1993). *Beethoven lives upstairs*. New York:
  Orchard Books.
Content Area: Music, Social Studies (History).
Connection: Beethoven's life

Book: Pallotta, Jerry. (1986). *The ocean alphabet book*. Watertown, MA:
  Charlesbridge.
Content Area: Science
Connection: The ocean

Book: Pallotta, Jerry. (1991). *The dinosaur alphabet book*. Watertown, MA:
  Charlesbridge.
Content Area: Science
Connection: Dinosaurs

Book: Pallotta, Jerry, & Bolster, Rob. (1999). *The Hershey's milk chocolate
  fractions book*. Needham, MA: Tidal Wave Press.
Content Area: Mathematics
Connection: Fractions

Book: Pinczes, Elinor J. (1993). *One hundred hungry ants*. Boston:
  Houghton Mifflin.
Content Area: Mathematics
Connection: Division

Book: Polacco, Patricia. (1994). *Pink and Say*. New York: Philomel Books.
Content Area: Social Studies (History)
Connection: Civil War

Book: Rey, H. A. (1988). *Find the constellations*. Boston: Houghton Mifflin.
Content Area: Science
Connection: Astronomy

Book: Ringgold, Faith. (1993). *Dinner at Aunt Connie's house*. New York: Hyperion Books.
Content Area: Art, Social Studies (History)
Connection: African American women

Book: Sabuda, Robert. (1994). *Tutankhamen's gift*. New York: Atheneum.
Content Area: Art, Social Studies (History)
Connection: Ancient Egypt

Book: San Souci, Robert. (1991). *N. C. Wyeth's pilgrims*. San Francisco: Chronicle Books.
Content Area: Art, Social Studies (History)
Connection: Plymouth Colony, Thanksgiving

Book: Say, Allen. (1993). *Grandfather's journey*. Boston: Houghton Mifflin.
Content Area: Social Studies (Geography, History)
Connection: Japanese immigration

Book: Schwartz, David M. (1985). *How much is a million?* New York: Lothrop, Lee & Shepard Books.
Content Area: Mathematics
Connection: Conceptualization of a million

Book: Scieszka, Jon. (1995). *Math curse*. New York: Penguin Books.
Content Area: Mathematics
Connection: Humorous look at math anxiety

Book: Sierra, Judy. (1998). *Antarctic antics: A book of penguin poems*. New York: Harcourt Brace.
Content Area: Social Studies
Connection: Geography

Book: Simon, Seymour. (1996). *The heart: Our circulatory system*. New York: Scholastic.
Content Area: Science
Connection: The heart

Book: Sis, Peter. (1996). *Starry messenger*. New York: Farrar, Straus, & Giroux.
Content Area: Science, Social Studies (History)
Connection: Galileo

Book: Soto, Gary. (1993). *Too many tamales*. New York: Putnam.
Content Area: Social Studies (Cultures)
Connection: Hispanic culture

Book: Steele, Philip. (1998). *The best book of mummies*. New York: Kingfisher.
Content Area: Science and Social Studies (History)
Connection: Mummies—their history and scientific secrets

Book: Taylor, Barbara. (1992). *Rain forest*. New York: Dorling Kindersley Books.
Content Area: Science
Connection: Rain forest

Book: Van Allsburg, Chris. (1990). *Just a dream*. Boston: Houghton Mifflin.
Content Area: Science
Connection: Environment

Book: Van Der Vol, Ruud, & Verhoweven, Rian. (1993). *Anne Frank: Beyond the diary*. New York: Viking.
Content Area: Social Studies (History)
Connection: Holocaust

Book: Volavkova, Hana (Ed.). (1998). *I never saw another butterfly.* New York: Schocken Books.
Content Area: Social Studies
Connection: Holocaust

Book: Wagner, David R. (1993). *In my own backyard*. Watertown, MA: Charlesbridge.
Content Area: Social Studies (Geography, History).
Connection: Historical and geological periods

Book: Wiesner, David. (1990). *Hurricane*. New York: Clarion Books.
Content Area: Science
Connection: Weather

Book: Wilcox, Charlotte. (1993). *Mummies & their mysteries*. New York: Scholastic.
Content Area: Social Studies (Geography, History)
Connection: Mummies

Book: Yolen, Jane. (1993). *Encounter*. Orlando, FL: Harcourt Brace.
Content Area: Social Studies (Geography, History)
Connection: Christopher Columbus

Book: Yolen, Jane. (1993). *Welcome to the green house*. New York: Putman.
Content Area: Science
Connection: Rain forest

Book: Zeldis-McDonough, Yona. (1997). *Anne Frank*. New York: Holt.
Content Area: Social Studies (History)
Connection: Holocaust

Other Book Resources

The Century, written by Peter Jennings and Todd Brewster, offers a remarkable variety of read-aloud possibilities. Many of these are eye-witness accounts of events such as the flight of the Wright brothers. *The Greatest Generation* by Tom Brokaw is also a valuable resource.

There are several published resources to help teachers locate discipline-specific titles. Three annotated bibliographies that provide extensive lists of books are *The Wonderful World of Mathematics: A Critically Annotated List of Children's Books in Mathematics,* edited by Diane Thiessen and Margaret Mattias (National Council of Teachers of Mathematics, 1998); *Eyeopeners I! How to Choose and Use Children's Books About Real People, Places, and Things* by Beverly Kobrin (Penguin Books, 1988); and *Eyeopeners II! Children's Books to Answer Children's Questions About the World Around Them* by Beverly Kobrin (Penguin Books, 1998). *Children's Literature & Social Studies: Selecting and Using Notable Books in the Class-room* by Myra Zarnowski and Arlese F. Gallagher (Kendall/Hunt) discusses criteria for selecting books and recommends specific titles for classroom use. *Fact and Fiction: Literature Across the Curriculum* edited by Bernice E. Cullinan (International Reading Association) offers suggestions for choosing and using books in many areas of the curriculum.

Magazines

Atlantic Monthly
Biography
Chicago (Most major cities have magazines)
Civil War History
Conde Nast Traveler
Fortune
Historical Traveler
National Geographic
National Geographic World
Natural History
New York Magazine
Omni
Psychology Today
Scientific American
Smithsonian
Southwest
Sports Illustrated
Sports Illustrated for Kids
The New Yorker
Time
Time for Kids
University Alumni Magazines
US Airways Attache
U.S. News and World Report

References

Cullinan, B. E. (Ed.) (1992). *Invitation to read: More children's literature in the reading program.* Newark, DE: International Reading Association.

Finley, F. N. (1991). Why students have trouble learning from science texts. In C. Santa & D. E. Alvermann (Eds.), *Science learning: Processes and applications* (pp. 22–27). Newark, DE: International Reading Association.

Freeman, E. B., & Person, D. G. (1998). *Connecting informational children's books with content area learning.* Boston: Allyn & Bacon.

Greenlaw, M. J. (1992). Interacting with informational books. In B. E. Cullinan (Ed.), *Invitations to read: More children's literature in the reading program* (pp. 41–47). Newark, DE: International Reading Association.

Kobrin, B. (1988). *Eyeopener I! How to choose and use children's books about real people, places, and things.* New York: Penguin Books.

Levstik, L. (1990). Research directions: Mediating through literacy texts. *Language Arts, 67,* 848–853.

Manzo, A. V. (1969). The ReQuest procedure. *Journal of Reading, 2,* 123–126.

McKeown, M. G., & Beck, I. L. (1993). Grappling with text ideas: Questioning the author. *Reading Teacher, 46* (7), 16–21.

McNergney, R. F., & Herbert, J. M. (1995). *Foundations of education: The challenge of professional practice* (2nd ed.). Boston: Allyn & Bacon.

Morrow, L. M., Cunningham, K., & Murray-Olsen, M. (1994). *Current strategies for literacy development in early childhood science texts* (Reading Research Report No. 11). College Park, MD: Reading Research Center.

Moss, B. (1991). Children's nonfiction tradebooks: A complement to content area texts. *Reading Teacher, 45* (1), 26–32.

Rosenblatt, L. (1994). The transactional theory of reading and writing. In R. B. Ruddell, M. R. Ruddell, & H. Singer (Eds.), *Theoretical models and processes of reading* (4th ed). Newark, DE: International Reading Association.

Savage, J. (1998). *Teaching reading and writing: Combining skills, strategies, and literature* (2nd ed.). Boston: McGraw Hill.

Short, K. G., Harste, J. C., & Burke, C. (1996). *Creating classrooms for authors and inquirers* (2nd ed.). Portsmouth, NH: Heinemann.

Smith, J. A., Monson, J. A., Dodson, D. (1992). A case study integrating history and reading instruction through literature. *Social Education, 56* (7), 370–375.

Tyson, H., & Woodward, A. (1989). Why students aren't learning very much from textbooks. *Educational Leadership, 47* (3), 14–17.

Vacca, R. T., & Vacca. J. (1999). *Content area reading* (6th ed.). New York: Addison Wesley Longman.

Informational Articles

Anderson, B. (1998), April). How the institution got its start. *US Airways Attache,* p. 69.

Bang! Went the doors of every bank in America. (1997, April). *Smithsonian,* p. 121.

Barry, D. (1997, November 14). The final exam. *Miami Herald.* [Online]. Available: http://www.herald.com/archive/barry/archive/nov.16/htm.

The battle was lost in a zone of silence. (1998, October 26). *U.S. News & World Report,* p. 59.

Begley, S. (1994, August 1). Why does traffic jam? *Newsweek,* p. 53.

Child, G. (1999, January). Hitting the wall. *National Geographic, 195* (1), 79–91.

Collins, J. (1998, June). What time is it? *US Airways Attache,* pp. 30–32.

Greene, B. *The elegant universe.* NY: Norton, 1999.

Keith, J. H. (1998, Fall). The search for the seafloor's secrets. *Bostonia,* pp. 24–27.

Leland, J. (1999, May 10). The secret life of teens. *Newsweek,* pp. 45–50.

Moving beyond the blame game. (1999, May 17). *Newsweek,* pp. 30–32.

Raymo, C. (1999, May 3). Peering through the Hubble telescope to our distant past. *Boston Globe,* p. C-2.

Ross, J. F. (1999, June). Discovering the odds. *Smithsonian,* pp. 133–142.

Tyson, N. de G. (1995, October). Death by black hole. *Natural History,* p. 20.

Widstrand, S. (1998, July/August). Perils in wonderland. *Scandorama,* pp. 31–35.

Chapter 8

Poetry: A Creative Resource for Teaching and Learning in the Content Areas

Elizabeth Paugh
Maureen McLaughlin
Barbara Call
Amy Vandever-Horvath

"A Beautiful Scene: A Cliff at Sunset by Claude Monet"
by Lauren Pigeon

As I look across the cool, calm water,
   A cliff stands tall,
The moon hangs lifelessly in the pale sky,
   A thin mist wraps around me.

As I look across the cool, calm water,
   Wisps of light gray clouds float together like a school of fish,
The stars that peek through the clouds are barely visible,
   The waves rock back and forth to the swaying of the wind.

As I look across the cool, calm water,
   I see the hopes and dreams of the human race,
The creativity of the mind,
   And the art of the soul.

We decided to open our chapter with this student-authored poem because it so beautifully illustrates the use of poetry in content area teaching and learning. While Lauren, a middle school student, has used poetry to express her thoughts about art, one need only consider Shel Silverstein's "Smart" or Carl Sandburg's "Arithmetic" to perceive poetry's connection to math; Jack Prelutsky's "New York Is in North Carolina" or Rosemary Carr and Stephen Benet's "Nancy Hanks" to understand its role in social studies; or Paul Fleischman's "Grasshoppers" or Robert Francis's "Like Ghosts of Eagles" to see its relationship to science. Poetry is a genre that permeates and enriches all subjects of content area study.

Perhaps one reason for poetry's amazing adaptability is its capacity to engage the reader. As Rosenblatt (1980) has observed:

> A poem is not a ready-made object to which a reader is passively exposed. A poem is a happening, an event, in which the listener or reader draws on images and feelings and ideas stirred up by the words of the text; out of these is shaped the lived-through experience. (p. 386)

This description appears to extend to the poet as well—the one who uses the words to document his or her "lived through experience." The dynamic nature of poetry invites students to participate in it as readers of poems written by others and as writers of their own poetry.

In this chapter, we begin by presenting a rationale for using poetry as a creative resource in the content areas. This is followed by a series of creative teaching ideas that focus on using poetry in social studies, science, and mathematics classes. Embedded in the discussion of each subject area is a list of additional content-related poems. Next, we present examples of student-authored poems written in response to content area learning. These include adapted song lyrics, collective impressions, repeated phrase collaborations, acrostics, cinquains, and diamantes.

Rationale for Using Poetry

The use of poetry as an instructional resource exemplifies a meaningful way in which language arts and content area instruction can be integrated. Both learning processes become mutually supportive in this type of creative application to instruction. In addition, poetry can be used to enhance textbook learning. Not only can it be used in conjunction with a motivational activity for a content area lesson, it can also aid students in activating or acquiring pertinent background knowledge before reading the more conceptually dense information contained in textbooks. Further, it can extend students' thinking about various content-related topics by offering different perspectives and encouraging critical thinking. These connections capitalize on the relevancy to the learner, encouraging the attachment of personal meaning as well as an emotional investment in the learning process.

Using poetry in the content areas has myriad benefits for both teachers and students. Teachers can use poetry to do the following:

- Motivate student learning
- Activate prior knowledge
- Encourage in-depth processing of concepts
- Encourage students to formulate personal interpretations
- Offer a different perspective
- Encourage students to take an aesthetic stance
- Extend students' thinking
- Assess student learning.

Poetry provides teachers with the means to capture attention, establish a focus, and encourage discussion before engaging in the lesson. Perhaps it is simply the cadence of the language or the visual images set free in one's imagination that make poetry such an important vehicle for motivating student interest. In any case, prereading activities such as Semantic Maps, Concept of Definition Maps, and Anticipation-Reaction Guides can all be used with poetry to activate knowledge and interest, and aid in organizing students' thoughts on a given topic. As such, poetry can be used to provide the necessary connections between the familiar and the unfamiliar, which is crucial if teaching for understanding is the goal. If understanding is defined as "going beyond the information given," then the metaphorical language of poetry encourages that type of response.

The simple act of reading a poem aloud can in itself serve as a model of explaining ideas in one's "own words" and creating analogies to define concepts. Poetry can encourage students to formulate personal interpretations, explore different perspectives on a given topic, extend thinking, and assess learning. Postreading activities that help to facilitate this process include completing Venn Diagrams, writing first-person narratives or poems, creating artistic representations, engaging in class discussions or debates, and using newspaper and magazine articles to support or develop concepts.

Textbooks serve as a valuable resource for content area instruction, but when they are used exclusively, students are encouraged to focus their attention only on what is to be extracted and remain as residue after the reading has taken place. On the contrary, in aesthetic reading, the reader focuses on the images, feelings, sensations, and ideas that the text evokes during the reading. Research has shown that the evocation of an emotional response signals a higher degree of personal relevance to the learning event

(Rosenblatt, 1980). It stands to reason that, as a result, learning is more memorable. Poetry, perhaps more than any other genre, encourages students to take an aesthetic stance, aiding in the development of their ability to interpret language, explore personal relevance, and identify connections to prior knowledge as well as to implications for further learning.

Poetry also has much to offer students. It enhances students' learning because it provides them with opportunities to do the following:

- Experience an alternative way of learning new information
- Develop communication skills, including active listening
- Gain new perspectives
- Establish personal relevance
- Explore personal interpretations
- Visualize difficult or abstract concepts. (For more information about visualization, see chapter 4).

The more connections that students can make between prior knowledge and new concepts, the more memorable, retrievable, and applicable those concepts become. By providing an alternative avenue to learning, poetry is probably best used to enhance textbook learning. As such, poems can be used to introduce a topic or a lecture, making more difficult concepts easier to visualize from the onset. Poetry can also be used quite effectively to introduce ideas that will be more fully developed in the lesson or reading assignments.

In addition, poetry can be used throughout lessons as a kind of universal language, tapping into the private as well as the public aspects of meaning. It offers students the opportunity to develop communication skills, to think critically, and to gain new perspectives.

Student learning is best supported in an environment that not only encourages connections among subject areas but also between mind and heart. Poetry stimulates the use of mental imagery and critical thinking in all students, but particularly with the hard-to-reach young adult. Within that context, science and math concepts can more easily be visualized, social issues can be discussed or debated, people or events of historical significance can be made authentic, alternate viewpoints can be explored, and connections between personal experiences and new concepts can be made.

Showing students how to learn by supplementing texts with creative instructional applications such as the use of poetry to motivate, enhance, or extend content area learning ensures that teaching and learning will be more memorable to students, more satisfying to teachers, and more enjoyable for both.

Creative Teaching Ideas for Using Poetry in the Content Areas

Because there is no way of knowing what students' past experiences with poetry have been, it is important to dispel any misconceptions before teaching. Among the most frequent student misperceptions are that poetry must always rhyme, poems have only one interpretation, and poetry is boring. Discussing these issues openly assures students that poetry has many formats, is open to personal interpretation, is content-related, and can engender responses ranging from laughter to tears.

The following sample lessons demonstrate how poetry can be used in conjunction with various strategies to engage, guide, or extend students' thinking. Subject areas, topics of study, poem titles, and suggested school levels are provided for each lesson. Examples include classroom applications in social studies, science, and mathematics.

Social Studies
Topics: Types of governments, war or prejudice
Poem: "Mending Wall"
Levels: Middle School, High School

Robert Frost's (1967) poem "Mending Wall" can be used in middle school or high school to introduce a unit on government study comparing and contrasting democracy with dictatorship. The poem also lends itself to a general exploration of man's inhumanity to man and may therefore be used as a prelude to any study involving war or prejudice, including American slavery, the Holocaust, international conflicts, the Iron Curtain, or Apartheid. To engage students' interest, consider using either the Concept of Definition Map (Figure 8-1) or Opinionnaire /Questionnaire (Figure 8-2).

In preparation for your reading of the poem, remind students that they expressed different ideas about walls in the prereading activities. Then ask students, while they are listening to the poem being read, to attend to the different opinions of the author and his neighbor concerning the importance of the wall that separates their properties. After you have read the poem aloud to the class, encourage students to reread the poem silently, highlighting the lines that best illustrate the different opinions. Follow this activity with a class discussion that relates to the opinionaire/questionnaire.

To extend students' thinking, ask them to choose from several activities, including the following:

- Write either a poem or a short narrative about a topic in the unit of study that relates to walls (discrimination, war, political domination, etc).

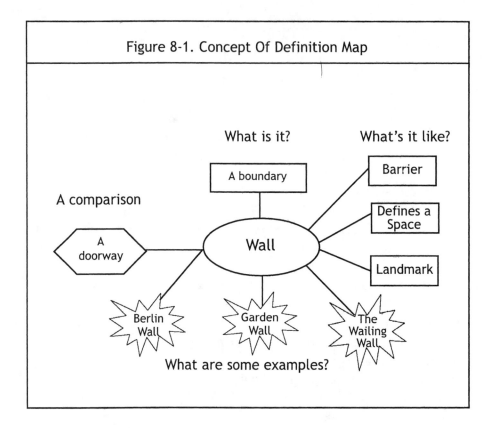

Figure 8-1. Concept Of Definition Map

- Visualize and sketch ways in which "invisible walls" can be broken down.
- Choose a person—such as Abraham Lincoln, Martin Luther King, or Rosa Parks, related to the unit of study—who has worked to break down walls. Research one of these people and create a First-Person Experience (For more information about First-Person Experiences, see chapter 3).
- Read "Mending Wall" and create an artistic representation of the text as it relates to the unit of study. This can be a drawing, a painting, or a collage. Students should then write their interpretation of the poem. When completed, these works can be displayed in the classroom.
- Find a current newspaper or magazine account of some type of "wall" (discrimination, war, political domination, etc.) and write a poem about that incident.

Figure 8-2. Opinionnaire/Questionnaire

1. When you hear the word *wall*, what is the first image that comes to mind?

   Please describe your "wall."

   What does it look like?
   What is it made of?
   Where is it?
   How did it get there?
   What is its purpose?

2. How do walls make you feel?
   Check all that apply. Include an explanation or example.

   _____ safe _____

   _____ confined _____

   _____ excluded _____

   _____ other _____

3. Think about relationships between people. Are there such things as invisible walls?
   _____ yes _____ no

   Explain your response.

Topic: American Slavery/Underground Railroad
Poem: "Harriet Tubman"
Levels: Middle School, High School

E. Greenfield's (1993) poem "Harriet Tubman" can be used in middle school or high school to teach about American slavery and the Underground Railroad. The focus of this lesson is to encourage students to formulate and express their opinions. The poem takes Harriet Tubman's experience out of the history book and allows the students to understand the significance of one person risking her life so that others may be free. To engage students' thinking, ask them to complete the Anticipation Guide (Readence, Bean, & Baldwin, 1998) (Figure 8-3) designed for the pre–Civil War time period.

Figure 8-3. Anticipation Guide

Agree	Disagree	
_____	_____	All people are equal.
_____	_____	When one is faced with an intolerable situation, it is better to run rather than to stay and fight for changes.
_____	_____	If I had been a slave who successfully escaped, I would not have risked my life to help others escape.

Follow this with a brief discussion of student responses. This can easily lead to an informal class debate focusing on risking your life to escape versus waiting to be freed.

After the debate concludes, invite students to join in a choral reading of "Harriet Tubman." Follow this with a class discussion about which side of the debate Harriet Tubman would have supported.

To extend students' thinking, ask them to select one of the following activities:

- Read a biography of Harriet Tubman's life and create a picture book, response journal, or collage focusing on different experiences (before or after escape, en route alone, en route with others, reaching safety).
- Read about other African Americans who escaped slavery or who helped others to escape. Use Venn diagrams to compare and contrast their experiences with Harriet Tubman's experience.

- Read "I Rise" by Maya Angelou and write a class poem using the following format: (a) Each pair of students writes two lines about Harriet Tubman's experiences and/or attitude. (b) Follow each student's verse with the line "I rise." (c) Combine each pair's efforts to create a class poem. (d) Display the poem in the classroom.

Other Poems that can be used as creative resources when teaching social studies include the following:

Poem: "Nancy Hanks"
Poets: Rosemary Carr and Stephen Benet
Connection: Abraham Lincoln
Source: Ferris, H. (1957). *Favorite poems: Old and new.* Garden City, NY: Doubleday.

Poem: "Incident"
Poet: Countee Cullen
Connection: Racial prejudice
Source: Hudson, W. (1993). *Pass it on: African-American poetry for children.* New York: Scholastic.

Poem: "The Pioneer"
Poet: Arthur Guiterman
Connection: The western expansion of the United States
Source: Schauffer, R. H. (1931). *Junior poetry cure.* New York: Dodd, Mead.

Poem: "Dancing Teepees"
Poet: Calvin O. John
Connection: Native Americans
Source: Sneve, V. D. H. (1989). *Dancing teepees: Poems of American Indian youth.* New York: Holiday.

Poem: "Abraham Lincoln Walks at Midnight"
Poet: Vachel Lindsay
Connection: War in general, Abraham Lincoln
Source: *Ferris, H. (1957).* Favorite poems: Old and new. *Garden City, New York: Doubleday.*

Poem: "Paul Revere's Ride"
Poet: Henry Wadsworth Longfellow
Connection: The Revolutionary War
Source: Ferris, H. (1957). *Favorite poems: Old and new.* Garden City, New York: Doubleday.

Poem: "New York Is in North Carolina"
Poet: Jack Prelutsky
Connection: Geography
Source: Prelutsky, J. (1984). *The new kid on the block.* New York: Greenwillow Books.

Poem: "Colors"
Poet: Shel Silverstein
Connection: Civil rights
Source: Silverstein, S. (1974). *Where the sidewalk ends.* New York: Harper Collins

Poem: "Ickle Me, Pickle Me, Tickle Me Too"
Poet: Shel Silverstein
Connection: Exploration
Source: Silverstein, S. (1974). *Where the sidewalk ends.* New York: HarperCollins.

Poem: "There Was an Indian"
Poet: Sir John Squire
Connection: Columbus's explorations
Source: Ferris, H. (1957). *Favorite poems: Old and new.* Garden City, New York: Doubleday.

Science
Topic: Insects
Poem: "Grasshoppers"
Level: Intermediate

Science offers many opportunities for students to read and write poetry using information they are involved in exploring. The poem "Grasshoppers" by Paul Fleischman (1988) from his book *Joyful Noise* may be used to extend the study of insects.

To engage students' thinking, begin by developing a KWLS chart: what students know, what they want to know, what they've learned, what they still want to know. Ask them to brainstorm what they think they already know about insects and what they want to learn about them. Alternatives to using this strategy include preparing a classroom insect display or inviting an entomologist to class to speak about the topic.

Before having the students read the poem, model the paired reader format. Once students have listened to the poem, invite them to read it out loud in pairs. Follow the reading with a discussion of the effectiveness of the format and a continuation of KWLS, in which students record what they have learned and what they still want to know.

To further extend their learning, have students create models of real or imagined insects and write descriptions of them or author poems about insects using the paired reading format or another format of their choosing.

Other science-related poems include the following:
Poem: "The Snake"
Poet: Emily Dickinson
Connection: Snakes.
Source: Elledge, S. (1990). *Wider than the sky: Poems to grow up with.* New York: Harper & Row.

Poem: "Something Told the Wild Geese"
Poet: Rachel Field
Connection: Study of animal migration
Source: Lawerence, M. (1967). *An invitation to poetry.* Menle Park, CA: Addison-Wesley.

Poem: "Like Ghosts of Eagles"
Poet: Robert Francis
Connection: Water pollution in North American rivers
Source: Friebert, S., & Young, D. (1989). *The Longman anthology of contemporary American poetry.* New York: Longman.

Poem: "Giraffes"
Poet: Mary Ann Hoberman
Connection: Study of jungle animals
Source: Whipple, L. (1989). *Eric Carle's animals, animals.* New York: Philomel.

Poem: "Snow Falling"
Poet: Gillian Hughes
Connection: Meteorology
Source: Phillips, N. (1990). *New treasury of poetry.* New York: Stewart, Taburi & Chang.

Poem: "Bats"
Poet: Randell Jarrell
Connection: Mammals or nocturnal animals
Source: Elledge, S. (1990). *Wider than the sky: Poems to grow up with.* New York: Harper & Row.

Poem: "A Jellyfish"
Poet: Marianne Moore
Connection: Marine life
Source: Kavanagh, P. J. (1985). *The Oxford books of short poems.* Oxford
   University Press.

Poem: "There's a Worm in My Apple"
Poet: Jack Prelutsky
Connection: A motivational tool in the study of insects
Source: Prelutsky, J. (1990). *Something big has been here.* New York:
   Greenwillow Books.

Poem: "American Wizard"
Poet: Lawrence Schimel
Connection: Thomas Edison, invention of electric light
Source: Hopkins, L. B. (Ed.). 1999. *Lives: Poems about famous
   Americans.* New York: HarperCollins.

Poem: "Boa Constrictor"
Poet: Shel Silverstein
Connection: Science
Source: Silverstein, S. (1974). *Where the sidewalk ends.* New York:
   HarperCollins.

Poem: "Rain"
Poet: Shel Silverstein
Connection: Science, Meteorology
Source: Silverstein, S. (1974). *Where the sidewalk ends.* New York:
   HarperCollins.

Mathematics
Topic: Problem Solving, Geometry
Poem: "The Roads of Math"
Level: Middle School, High School

Poetry often challenges the reader to solve problems, which makes it a
perfect companion to topics in mathematics. "The Roads of Math" by J.
Dielle (1988) has several applications to problem solving in geometry at the
middle school or high school level.

Begin by engaging students in the creation of a Semantic Map focusing
on geometry. Incorporate and classify students' ideas. Discuss the final map

with the class. Then read the poem to students twice. For the first reading, ask them simply to listen to the author's message. For the second reading, ask them to sketch the geometric figures described in each stanza.

Once the readings are finished, the poem can be discussed, offering students an opportunity to share their personal interpretations as well as their sketches. Students can then choose a partner and create photographic essays on "Geometry in Everyday Life." To create the essay, students should take photographs of geometric shapes they see in their everyday experiences. Once the photo project is complete, students can use it as an information source to write a poem in the format of their choice.

Other poems related to mathematics include the following:

Poem: "The Storm Snapped Its Fingers"
Poet: Elizabeth Coatesworth
Connection: Problem solving
Source: Hall, D. (1985). *The Oxford book of children's verse in America.* New York: Oxford University Press.

Poem: "The Wise Triangle"
Poet: Vasko Popa
Connection: Geometry
Source: Haughton, H. (1988). *The Chatto book of nonsense poetry.* London: Chatto & Windus.

Poem: "Arithmetic"
Poet: Carl Sandburg
Connection: The functions of mathematics
Source: Lawerence, M. (1988). *An invitation to poetry.* Menlo Park, CA: Addison-Wesley.

Poem: "One Inch Tall"
Poet: Shel Silverstein
Connection: Measurement
Source: Silverstein, S. (1974). *Where the sidewalk ends.* New York: HarperCollins.

Poem: "Smart"
Poet: Shel Silverstein
Connection: Money, base ten system
Source: Silverstein, S. (1974). *Where the sidewalk ends.* New York: HarperCollins.

Other Poetry Resources

In addition to the volumes cited throughout this chapter, there are numerous other poetry books that contain a variety of content-related titles. The following are among our favorites.

Berry, J. (1995). *Classic poems to read aloud*. New York: Larousse Kingfisher Chambers.

Prelutsky, J. (1990). *Something big has been here*. New York: Greenwillow Books.

Prelutsky, J. (1991). *For laughing out loud: Poems to tickle your funnybone*. New York: Greenwillow Books.

Prelutsky, J. (1994). *A pizza the size of the sun*. New York: Greenwillow Books.

Ryder, J. (1996). *Jaguar in the rainforest*. New York: Morrow.

Rylant, C. (1996). *The whales*. New York: Blue Sky/Scholastic.

Silverstein, S. (1981). *A light in the attic*. New York: HarperCollins.

Silverstein, S. (1996). *Falling up*. New York: HarperCollins

Yolen, J. (1996). *Sea watch: A book of poetry*. New York: Philomel Books.

Student-Authored Poetry

Creating their own poems expands the students' role from reader to author and further engages them in critical thinking processes. It also offers multiple opportunities for student choice: They may self-select their topics, write in response to something they've read or reflect on personal content-related experiences, choose from a variety of formats to express their ideas, write collaboratively or individually, and express perspectives ranging from humorous observations to serious contemplations.

If reader response is viewed as the basis for understanding and critically interpretating what is read, then student-authored poetry encourages such an outcome by the very nature of the exercise. Student-authored poetry, a response as personal as a signature, individualizes the connections made between the learner and the learning event. These connections make learning applicable and therefore memorable for each student.

In the examples that follow, students at various grade levels have created poems by using adapted song lyrics and the repeated-phrase technique. After these, more common poetry formats, including acrostics, cinquains, and diamantes, are presented.

Teaching Idea: Adapted Song Lyrics
Content Area: Social Studies: The decade of the 1950s
Level: High School

In this instance, high school social studies students were asked to work cooperatively in small groups to design an alternative means of sharing information on a recently completed unit on the 1950s. The teacher offered options but encouraged students to make a creative, personal response. She explained that evaluation would be based on factual content and format…and that upon completion of the project students would be given an opportunity to share their writing with the rest of the class. The students who wrote this variation of lyrics to a familiar song ("Happy Together" by the Turtles) share an affinity for musical expression, which makes this format meaningful to them. This assignment allowed for student choice and, as such, accommodated a variety of needs, abilities, and interests in student products in meeting the instructional goal.

"So Happy Together in the 1950s"
by Suzanne Paugh and Nicole Borasso

1. Imagine rising up from debt and war
   Not knowing what the next day brings we'll fear no more.
   And now it's time to settle down and start anew
   We'll do it together.

2. With no expense to spare and cars to roam
   We'll move out to suburbia and start our home
   With luxuries like dishwashers and telephones
   We'll do it together.

   Chorus:
   I can't help lovin' the life that I do, as a homemakin' mom
   In the '50s baby the skies are all blue, as the breadwinnin' dad.

3. Sue Johnson calls me up invites to dine
   We'll meet down at the local park your kids and mine
   Imagine how the world could be so very fine
   So happy together.

   Repeat Chorus

4. Productions booming up and money's good
   We got a baby on the way just like we should

John Levitt built our premade house fast as he could
They did it together.
Ba, ba, ba. ba. ba…

5. We preach conformity on the same tones
    We keep our standards up with Mr. Jones
    We're working to build social norms all our own.
    We'll make it together.

    Repeat Chorus

6. We join to pray each week in Sunday's best
    Newcomers come from north and south to meet the west
    The spectrum's moving further right without a rest
    We'll do it together.

7. The TV's always on with ads to sell
    We meet boys at the drive-in films hair slicked with gel
    They never fail to pay the bill 'cause money's swell
    We love it together
    We made it together
    They did it together
    We love it together
    We made it together
    They did it together
    We love it together
    We made it together
    They did it together!

Teaching Idea: Collective Impressions Poems
Content Area: Social Studies
Level: High School, College

This poem was written collaboratively by a group of college students studying social development in cities of third world countries. A clipboard was passed from seat to seat in various bus stations and airport terminals as the students traveled. Each student read all previous verses before adding his or her own. The final compilation of all the verses created a collective impression of Bombay while retaining the personalized responses of each student. Reading this poem at their final program before leaving Bombay provided closure to their experiences and a pathway for evoking vivid memories inherent to those experiences.

This same exercise would have a similar application for high school social studies students in response to textbook reading, the viewing of films or videos, or as a response to a field experience. It provides an avenue for establishing personal relevance and visualizing abstract concepts.

"Mumbai Meditations"
by Melissa Paugh

Inside my mosaic of thoughts swirl until the
Colors are muffled. Desperately, I try to arrange my window
Into a stained-glass depiction of Bombay life.
Just when a picture is about to emerge,
My thoughts are interrupted by the shouts of
A vendor selling peddling pushing drums.
And so I return with my kaleidoscoped impressions,
Kept spinning by the uniqueness of the experience.

The old against the new,
The traditional wedged among the modern,
Growing, forming, emerging
Against the dingy expanse of concrete, corrugated boards, and brick
The blues, pinks, oranges, and purples of freshly cleaned saris
Head held high, she steps into her well-kept abode.

Dust, people, more dust, more people
Bright sun, shiny sea
Small children running barefoot
Young boy asleep on the wet street
With his worn shoeshine box,
Hawkers go home!
More nutties please…

So much humanity, so much beauty.
A grandmother teaches her granddaughter
A lesson as the small girl sits watching
The trains go by. A man murmurs a few words
In Hindi or Marathi,
And broad smiles under well-kept whiskers
Grow into warm laughs,
Random PO-lice wearing berets, artillery
And sneering eyes. Midnight special, never fully clean,
Us or the cabdrivers, but tougher than leather all the same.

Three weeks of connection and dialogue
About our lives before entering the smog
And your lives revealed bit by bit
To feel the excitement between us and
The future that promises reunion.

Teaching Idea: Repeated-Phrase Collaborative Poems
(adapted from Kaywell, 1993)
Content Areas: All
Levels: Intermediate, Middle, High School

After reading a text chapter or a content-related novel, have students choose three passages of one to three lines that they found especially meaningful or powerful. Working in small groups, they should organize the passages to evoke a mood and place the same phrase after each passage. For example, for the Great Depression in the United States, the repeated phrase might be "We will survive." For scientific discoveries, the repeated phrase might be "We will discover."

Teaching Idea: Acrostic Poems
Content Areas: All
Levels: Intermediate, Middle, High School

When writing acrostic poems, students write vertically the word or phrase that is the focus of their poem. Then they use each letter of the word to start a line of the poem. In the first example, a fourth-grade science student writes about his understanding of watersheds. In the second example, middle school students write about their field trip to a science museum.

"Watershed"
by Nathaniel Wiley Taylor

Watershed

A lot of bodies of water

Tumble through stony valleys

Enter

Rivers and

Streams

Have a lot of water

Ends at the ocean's

Door

"Science Museum"
by Chad Rinker, Mike Teible, Nate Brosius

So very
Cool
It
Entertains
New
Comers
Everywhere

Many things for
Us to
See and become
Educated
Until we
Move on.

Teaching Idea: Cinquains
Content Areas: All
Levels: All

The cinquain is another poetry format that can be used at all levels in all content areas to write a poem about a person, place, or issue. The format for the cinquain and a middle school example follow.

_____
One-word Noun

_____   _____
Two adjectives describing line 1

_____   _____   _____
ing words telling actions of line 1

_____   _____   _____   _____
Four-word phrase describing a feeling related to line 1

_____
One word—Synonym
or reference to line 1

"Green House"
by Alicia Wagner, Amanda LaBar, Krystal Funk

Reptile
Scaly, fast
Slithering, twisting, writhing
Clever, cold-blooded animal
Snake

Teaching Idea: Diamante
Content Areas: All
Levels: Intermediate, Middle, High School

The diamante encourages the writer to contrast a topic with its opposite. The following example addresses peace and war.

"Peace"
by Beth Gress

Peace
Subject—One noun

Quiet Agreeable
Two adjectives describing the subject

Calming Nurturing Inspiring
Three participles (*ing* words) telling about the subject

Contentment Freedom Conflict Weapons
Four nouns—First two relate to subject—Last two relate to the opposite

Crushing Storming Debilitating
Three participles (*ing* words) telling about the opposite

Harmful Dangerous
Two adjectives describing the opposite

War
Opposite of subject—One noun

Concluding Thoughts

As an instructional resource, poetry provides an array of ideas to encourage critical and creative thinking in the content areas. The variety of poems available and the possibilities of student-authored poems provide not only stimulating instruction but also meaningful learning.

We support Rosenblatt's (1980) thinking that poems are events. They invite us to participate, give us cause for reflection, enrich our experiences, and emerge as essential to life.

References

Angelou, M. (1994). *The complete collected poems of Maya Angelou.* New York: Random House.

Dielle, J. (1988). The roads to math. In M. Lawerence (Ed.), *An invitation to poetry.* Menle Park, CA: Addison-Wesley.

Fleischman, P. (1988). *Joyful noise: Poems to grow up with.* New York: Harper & Row.

Frost, R. (1967). *Complete poems of Robert Frost.* New York: Holt, Rinehart, & Winston.

Greenfield, E. (1993). Harriet Tubman. In W. Hudson (Ed.), *Pass it on: African-American poetry for children.* New York: Scholastic.

Kaywell, J. F. (1993). Anne Frank's *The Diary of a Young Girl*: World War II and young adult literature. In *Adolescent literature as a complement to the classics.* Norwood, MA: Christopher-Gordon.

Readence, J. E., Bean, T. W., & Baldwin, R. S. (1998). *Content area literacy: An integrated approach* (6th ed.). Dubuque, IA: Kendall/Hunt.

Rosenblatt, L. (1980). What facts does this poem teach you? *Language Arts, 57* (4), 386–394.

Chapter 9

Celebrating Mathematics: Innovative, Student-Centered Approaches for Teaching and Learning

Maureen McLaughlin
Rita Corbett
Cynthia Stevenson

When we walked into the classroom, it was abuzz with voices and music—both computerized and human. Bright, attention-grabbing colors sprung from the student-designed posters that covered the walls and hung from the ceiling. Desks were in a circle and discussion was lively. The focus of the day's activities was prime and composite numbers. Some students were seated, creating word-works posters to explain the mathematical terminology. Others were busy writing song lyrics based on math metaphors they had created. Some were investigating the topic on an algebra-based CD-ROM. Still others were representing their understanding through visualization and drawing. A sign read WELCOME TO MATH 10. We were mesmerized, yet we all had the same thoughts: What a wonderfully innovative educational setting! The teacher is teaching, the students are learning, and all are feeling mathematically empowered!

As we focus on 21st-century mathematics, scenarios such as this are becoming increasingly common at the intermediate, middle school and high school levels. These classrooms are constructivist in nature, conscious of individual students' strengths, and aware of the value of student-teacher and peer interaction.

This chapter is about such student-centered teaching and learning in mathematics. It begins by exploring mathematical literacy and its theoretical underpinnings. This is followed by the characteristics of math students of the 21st century and a lesson format designed to engage, guide, and extend students' thinking. Finally, it presents a series of creative teaching ideas for integrating innovative, active learning in mathematics classrooms at the intermediate, middle school, and high school levels.

The Rationale for Creative and Innovative Teaching

The days of having only one way to solve a problem and fearing to speak in math class because you might utter the wrong answer have transitioned into times of personal interpretation, response-centered classrooms, and social construction of mathematical knowledge. The primary goal of mathematics teachers is to help students achieve their mathematical potential; the primary goal of math students is to achieve that potential through mathematical literacy and self-esteem.

To understand mathematical literacy, it is necessary to have (a) an operational definition of mathematics and (b) an understanding of the National Council of Teachers of Mathematics (1989) publications, *Curriculum and Evaluation Standards for School Mathematics*. To accommodate the former, Battista (1999) suggests the following:

> Mathematics is first and foremost a form of reasoning. In the context of reasoning analytically about particular types of quantitative and spatial phenomena, mathematics consists of thinking in a logical manner, formulating and testing conjectures, making sense of things, and forming and justifying judgments, inferences, and conclusions. We do mathematics when we recognize and describe patterns; construct physical and/or conceptual models of phenomena; create symbol systems to help us represent, manipulate, and reflect on ideas; and invent procedures to solve problems. (p. 428)

To accommodate the latter, Reys, Robinson, Sconiers, & Mark (1999) report the following:

> The *NCTM Standards* call for curriculum and instruction that engage and challenge students and prepare them for continued study and growth in mathematics skill and understanding. They call for the development of mathematical habits of mind and of understanding and appreciation of the important role of mathematics in scientific applications and in daily life. (p. 455)

Whitin and Whitin (1997) further observe that the NCTM standards "emphasize the constructive nature of knowledge and the importance of language in understanding and exploring mathematical ideas" (p. 108). This constructive nature of knowledge refers to students' ability to create personal meaning by actively relating new learning to prior knowledge and experiences (Alper, Fendel, Fraser, & Resek, 1996; Mercer, Jordan, & Miller, 1996).

Having an authentic context for learning is another significant feature of constructivism. This encourages students to make connections between classroom learning and experiences outside of school (Alper et al., 1996; Mercer et al., 1996; Whitin & Whitin, 1997). This greatly benefits students because, as Alper et al. note, "Students construct ideas in context; instead of just memorizing definitions, mathematical concepts and methods have real meaning for them" (p. 20).

Although the term *literacy* has historically been connected to the ability to read and write, the word is now being used to describe students' abilities to successfully function in other areas. Technological literacy and mathematical literacy are just two examples of the term's new use. Reys et al. (1999) note that the NCTM Standards and mathematical literacy are inextricably linked. "The intent of the *Standards* is to help students become mathematically literate, which includes being able to explore, to conjecture, to reason logically, and to use a variety of mathematical methods to solve problems"(p. 455). Steele and Arth (1998) concur noting, "Society is increasingly dependent on mathematical literacy" (p. 44).

In order to achieve mathematical literacy, students first need to value math. "They need to understand mathematics in ways that will give them the power to make sense of the world around them and to confront and solve new problems" (Steele & Arth, 1998, p. 44). This understanding gives students confidence and empowers development of mathematical self-esteem.

Connecting Theory and Practice: Teaching Mathematics in the 21st Century

Inquiry, multiple intelligences, learning styles, critical and creative thinking, flexible grouping, standards-based assessment, and a student-centered paradigm are all components of innovative mathematics instruction. In addition, instructional processes such as modeling and scaffolding facilitate students' understanding. All of these elements contribute to intermediate, middle school, and high school students' development of the following characteristics. Math students of the 21st century:

- Are active learners
- Engage in critical and creative thinking
- Experience teacher modeling and scaffolding
- Learn through social experiences

- Learn authentically—connecting learning to life beyond the class-room
- Self-reflect as a natural part of learning
- Are strategic problem solvers
- Transfer math skills and strategies to other areas of study
- Value math as a necessary life skill
- Are technologically engaged
- Possess mathematical self-esteem
- Are mathematically empowered.

As teachers of 21st century mathematics, we need to provide contexts that nurture these characteristics in order to help students experience their mathematical potentials. The following strategies and activities facilitate that process.

Creative Teaching Ideas

Mathematical literacy encompasses many aspects of thinking and communication. For this reason we have included a variety of strategies in this section that are appropriate for all levels. Each has unique qualities that help students to focus their thinking. The ideas provide ways for students to engage in reading math problems and then extend the process to provide continuing steps to work through the problem solving. Teacher modeling is an essential component of successful strategy use. Taking time to model each step of the process has several benefits. First, it shows students that the teacher has ownership of the concept. Second, teacher modeling helps students to understand how the strategy works. Third, it offers students the opportunity to ask questions to clarify aspects of the strategy. Modeling also helps students to remember how the process functions as they begin using it themselves.

Teaching Idea: Paraphrasing
Content Area: Mathematics
Levels: Intermediate, Middle, High School

Paraphrasing helps students to translate mathematical language into conversational terms. It gives students an opportunity to hear problems or directions as they are written, as well as in the language of their peers.

To use Paraphrasing at the intermediate level, do the following:
- Ask a capable reader to read a problem or set of directions.
- Direct the class to cover the problem or directions with their hands.
- Then ask, "Who can tell us what we are supposed to do?"
- Have a volunteer paraphrase, or restate, the problem or directions in his or her own words.

- Students then work individually or with a partner to solve the problem or begin the activity.

An additional step to this strategy might occur after a volunteer paraphrases the words read by a capable reader. Students can then turn to a partner and repeat or restate the problem or directions before beginning the work.

For Paraphrasing at the middle and high school levels, students can jot down the directions at the top of their papers and then discuss them with a peer. When this strategy is used often, students soon become savvy and both read along and listen carefully as directions or problems are being read. In addition, paraphrasing is a skill that benefits students across the curriculum, so learning it in math will help the students become more proficient learners in all academic areas.

Teaching Idea: What's the Question?
Content Area: Mathematics
Levels: Intermediate, Middle, High School

An old joke about a bus route is often used to demonstrate how programmed we are to think of math as simply the manipulation of numbers. The joke begins with the statement "You are the bus driver" and goes on to describe the distance between stops on the bus route and the number of passengers who get on or off at each stop. For example, "The bus leaves the station with 18 passengers, travels 2 miles to the first stop, drops off 6 passengers, and picks up 5 more. At the second stop, which is 3 miles away, 7 passengers get off and 9 more get on." By the time that four or five stops on the bus route have been described, the students are either totally immersed in attempting to keep both distances and number of passengers straight, or they have totally given up trying to keep track. The punch line is delivered in the form of the question "How old is the bus driver?" Usually about 95% of the students respond with either a completely blank look or a numerical guess based on some set of number combinations from the problem, but a few people will remember the original statement, "You are the bus driver," and know that the answer is their own age.

The point is that knowing the question would have saved the students a great deal of work. Often, students in math class read problems, then simply begin manipulating numbers without really identifying the question being asked. The What's the Question? strategy provides students with a focus as they interpret problems or directions. This strategy works at all grade levels.

When students are directed to "look for the question" in math , they discover a purpose for reading. By setting a purpose, students focus on a particular idea and make reading an active, meaning-constructing process. Mitchel, a 5th grader, describes the What's the Question? strategy in Figure 9-1.

Figure 9-1. Mitchel Using "What's the Question"

Mr. Erler taught us a uniquike way to do word problems. for example, telephones are packaged 20 to a crate. The Kelso Building needs 150 telephones. How many crates have to be opened to fill the order?

1. First you read and look at the problem.
2. Then you find the question and write it down. The question is, How many crates have to be opened to fill the order?
3. Then you find the facts, and the facts are, Telephones are packaged 20 to a crate, and The Kelso Building needs 150 telephones. Then write them down.
4. Then you find wether you are going to +, -, x, or ÷.

(On this problem you ÷. This is the prosses.)

5. Then you write the problem, The problem is:

$$20\overline{)150}$$

6. Then you figure out the answer. The answer is:

$$20\overline{)150}7\,r10$$
$$-140$$
$$10$$

$$\begin{array}{r}20\\ \times 7\\ \hline 140\end{array}$$

$$\begin{array}{r}20\\ \times 8\\ \hline 160\end{array}$$

7. The answer is The Kelso Building needs to open 8 crates to fill the order.

The need to focus on the question being asked before attempting to solve the problem may seem obvious to adults, but often it is not obvious to students. Students concentrate on simply "doing something" with the numbers presented in a problem rather than on understanding what is being asked. Fifth graders who have worked with the "What's the question?" strategy indicate that it is helpful to them:

> "You will find out that these steps will help a lot. It helps me understand and it helps me organize everything."—Danielle

> "It helped me a lot. I started to get the problems. It helped me slow down."—Willie

> "It helped me a lot. When I did not know how to do this, I was terrible at word problems, but now I am very good."—Jessica

Teaching Idea: What's Happening?
Content Area: Mathematics
Levels: Intermediate, Middle, High School

The second thing that students need to recognize when they are working with mathematical text is what, if anything, is happening. There are times in math when we are merely *observing* or *describing*. Examples of this include "What are the characteristics of a hexagon?" and "What does the expression $5n - 2$ represent?" At other times we are *comparing*. Examples include "How are a hexagon and a pentagon alike and different?", "List the following integers from greatest to least value," and "What is the tangent ratio of angle A?" At still other times we are *combining* or *separating* groups or amounts. Examples of this include all operation and equation work.

After determining what the question is, students need to determine what if anything is happening. When observing, a list is in order; when comparing, a diagram or table is in order; when combining or separating groups, three questions become essential: Have? Happen? Result? (These are explained in the next strategy.)

Teaching Idea: Have? Happen? Result?
Content Area: Mathematics
Levels: Intermediate, Middle, High School

No matter how complex a mathematical question, operational problems are solved in a series of one action at a time. A simple problem like $3 + 5 = ?$ is completed by asking What do I have? A group of three. What happened to it? A group of five was added. What is the result? A total of eight. Similarly, a complex algebraic equation like $d = \sqrt{12{,}800h + h^2}$ is nothing more than a series of the same questions to arrive at a solution.

The following problem and solution illustrate this thinking strategy:

Find the distance to the horizon from a satellite 4,200 km above the Earth. Using the "Have? Happen? Result?" formula, tell the distance in kilometers to the horizon, from a satellite h km above the Earth.

What do we have?	A formula and a height.
What is happening?	We will square the height.
What is the result?	We now have $\sqrt{12,800\,h + 17,640,000}$
What is happening?	We need to multiply 12,800 h.
What is the result?	We now have $\sqrt{53,760,000 + 17,640,000}$
What is happening?	We need to add.
What is the result?	We now have $\sqrt{71,400,000}$
What is happening?	We need to find the square root (calculator!)
What is the result?	8449.852 or about 8500 km to the horizon.

Giving students a quick and consistent pattern to look for as they read mathematical text facilitates their thinking. No matter what the problem contains, ask them to determine *what they have, what has happened* or is happening to what they have, and *what the result of the action is.* A complex problem is nothing more than a series of simple steps repeated over and over again until one finds the result.

Teaching Idea: K-W-L: What We Know, What We Want to Know, What We Learned
Content Area: Mathematics
Levels: Intermediate, Middle, High School

Recent information about learning and the brain reinforces the idea that in order for new information to be remembered, it must be linked to what the learner already knows. According to Jensen (1997), the more links the brain establishes . . . the firmer the information is woven in neurologically. The K-W-L technique (Ogle, 1986), which was developed to improve reading comprehension, may also be used effectively in mathematics instruction to activate prior knowledge about a particular math topic. As you begin a new chapter, theme, or topic in math, ask students to brainstorm and discuss what they think they already know about that topic. For example, if you are about to begin work with basic fraction concepts, one student may remember that there are always pictures of pizzas in the math book when you work on fractions. Other students may already know that fractions are about parts, that they have a top number and a bottom number, that you can add them, and that they are used in recipes.

Figure 9-2. K-W-L—Fractions		
K—what we think we KNOW	W—what we WANT to know	L—what we LEARNED
- pictures of pizzas - about parts - top number and bottom number - used in recipes		

A chart, such as the one in Figure 9-2, is used to record student responses. Use of the title "what we think we know" in the first column allows for what students already know about fractions to be listed, then corrected later as misconceptions are clarified. In the second column, record what students want to know about fractions. After they have completed work on the topic, the third column of the chart may be used during a review session to record what they learned.

The K-W-L chart may initially be used for whole-class responses. After students become familiar with this strategy, it may be used for group, paired, or individual responses.

Teaching Idea: K-W-D-L
Content Area: Mathematics
Levels: Intermediate, Middle, High School

A modified K-W-L chart, described by Shaw, Chambless, Chessin, Price, and Beardain (1997) at the University of Mississippi, may be used as an organizational tool for group problem solving (Figure 9-3). In addition to the original "what we think we know, what we want to know, and what we learned" categories, another step is inserted in which students describe "what we did."

Figure 9-3. K-W-D-L Problem Solving	
K—what we think we **know**	W—what we **want** to know
D—what we **did**	L—what we **learned**

To use the K-W-D-L strategy for group problem solving, students begin by reading and paraphrasing a problem. Next, they list information provided in the problem in the K quadrant (what we think we know) on the chart. In the W quadrant (what we want to know), the group comes to agreement on what is being asked and records the question. These two steps provide structure for students as they interpret the problem and plan how to solve it. Shaw et al. inserted the D step to the original strategy to create a quadrant to record "what we did." Here, students identify and illustrate their plans and processes for solving the problem. The L, or final step, is used to record and defend the answer or answers to the problem.

Teaching Idea: Write and Draw
Content Area: Mathematics
Levels: Intermediate, Middle, High School
Some learners prefer to process information verbally, while others process visually. The Write and Draw strategy allows students to use both language and symbols to make their thinking about problem solving visible to themselves and others. To begin this strategy, a problem is posed. Students read or listen to the problem and paraphrase if desired. Then students record their thinking about how to solve the problem on a paper that has been divided in half vertically. On one side of the paper, students draw a picture to show how they would solve the problem. On the other side of the paper, they use words to describe how they solved the problem. Emily W. is a third grader whose use of the Write and Draw strategy has improved her prob-

lem-solving ability (See Figure 9-4a). Justin, a middle school student, makes a more sophisticated use of this strategy by analyzing his drawing to determine the best problem solution (See Figure 9-4b). At the high school level, the additional requirement of writing a math sentence further enhances mathematical communication (See Figure 9-4c).

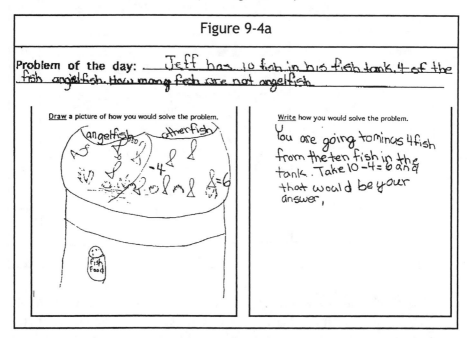

Figure 9-4a

Problem of the day: _Jeff has 10 fish in his fish tank. 4 of the fish angelfish. How many fish are not angelfish_

Draw a picture of how you would solve the problem.

Write how you would solve the problem.

You are going to minus 4 fish from the ten fish in the tank. Take 10−4=6 and that would be your answer.

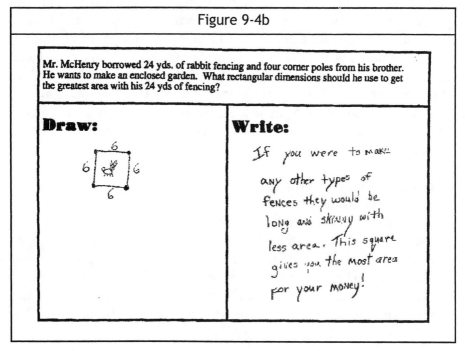

Figure 9-4b

Mr. McHenry borrowed 24 yds. of rabbit fencing and four corner poles from his brother. He wants to make an enclosed garden. What rectangular dimensions should he use to get the greatest area with his 24 yds of fencing?

Draw:

Write:

If you were to make any other types of fences they would be long and skinny with less area. This square gives you the most area for your money!

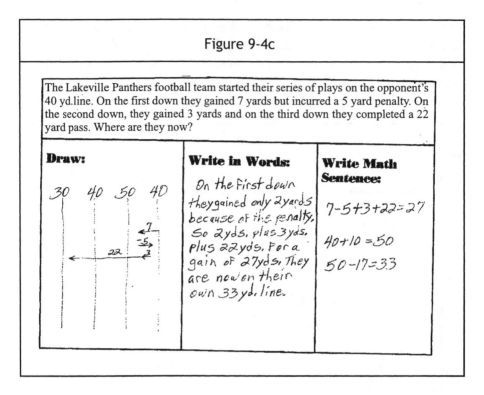

Figure 9-4c

The Lakeville Panthers football team started their series of plays on the opponent's 40 yd.line. On the first down they gained 7 yards but incurred a 5 yard penalty. On the second down, they gained 3 yards and on the third down they completed a 22 yard pass. Where are they now?

Draw:	Write in Words:	Write Math Sentence:
30 40 50 40 22	On the first down they gained only 2yards because of the penalty. So 2yds, plus 3yds, plus 22yds. For a gain of 27yds. They are now on their own 33yd. line.	7-5+3+22=27 40+10 =50 50-17=33

The Write and Draw strategy offers a vehicle for linking the symbols and the language of mathematics. If we could see inside the brains of students as they are using this strategy, we would see the frontal lobe, or front part, of the brains working as they engage in thinking about problem solving. We would also see a great deal of activity in the right hemisphere as they use symbols or pictures to illustrate their thinking and in the left hemispheres as they use words to describe their thinking. In a classroom where students are using both symbols and language to reflect their mathematical thinking, one can almost hear the snapping and crackling of brain connections happening! (For more information about visualization and sketching, see chapter 4.)

Teaching Idea: Be a Math Author
Content Area: Math
Levels: Intermediate, Middle, High School

When students create their own math problems, they become more interested and engaged in solving problems. Designing written problems is an effective way to tap into students' personal experiences and bridge the gap between existing and new knowledge. In addition, practice in interpreting problems invented by peers helps them to better interpret formal math problems presented in textbooks or by teachers. When engaging in the Be a Math Author strategy, students create problems to be solved by classmates. Problem topics may be left open to the imagination of the students or be directed by a topic currently being studied in math class (see Figure 9-5).

Figure 9-5. Student – Authored Math Problems

Intermediate Examples

Warren likes to bike ride to school. His school has 6 bike racks. Each bike can hold 12 bikes. One day 65 kids rode their bikes to school. Can all of their bikes fit in the bike racks?

-Maren G.

The Broncos have won 12 games this year. They have played 16 games. How many games have they lost? How many will they have won if they win one-sixth of the 6 playoff games?

-Ryan H.

Middle School Example

Dana had a babysitting job each weekend for 6 weeks. She made $12 the first weekend, $18 the second weekend, and then $30, $42, $6 and $18. What is the average amount of money she earned each weekend?

-Cristin M.

High School Example

Mel's Music Mart has a special CD club. If you join the club for $39.00 a year, you can buy CDs for $9.95 each instead of $14.95 each. Would it be wise to join the club if you buy about 20 CDs per year?

-Jamel G.

Next, have students exchange problems and solve a partner's created problem. Answers are then submitted to the author to be checked. Problems may be exchanged several times. Problems may also be exchanged with students in another classroom.

Anticipation-Reaction Guide

The Anticipation-Reaction Guide (Readence, Bean, & Baldwin, 1998) is designed to activate students' prior knowledge about a topic before reading and serves as a guide for subsequent reading.

To use the Guide, begin by identifying the major concepts. Then write three to five general statements that relate to these concepts. Students need to be able to connect the statements to their background knowledge.

Share the directions orally. Explain to students that they will need to agree or disagree with the statements and defend their responses. Students then respond, either individually or in small groups, and a class discussion ensues, with students sharing their opinions.

In Figure 9-6, fractions are the topic of the Anticipation-Reaction Guide.

Figure 9-6. Anticipation/Reaction Guide

Agree   Disagree

_____   _____   Fractions are always less than 1.

_____   _____   Fractions are hard to use.

_____   _____   People use fractions in everyday life experiences.

After students have learned about the topic, they may revisit the Anticipation-Reaction Guide and explain how their thoughts have changed because of discussion or text content. As an alternative reaction, students may select a guide statement to respond to in their journals.

Teaching Idea: Paired or Trio Retellings
Content Area: Mathematics
Levels: Intermediate, Middle, High School

Wood (1992) suggests using the retelling strategy in mathematics. Students in pairs or trios are given different computational problems. Each student writes out the process used in solving his or her problem and presents it in an enlarged version on poster paper to the group. Each student then retells his or her problem-solving method to the partner(s).

This activity reminds students that there are multiple ways to approach problem solving and offers them a forum for sharing their reasoning with their peers. It also encourages them to be analytic as they listen to the retellings. After the problems have been retold, the posters can be displayed for other students to see.

Teaching Idea: Math Journals
Content Area: Mathematics
Levels: Intermediate, Middle, High School

When maintaining journals, students may write about a self-selected topic or respond to a prompt provided by the teacher. When reflecting on their students' journals, Gordon and MacInnis (1993) observed, "Students saw the math journal as a place to take risks, to make mistakes, to sort out and be open about problems they had in learning mathematics" (p. 41).

Journals provide an informal way to promote meaningful communication between student and teacher. It is important to note that while we acknowledge the value of conventional spelling and correct grammar, we do not evaluate journals for these elements. This is one of several factors that contribute to students being much more open when writing in a journal than they may be at other times.

Journal prompts can be related to any aspect of math. Figure 9-7 offers a list of generic prompts that can be adapted for use at the intermediate, middle, and high school levels. These prompts are particularly effective when modeling the journal process.

Figure 9-7. Journal Prompts

1. Explain what you know about_____ (a particular math operation).

2. (a) Create, solve, and explain a math problem using a math concept we studied in class this week. (b) Explain how you used technology to facilitate your work.

3. Explain how you could use_____ (fractions, algebraic equations, geometry, etc.) in another class or outside school.

4. Use the newspaper to find an example of how a business in our community uses math. Respond to the article in your journal, citing the math concept(s) used and your thoughts on other ways that math might benefit the company.

cont.

5. Create a poem about a particular math concept.

6. Write a story or a song that incorporates mathematical concepts.

7. What are_____(fractions, decimals, algebraic equations, geometric principles, etc.)?

8. Write questions about something in math that you are having difficulty understanding or write questions about something we haven't studied yet that you would like to know about.

9. Draw a mathematician. How might he or she be employed in our community?

10. Describe a mathematically talented character from a book or television series.

Adapted from McLaughlin (1995)

Teaching Idea: Math Metaphors
Content Area: Mathematics
Levels: Intermediate, Middle, High School

Creating Math Metaphors helps students to make connections to life experiences. According to Whitin & Whitin (1997), "metaphors connect abstract concepts to personal experiences, support an aesthetic stance toward mathematics, and foster a sense of intellectual play that is the root of invention" (p. 109).

Pollina (1995) offers the following example of a Math Metaphor created by a ninth-grade algebra student. The student was completing the following metaphor: "If mathematics were a food, for me it would be _____ because _____." Her response was, "If mathematics were a food, for me it would be a sandwich, because sometimes I like what's on a sandwich and sometimes I don't. When there's too much stuff on a sandwich, I can't fit it all in my mouth" (p. 31).

Metaphors challenge students to express their thoughts about math in a different way. In turn, completed metaphors offer teachers insight into students' thinking.

Teaching Idea: Math Histories
Content Area: Mathematics
Levels: Intermediate, Middle, High School

A Math History chronicles a student's math experiences from earliest memory to the present (McLaughlin, 1995). Students are encouraged to reflect on math's positive and negative interactions with their lives. They may recall their parents reading a book about numbers to them at an early age, or they may comment on a text they used at a particular grade level. They may note that math has always been an integral part of their lives or that they've always felt totally disconnected from it.

Math histories celebrate student individuality and offer a wealth of information that is usually not available from other sources. Figure 9-8 lists some math history prompts that facilitate thinking when creating an individual history.

Figure 9-8. Math History Prompts

- What is your earliest math memory?
- Can you recall how/if you used numbers before you started school?
- Can you recall any specific positive or negative memories from your study of math in elementary school? Middle school? High school?
- Do you remember any particular characteristic of any of your math teachers?
- Do you recall any specific ways in which you used math outside of school during your elementary, middle or high school years?
- Do you remember enjoying math at any particular grade level? Why did you enjoy it? Why not?
- Do you feel comfortable using math now? Why? Why not?
- Do you consider yourself to be a mathematician?
- If you could change one thing about your math experiences, what would it be? How would you change it?

(McLaughlin, 1995)

This activity is best introduced by the teacher sharing his or her own math history. It is also important to note that math histories may have a variety of formats, including written narratives, audiotapes, scrapbooks, poems, and dramatizations captured on videotape. These possibilities accommodate students' modality preferences.

Teaching Idea: Tickets Out
Content Area: Mathematics
Levels: Intermediate, Middle, and High School

Tickets Out gives students an active role in their learning and offers teachers insight into students' understanding. An added advantage of this activity is that it requires very little time.

Five minutes before the end of class, distribute 3 x 5 index cards or paper cut to a similar size. Ask students to write something they learned today on one side. Then ask them to write one question they have about what they've learned on the other side. Students do not need to put their names on the cards. As the students leave the classroom, stand at the door and collect the students' Tickets Out.

After collecting the cards, read side 1 of all the cards first. This will give you information about what students learned. Then read side 2, noting which questions may have been raised by more than one student. Select what you perceive to be questions that are representative of all that have been raised. Open the next day's class by responding to the student-authored questions.

This strategy offers students an opportunity to reflect on what they have learned and to ask questions without pressure. It also affords teachers the opportunity to monitor students' learning and to reflect on the effectiveness of their teaching. Finally, it provides valuable connections from one class session to the next.

Teaching Idea: Modeling Vocabulary
Content Area: Mathematics
Levels: Intermediate, Middle, High School

Students often need help in relating difficult vocabulary to understandable wording. As teachers, we can model how difficult wording can make sense by relating it to something the student can easily understand. This will also encourage students to use this approach whenever they encounter other problems with difficult vocabulary.

The following problem illustrates this strategy.

The elasticity coefficient e of a ball relates the height r of its rebound to the height h from which it is dropped. You can find the elasticity coefficient using the function $e = \sqrt{r/h}$. What is the elasticity coefficient for a tennis ball that rebounds 3 feet after it is dropped from a height of 3.5 feet?

To relate this to something students can easily understand, bring two balls into class, perhaps a basketball and a soccer ball. Drop them both from the same height and relate the terminology of elasticity and rebound to the demonstration. The word *coefficient* then becomes "how much elasticity."

After doing multiple examples of relating difficult terminology to an everyday activity that they can observe, students will be able to translate problems either concretely or eventually abstractly into their own understandable scenarios.

Teaching Idea: Terminology Journal Entries
Content Area: Mathematics
Levels: Intermediate, Middle, High School

Instead of asking students to write the terminology and definitions in their notebooks, have them set aside a section of their journal as a vocabulary resource. As you begin a chapter or module of instruction, provide a short list of terms for students to enter into this resource area. Ask students to leave a space of five lines between each entry. Then, as they work through the materials and activities, have students look for the words they have entered. As they locate each term, students write their own definition and draw a sketch or diagram depicting the meaning. On a designated day, a "words found" discussion allows students to share their definitions and illustrations, revising them as needed.

Teaching Idea: Mathematical Conversations
Content Area: Mathematics
Levels: Intermediate, Middle, High School

Mathematical Conversations encourage the active involvement of all participants. The speaker must organize thoughts, use appropriate terminology, and state a sequentially developed case. The listeners must mentally visualize the steps of the case, comprehend them, and compare and contrast them to their own thinking.

To enhance the power of mathematical conversations, teachers can do the following:

- Pose open-ended questions that require students to engage in critical and creative thinking.
- After asking a question, wait 14 seconds before accepting a response from any participant. This provides time for all students to organize their thoughts and offer better quality responses.
- As the discussion leader, do not comment on the answer received. Instead, keep the students involved by asking questions such as "Do you agree or disagree with that response? Explain why." or "Can anyone add to this response?" or "Would that be true in all cases?" or "Is there an alternative to this response?"
- Encourage the conversation to continue through liberal use of the question "Why?"

Mathematical conversations benefit both teachers and students. According to Atkins (1999), they "provide a tool for measuring growth in understanding, allow participants to learn about the mathematical constructions of others, and give participants opportunities to reflect on their own mathematical understandings" (p. 294). This type of oral discourse in math also affords students the opportunity to gain practical experience in a mode of communication that they will use throughout their lives.

Teaching Idea: Word Works
Content Area: Mathematics
Levels: Intermediate, Middle, Level

Making a quick sketch or diagram helps students to remember more effectively, but creating an elaborate poster is even more fun. Students enjoy creating these Word Works and the sketching makes retention much easier. A major advantage of students creating Word Works is the combination of several different terms in one drawing, which allows students to compare and contrast terminology rather than dealing with it in isolation. Doing each term in a different color of marker creates a clear distinction, both visually and verbally. Figure 9-9 shows one student's work. (For more information about visualization and sketching, see chapter 4.)

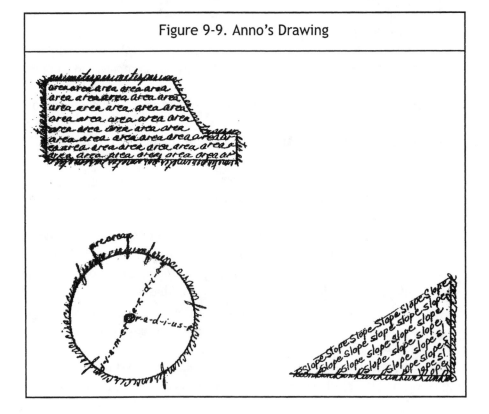

Figure 9-9. Anno's Drawing

Teaching Idea: Reading Visuals
Content Area: Mathematics
Levels: Intermediate, Middle, High School

Mathematical text utilizes pictures, tables, graphs, or diagrams to convey important information. A picture is often the culmination of what the words express. Reading the visuals as well as the words enhances students' understanding of the concept in mathematics as well as in other content areas. An example of this can be seen in the following problem.

You have received a $50.00 gift certificate to City Side Music and Books. You want to buy some books and at least one CD. How can you spend your gift certificate on X paperbacks and Y CDs?

In this problem students need more information. Often that data is contained in visuals such as the one found in Figure 9-10.

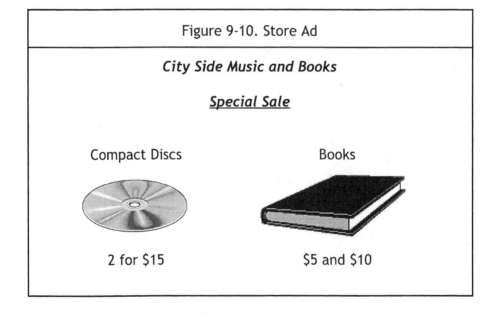

Figure 9-10. Store Ad

City Side Music and Books

Special Sale

Compact Discs

Books

2 for $15

$5 and $10

When students learn to read the words and the visuals, their understanding of the problem and its solution are enhanced.

Students also need to be able to create their own visuals when problem solving. For this problem, one student may write and graph a series of linear inequalities, while another may use a simple sketch of rectangles and circles to represent the books and CDs. Either visual can help solve the problem.

Modeling these sketching activities for students offers a dynamic example of the approach and helps them to see that you value what you're asking them to do. It also takes away any stigma that only very young children use drawing as part of the learning process.

Teaching Ideas: Student-Constructed Reviews
Content Area: Mathematics
Levels: Intermediate, Middle, and High School

A small-group cooperative learning activity can be used to facilitate development of student-constructed reviews. Each group is responsible for developing a complete review of material for a test. The students use their texts, notebooks and others resources as information sources. They decide who will be responsible for which segment of the information.

Students then work individually to complete their section of the review. On a specified day, students bring multiple copies of their reviews to the small group. Each student then conducts a review of his or her segment for the other group members. The reviews may include oral questions, student-designed problems to complete, or requests for students to apply particular mathematical concepts. After all segments of the review have been completed and discussed, the students keep the reviews as additional study sources.

While engaging in this activity, students become teachers. They examine what has been learned and select what they believe are the most important concepts. Then they develop appropriate tasks to prepare fellow students to take a test. Another interesting aspect of this activity is students' willingness to participate. Each is motivated and keenly aware of individual responsibility. If any student fails to meet his or her responsibility, the entire group misses the review of that material.

In addition to all of the ideas presented in this chapter, trade books, informational articles, poetry, music, drama, and technology can be used as resources in the creative and innovative teaching of mathematics. For more information about these topics, see chapters 5, 6, 7, 8, and 10.

Concluding Thoughts

Shifting the paradigm to student-centered learning is challenging in all subject areas, but the greatest challenge may be in mathematics. While the National Council of Teachers of Mathematics promotes meaningful national standards and encourages innovative instructional practices, many math educators continue to feel unprepared to teach the subject in meaningful ways. Several contributing factors can be cited. One is teacher certification programs that require minimal course work in mathematics. Another is Merseth's (1993) observation that society as a whole has become comfortable acknowledging that math is not its strength. Finally, when instructional innovations such as thematic instruction are introduced, examples offered are usually applications in social studies, science, and language curriculums. Math appears to be an add-on covered by phrases such as "This can also be used in mathematics." It is time for this to change. The demands placed on graduates in the 21st century require the educational process to address mathematical literacy for all students.

The reality is that strategy-based, student-centered contexts enhance mathematics instruction and foster students' mathematical literacy. As a result, students become critical and creative thinkers, engage in the social construction of knowledge, and link their learning to their life experiences. In these situations, both teachers and students become mathematically empowered.

Bussey (cited in Alper et al., 1996, p. 21) seems to have summarized it best when she wrote the following:

> When I'm in my classroom and witness students working in groups, debating mathematical principles, and developing their own ideas to solve meaningful problems, that is when I feel most successful. My students have proven to me that they can learn, that learning can be meaningful and relevant—and fun. What more can anyone ask of the educational process?

References

Alper, L., Fendel, D., Fraser, S., & Resek, D. (1996). Problem-based mathematics: Not just for the college bound. *Educational Leadership, 53* (8), 18–21.

Artzt, A. (1994). Integrating writing and the cooperative learning classroom. *Mathematics Teacher, 87* (2), 80–85.

Atkins, S. L. (1999). Listening to students: The power of mathematical conversations. *Teaching Children Mathematics, 5* (5), 289–295.

Battista, M. (1994). Teacher beliefs and the reform movement in mathematics education. *Phi Delta Kappan, 75* (6), 462–470.

Battista, M. (1999). The mathematical miseducation of America's youth: Ignoring research and scientific study in education. *Phi Delta Kappan, 80* (6), 425–433.

Borasi, R., Siegel, M., Fonze, J., & Smith, C. (1998). Using transactional reading strategies to support sense-making and discussion in mathematics classrooms: An exploratory study. *Journal for Research in Mathematics Education, 29*, 275–305.

Braselton, S., & Decker, B. C. (1994). Using graphic organizers to improve the reading of mathematics. *The Reading Teacher, 48* (3), 276–281.

Coxford, A. F., & Hirsh, C. R. (1996). A common core for all. *Educational Leadership, 53* (8), 22–25.

Fernandez, M. L. (1999). Making music with mathematics. *Mathematics Teacher, 92* (2), 90–95.

Gordon, C. J., & MacInnis, D. (1993). Using journals as a window on students' thinking in mathematics. *Language Arts, 70*, 37–43.

Greenes, C. (1997). Honing the abilities of the mathematically promising. *Mathematics Teacher, 90* (7), 582–586.

Hansbarger, J. C., & Stewart, E. L. (1996). Merging mathematics and English: One approach to bridging the disciplines. *Mathematics Teacher, 89* (4), 294–297.

Jensen, E. (1997). *Teaching with the brain in mind*. Reston, VA: Association for Supervision and Curriculum Development.

Maurer, M. M., & Davidson, G. (1999). Technology, children, and the power of the heart. *Phi Delta Kappan, 80* (6), 458–460.

McLaughlin, M. (1995). *Mathematics performance assessment: A practical guide to implementation*. Boston: Houghton Mifflin.

Mercer, C. D., Jordan, L., & Miller, S. P. (1996). Constructive math instruction for diverse learners. *Learning Disabilities Research & Practice, 11* (3), 147–156.

Merseth, K. K. (1993). How old is the shepherd? *Phi Delta Kappan, 74* (7), 548–554.

National Council of Teachers of Mathematics. (1989). *Curriculum and evaluation standards for school mathematics*. Reston, VA: Author.

Odage, V. U. (1998). Students generating test items: A teaching and assessment strategy. *Mathematics Teacher, 91* (3), 198–202.

Ogle, D. (1986). K-W-L: A teaching model that develops active reading of expository test. *The Reading Teacher, 39*, 564–570.

Oleson, V. L. (1998). Incredible comparisons: Experiences with data collection. *Teaching Children Mathematics, 5* (1), 12–17.

Pollina, A. (1995). Gender balance: Lessons from girls in science and math. *Educational Leadership, 53* (1), 30–33.

Pugalee, D. K. (1997). Connecting writing to the mathematics curriculum. *Mathematics Teacher, 90* (4), 308–310.

Readence, J. E., Bean, T. W., & Baldwin., R. S. (1998). *Content area reading: An integrated approach*. (6th ed.). Dubuque, IA: Kendall & Hunt.

Reys, B., Robinson, E., Sconiers, S., & Mark, J. (1999). Mathematics curricula based on rigorous national standards: What, why, and how? *Phi Delta Kappan, 80* (6), 454–456.

Schoen, H. L., Fey, J. T., Hirsch, C. R., & Coxford, A. F. (1999). Issues and options in the math wars. *Phi Delta Kappan, 80* (6), 444–453.

Shaw, J., Chambless, M., Chessin, D., Price, V., & Beardain, G. (1997). Cooperative problem solving: Using K-W-D-L as an organizational technique. *Teaching Children Mathematics, 3*, 482–486.

Shigematsu, K., & Sowder, L. (1994). Drawings for story problems: Practices in Japan and the United States. *Arithmetic Teacher, 41* (9), 544–547.

Steele, D. F., & Arth, A. A. (1998). Math instruction and assessment: Preventing anxiety, promoting confidence. *Schools in the Middle, 6* (5), 44–48.

Stokes, J. (1999). Problem-solving software, equity, and the allocation of roles. *Learning & Leading With Technology, 26* (5), 6–9, 30–31.

Thompson, D. R., & Senk, S. L. (1998). Using rubrics in high school mathematics courses. *Mathematics Teacher, 91* (9), 786–793.

Whiteford, T. (1998). Math for moms and dads. *Educational Leadership, 55* (8), 64–66.

Whitin, P. E., & Whitin, D. J. (1997). Ice numbers and beyond: Language lessons for the mathematics classroom. *Language Arts, 74*, 108–115.

Wood, K. D. (1992). Fostering collaborative reading and writing experiences in mathematics. *Journal of Reading, 36* (2), 96–102.

Chapter 10

Developing New Literacies: Using the Internet in Content Area Instruction

Donald J. Leu

The nature of literacy and learning is rapidly changing as new technologies for information and communication such as the Internet appear, providing us with new challenges and opportunities as we consider how best to prepare students for their futures. While the complete definition of these new literacies is not yet complete (see preliminary descriptions in Leu, in press–a; Leu, in press–b; Reinking, Labbo, & McKenna, 1997), it is clear that new technologies require new literacies. In fact, if there is one thing that is certain in these uncertain times, it is that the technologies of information and communication will regularly and repeatedly change, constantly redefining what it means to be literate (Leu, 1997; Leu, in press–a). This presents particular problems to those of us charged with preparing students for the future. How can we best prepare students for the new literacies that will be needed for the new technologies of information and communication that regularly appear?

Some argue that the new technologies for information and communication are harmful, too expensive, or lead to surface-level, rather than deeper and more complex thinking (Birkerts, 1994; Oppenheimer, 1997; Rochlin, 1997; Roszak, 1994; Stoll, 1995). Nevertheless, a growing body of work suggests that one's ability to effectively use Internet technologies will be central to the workplace demands in an information economy (Bruce, 1997; Harrison & Stephen, 1996; Johnson, 1997; Leu, in press–a; Mikulecky & Kirkley, 1998; Negroponte, 1995). Preparing students for their futures in an information age will profoundly change content area instruction, for it will require that we integrate Internet technologies into our instructional programs. Indeed, the convergence of literacy instruction with the technologies of information and communication will be a defining aspect of education in the new millennium (Leu & Kinzer, in press).

This chapter will begin by describing the changes taking place in content area reading instruction and explain why these changes are taking place. It will then explore answers to a series of instructional questions that teachers often ask as they consider their new roles within the new literacies required by the Internet:

- How can I use the Internet to quickly find useful information for my class?
- How can I integrate the Internet into classroom teaching?
- How can I protect students as they begin to explore the wider world of the Internet?
- How can I keep up with all the changes taking place on the Internet?

Finally, it will conclude by providing windows to the world of your future, showing you the wonderful work that a number of teachers are accomplishing as they integrate these new technologies into their classrooms.

The World of Content Area Reading Instruction Is Changing

If you have any doubts that the world of content area reading instruction is changing, consider the following observations:

- In the fall of 1998, 51% of the K–12 instructional classrooms in the public schools of the United States contained at least one computer with an Internet connection (National Center for Educational Statistics, 1999). By the fall of 2000, it is expected that nearly every K–12 classroom in the United States will have at least one computer with an Internet connection.
- The percentage of classrooms connected to the Internet in the United States has nearly doubled each year during the past several years.
- During fiscal year 1998–99, the Federal Communications Commission provided approximately $1.7 billion in financial support to schools and libraries for Internet access, based on indicators of financial need. The Schools and Libraries Division (SLD) administer this e-rate program of the Universal Service Administrative Company (http://www.sl.universalservice.org/), a nonprofit organization established by the FCC for this purpose.
- The e-rate funding level for fiscal year 1999–2000 was recently set at $2.25 billion. This yearly support for schools and libraries will

speed up the already rapid integration of Internet technologies into school classrooms.

- At the same time that they are raising literacy standards, nations such as Great Britain, Australia, Finland, and New Zealand are formally integrating the use of Information Technologies (IT) or Information and Communication Technologies (ICT) into their curriculum (Leu & Kinzer, in press).
- Teachers and students around the world are sharing the results of content area research projects at classroom web sites, creating wonderful new curriculum resources for all of us (Leu, Karchmer, & Leu, 1999).

You may wish to visit examples of the latter. They include a wonderful collection of student projects on the Modern American Presidency (Figure 10-1) (http://www.vcsc.k12.in.us/staff/mhutch/modpres/mainpage.htm) created by Michael Hutchinson, a high school social studies teacher at Vincennes Lincoln High School in Indiana; the many exceptional content area projects (K–13) taking place in Canadian schools found at Grassroots—Project Centre (http://www.schoolnet.ca/grassroots/e/project.centre/index.html); the Earth Day Groceries Project (http://www.earthdaybags.org/) developed by Mark Ahlness, a third-grade teacher at Arbor Heights Elementary School in Seattle, Washington; and the many exciting social studies resources for middle and high school classes developed by Gary Cressman and other teachers in the state of Washington at Washington Social Studies Home Page (http://www.learningspace.org/socialstudies/).

The changes to content area instruction resulting from the integration of Internet technologies into classroom instruction are nothing short of revolutionary. They drastically change the information resources available to our students. The Internet opens a wonderful window on the world to new information resources, new people, and new perspectives about content area information.

In addition, however, they also reshape the traditional relationship between teachers and students. Because the technologies for information and communication are increasingly powerful, complex, and continually changing, our students quickly become more knowledgeable than we are in many aspects of information technologies. As a result, our role as teacher is changing from being the central source of information in the classroom to becoming a facilitator and guide, putting students together with other students who possess various types of expertise in order to exchange information and solve common problems.

Internet technologies also raise new issues about our relationship to content area information. In a world where anyone may publish anything,

Figure 10-1. The Modern American Presidency Site

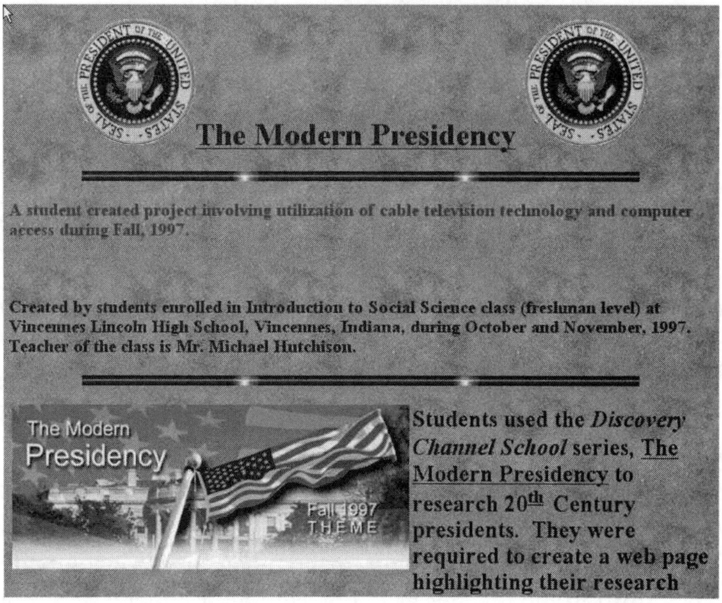

how does one evaluate the accuracy of information that one finds? In a world where there is too much information, rather than too little, how do we prepare students to quickly locate the most useful information resources? In a world where new juxtapositions of multiple media forms may be created, how do we help students to critically evaluate the variety of meanings inherent in the multiple media forms in which messages appear (Flood & Lapp, 1995)? Clearly, what has traditionally been referred to as critical reading or critical thinking assumes greater importance and new meaning with the introduction of Internet technologies into the content area classroom.

All of these changes require us to consider how best to prepare students for the new literacies necessary for success in the complex world they will enter as working adults. As teachers, we need to help students to develop the new composing, comprehension, and response abilities that the Internet demands for its effective use (Leu, in press–b).

Why are these changes happening? Reich (1992), Rifkin (1995), and many others argue that we have entered an information age where success is often defined by one's ability to use information for solving important problems. Moreover, it is increasingly clear that networked, digital technologies provide rapid access to vast amounts of information, increasing the importance of effective information use (Harrison & Stephen, 1996). As individuals or organizations identify problems, gather information, and seek solutions, digital bits become faster and cheaper than atoms (Negroponte, 1995), and in a highly competitive context speed, information, and cost become paramount. These global forces in the nature of work largely drive the changing definitions of information, literacy, and content area reading instruction. Moreover, the globally competitive context in which we find ourselves ensures that new technologies for information and communication will continually be developed, resulting in constantly changing literacies (Leu, in press–a). As a result, content area literacy instruction becomes even more important to our students than in the past. In an information age, success will be determined largely by our students' ability to use information and information technologies in effective ways.

How can we prepare students for their literacy futures by using networked technologies such as the Internet? The rest of this chapter will address this important issue. I will organize this discussion around the most common questions teachers ask as they begin to consider the use of Internet technologies in their classrooms.

"I Don't Have Much Time. How Can I Use the Internet to Quickly Find Useful Information for My Class?"

A common challenge for busy teachers is to quickly locate useful information resources on the Internet. No one has large amounts of time to spend finding classroom resources. Yet, search engines often turn up hundreds of thousands of locations when one uses a keyword such as *Jefferson, tessellation, geometry, physics, cell structure,* or *Shakespeare.* Moreover, many of these sites are not developed with the needs of students and classrooms in mind. As a result, we have to search through hundreds of sites in order to find one that is useful for classroom instruction.

Instead of using a search engine, teachers often rely on central sites for content areas (Leu & Leu, 1999). Central sites contain extensive and well-organized links to resources designed for use in content area classrooms. Visiting a central site will quickly provide you with many resources for your instructional units and save you valuable time. Table 10-1 lists a number of exceptional central sites for content areas. Most have been designed for busy teachers. As a result, they are organized to make it easy to locate useful resources for your class. Many teachers find it useful to set bookmarks on their Internet browser (e.g. Netscape Navigator or Internet Explorer) for central sites such as these. This permits them to quickly find classroom resources throughout the year as they begin different instructional units. Figure 10-2 shows an example of a central site.

Table 10-1. Central Sites on the Internet for Content Areas

Content Areas	Central Internet Sites
Literature	**Children's Literature Web Guide** http://www.ucalgary.ca/~dkbrown/index.html
	The Complete Works of William Shakespeare http://the-tech.mit.edu/Shakespeare/works.html
	Cyberguides http://www.sdcoe.k12.ca.us/score/cyberguide.html
Science (general)	**Action: Eisenhower National Clearinghouse** http://www.enc.org:80/classroom/index.htm
	Science Learning Network http://www.sln.org/
Math (general)	**Action: Eisenhower National Clearinghouse** http://www.enc.org:80/classroom/index.htm
	The Math Forum http://forum.swarthmore.edu/
	Canada's SchoolNet: Mathematics http://www.schoolnet.ca/home/e/resources/ mathematics/
Social Studies (general)	**American Memory** http://memory.loc.gov/ammem/amhome.html
	History/Social Studies Web Site for K-12 Teachers http://www.execpc.com/~dboals/boals.html
	Nebraska Department of Education Social Science Resource HomePage http://www.nde.state.ne.us/SS/ss.html
	People Past and Present http://www.ala.org/parentspage/greatsites/ people.html#b
Multicultural Resources	**Multicultural Pavilion** http://curry.edschool.Virginia.EDU:80/go/multicultural/
	Diversity http://www.execpc.com/~dboals/diversit.html
	Cultures of the World http://www.ala.org/parentspage/greatsites/ people.html#b
African American Culture	**Multicultural Paths: African American Resources** http://curry.edschool.Virginia.EDU:80/go/ multicultural/sites/afr-am.html
Chicana/o Latina/o Culture	**LANIC** http://www.lanic.utexas.edu/ **CLNET** http://clnet.ucr.edu/
Native American Culture	**Native American Resources** http://indy4.fdl.cc.mn.us/~isk/mainmenu.html

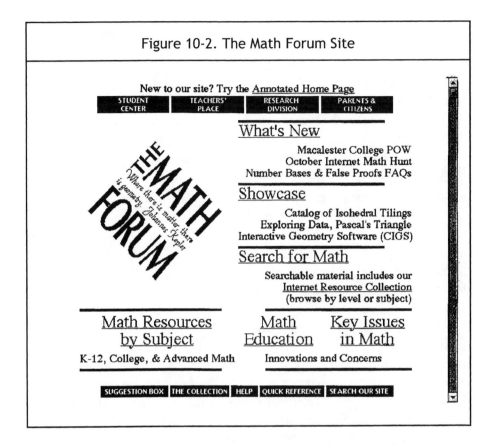

Figure 10-2. The Math Forum Site

"How Can I Integrate the Internet Into Classroom Teaching?"

The answer to this question is one of the greatest challenges we face. Increasingly, Internet connections are appearing in school classrooms. Unfortunately, however, funds are not always provided for the staff development and teacher education necessary to effectively use these technologies (President's Committee of Advisors on Science and Technology: Panel on Educational Technology, 1997). Three instructional models are especially useful as you begin to integrate Internet resources into your classroom: Internet Workshop, Internet Project, and Internet Inquiry (Leu & Leu, 1999).

Teaching Idea: Internet Workshop
Content Areas: All
Levels: Intermediate, Middle School, High School

If you are just beginning your journey with the Internet, you may wish to start by using Internet Workshop in your classroom. Internet Workshop is especially useful to introduce students to sites for an upcoming unit and to develop useful background knowledge.

Internet Workshop has many variations. Generally, though, it contains the following steps:

1. Locate a site, or several sites, on the Internet with content related to a classroom unit of instruction and set a bookmark for the location(s).
2. Develop an activity requiring students to use the site(s).
3. Assign this activity to be completed during the week.
4. Have students share their work, questions, and new insights at the end of the week during a workshop session.

Using one of the central sites identified earlier, you prepare for Internet Workshop by locating an Internet site containing information related to your classroom unit and setting a bookmark for your students. This limits random "surfing" and exploration of sites unrelated to your unit, an important student safety issue.

Next, develop an activity related to the learning goals of your unit that requires students to use this site on the Internet. Sometimes this will be used to introduce students to a site you will be exploring in your upcoming instructional unit, and sometimes it will be used to develop central content during your unit. Often, teachers will have students write down interesting information they find at this site in an Internet journal and then bring their journals and share this information during a workshop session at the end of the week. Sometimes teachers will prepare an activity page for students to complete and bring to the workshop session.

Figure 10-3 shows an example of an activity page developed by a teacher to introduce a social studies unit on Japan in a sixth-grade class. It was designed to allow students to develop wide-ranging background knowledge about Japan and then share what they discovered with the class during a workshop session at the end of the week. The teacher used this session to launch a cross-curricular unit on Japan. A similar set of activities could be developed for students at lower levels by using another, more age appropriate, site, Kids Window (http://www.jwindow.net/OLD/KIDS/kids_home.html). At the high school level, one might choose a more advanced site, such as Japan Window (http://www.jwindow.net/).

Figure 10-3. Internet Activity Page for Sixth-Grade Unit on Japan

Exploring Japan

Internet Researcher:_____ Date:_____

News About Japan

1. Go to the bookmark I have set for Kid's Web Japan (http://www.jinjapan.org/kidsweb/) and scroll down to the bottom of this page. Now click on the button "Monthly News" and read several recent news stories from Japan. Write notes about some of the news you discovered and be ready to share this with us during Internet Workshop.

Nature and Climate

2. Click on the button "Nature and Climate" and read a description of what it is like to live in Japan. Be certain to read answers to some of the questions at the bottom of this article. Write down notes about what you learned about the nature and climate of Japan. We will share these during Internet Workshop.

What's Cool in Japan?

3. Now let's find out what are some of the biggest fads among students your own age in Japan. Visit "What's Cool in Japan" and find out what kids are doing. Write down notes about what you discovered is most popular among kids and be ready to share this information during Internet Workshop.

Virtual Japanese Culture: Origami

4. Now let's discover a small piece of Japanese culture. Visit "Virtual Japanese Culture" and follow the directions to make an origami (folded paper) object. Use the special origami paper I placed next to the computer. Read the directions and make an airplane, a crane, or a soldier's helmet. Bring this to Internet Workshop so we can see how well you followed directions.

Your Choice

5. Visit at least one of the many other locations at Kids Web Japan. You decide where to go! Write down notes of what you discovered and share your special discoveries with all of us during Internet Workshop.

The third step is to assign the activity to be completed during the week. If you have only a single Internet connection in your classroom, you may wish to have students work in pairs to complete the assignment. If you have access to a computer lab with multiple Internet connections, this could be completed during your weekly computer lab session.

The fourth step is to have students share their work, questions, and new insights at the end of the week during a workshop session. This is a time for the class to get together and share the learning they completed during their Internet activity. It is also a time to ask questions about issues they have about their work on the Internet. Often, teachers conduct this workshop session similar to a grand conversation (Eeds & Wells, 1989; Peterson & Eeds, 1990; Tompkins & McGee, 1993) where students participate and share information in a collaborative process of meaning construction.

Teaching Idea: Internet Project
Content Areas: All
Levels: Intermediate, Middle School, High School

After you have used Internet Workshop in your classroom, you may wish to try Internet Project, a more complex instructional model. Internet Project is a collaborative learning experience between two or more classrooms that takes place over the Internet (Leu & Leu, 1999). Two basic types of Internet Project exist and are used by teachers: Web-site internet projects and spontaneous projects developed by teachers who find one another on the Internet.

Web-site projects are the easiest to use and a good way to begin, but they are less common than spontaneous projects developed by teachers and are sometimes hard to locate. Web-site projects are coordinated through a Web site developed by the originator. They are usually precisely defined with clear directions for participation. Because they are more precisely defined, however, Web-site projects are sometimes more limited in scope and learning potential. There is not yet a central internet site for Web-site internet projects. You will discover them in your explorations on the Internet. Examples of Web-site projects include the following:

- **Journey Exchange Project**
  http://www.win4edu.com/minds-eye/journey/
  Students conduct research about geographical locations and then develop a five-city journey around the world. They exchange clues to the locations with their Internet partner. Each attempts to discover the cities and the travel itinerary. A great project for grades 3–12.

- **Monarch Watch**
  http://www.keil.ukans.edu/~monarch/
  Raise Monarch butterflies, tag them, release them, record observa-

tions about Monarchs in your area, then watch as your data and those compiled by others are used to track the annual migration of this wonderful creature! A project for grades K–12.

- **Good News Bears**
  http://www.ncsa.uiuc.edu:80/edu/RSE/RSEyellow/gnb.html
  An excellent stock-market activity for middle school students. Students manage a portfolio and compete with others to see who manages their portfolio best.
- **Global Schoolhouse Projects and Programs Main Page**
  http://www.gsn.org/project/index.html
  Here you will find a number of permanent, ongoing projects for grades 3–12.

In addition to Web-site projects, there are also spontaneous projects between collaborating classrooms. These are more common than Web-site projects. During collaborative projects you work with another class on a common project, with students and teachers communicating extensively about the topic both classes are exploring. Collaborative projects also take place when classes contribute data to a common site and then, after the data are analyzed, see how their data compare with others. Often there will also be discussion between participating classes about the meaning of the results and even opportunities to use the data for further analyses. Each leads to rich learning opportunities.

Generally, spontaneous Internet projects follow these procedures (Leu & Kinzer, 1999; Leu & Leu, 1999):

1. Develop a collaborative project with a summary of the project, a clear list of learning goals, expectations you have for collaborating classrooms, and a projected timeline for beginning and ending the project.
2. Post the project description and timeline several months in advance at one or several locations, seeking collaborative classroom partners.
3. Arrange collaboration details with teachers in other classrooms who agree to participate.
4. Complete the project, exchanging information with your collaborating classrooms.

The first step requires some advance planning, often several months before you wish to begin a project. You should develop a clear description of the project that includes a summary of the project, the goals you wish to accomplish through the project, the expectations you have for collaborating classrooms, and a timeline for the project. A clear description with explicit goals and timelines will make it easier for everyone to understand what will be expected of them.

Next, post your project description and timeline several months in advance of your starting date at one of several locations designed for this purpose. One of the better locations for posting project descriptions and finding collaborative classrooms may be found at Global SchoolNet's Internet Projects Registry (http://www.gsn.org/pr/index.cfm). If you are looking for collaborative projects with schools in other countries, pay a visit to Intercultural E-mail Classroom Connection (http://www.stolaf.edu/network/iecc/), a wonderful resource provided by St. Olaf College.

The third step is to arrange collaboration details with teachers in other classrooms who agree to participate. Projects require careful coordination between teachers so that information is exchanged in a timely manner. Planning these exchanges in advance helps to eliminate difficulties.

After collaboration details have been worked out, you only need to complete the project. This is the exciting part, as you and your class connect with other classes around the world and discover how common and how different our perceptions of the world around us.

One example of Internet Project, "Passage to Hiroshima," took place recently between a classroom in Nagoya, Japan, and high school classrooms in several other countries around the world. The classroom in Nagoya sought collaborating classrooms interested in studying about the importance of peace and international cooperation. They proposed to exchange useful sites on the World Wide Web related to world peace. They also asked participating classrooms to develop interview and research questions that the Nagoya class could use during their upcoming trip to Hiroshima. The class in Japan volunteered to interview citizens of Hiroshima and then share the results, including photos, upon their return.

Thousands of projects similar to this one take place each day on the Internet between collaborating classrooms. If you are interested in a project approach to using the Internet, pay a visit to NickNacks Telecollaborate! (http://www1.minn.net:80/~schubert/NickNacks.html), where you can discover more information about this approach.

Internet Project is especially useful for several reasons. First, it provides opportunities for students to work together, a skill increasingly important in an interdependent world. Internet Project also provides unique opportunities to learn about different cultural contexts; sharing a learning experience with students in other parts of the world leads to important insights about cultural differences. Finally, Internet Project provides special opportunities to integrate the language arts with other subject areas, such as science, math, and social studies; communicating via Internet technologies is often a central part of Internet Project.

Teaching Idea: Internet Inquiry
Content Areas: All
Levels: Intermediate, Middle School, High School

A third instructional model often used with Internet technologies in the classroom is Internet Inquiry (Leu & Kinzer, 1999; Leu & Leu, 1999). During Internet Inquiry, individuals or groups identify an important question and then gather information as they seek answers to their question. Internet Inquiry is a student-directed activity because it turns over much of the responsibility for learning to students who explore issues important to them.

Internet Inquiry includes five phases: (a) question, (b) search, (c) analyze, (d) compose, and (e) publish. Each phase provides important opportunities to support traditional reading comprehension as well as the new literacies required in networked information contexts such as the Internet. Often this will take place during workshop sessions when useful strategies are exchanged.

For example, as students determine the question they will explore during the question phase, you might help them to brainstorm different questions and record these on the chalkboard. Afterwards, a discussion about each question helps students to clarify what they know and what they need to know related to each topic. Initial K-W-L techniques (Ogle, 1989) might be used. Exchanging information about these topics during conversations is often helpful to developing appropriate background knowledge before students begin their research.

As students engage in the search phase, you might support their work by calling them together for a short workshop session. This helps them to exchange research strategies. Students can exchange library resources, World Wide Web locations, and strategies for finding information. Each is important to students unfamiliar with independent inquiry and the use of the Internet.

During the analysis phase you should help students to determine the accuracy of information they locate on the Internet and also help them with other, traditional resources. Critically evaluating information accuracy is an especially important issue with networked information resources. Anyone may publish anything on the Internet. As a result, students may sometimes encounter Web pages created by people with political, religious, or philosophical stances that distort the nature of the information they present to others. At other times, a person simply gets the facts wrong on a Web page. This requires us to help our students become "healthy skeptics" about the accuracy of the information they encounter. Literacy on the Internet requires new forms of critical thinking and reasoning about the information that appears in this venue. Some of these include considering the different motivations behind information posted at Internet locations ending in ".com," ".org," or ".edu"; evaluating which information is likely to be most accurate in a world where contradictory factual content is increasingly likely; or how best to use a search engine when searching for either broad or narrow topics. Such skills have not always been central in classrooms where textbooks and other traditional resources are often the only source of information and they are often assumed to contain factually accurate information.

The composing phase of Internet Inquiry often relies on writing-process stages. Peer revision conferences help authors to become more sensitive to the comprehension needs of their readers. These conversations can lead to important insights about reading comprehension.

The publishing phase of Internet Inquiry may also be used to heighten awareness about useful comprehension strategies. As students share their work in your class, you might direct the audience to share what elements of the presentation they found especially useful as a listener or reader. Discussion about these elements often leads to important insights about useful comprehension strategies.

Following a classroom presentation, teachers sometimes publish the results of independent inquiry projects at their classroom Web sites. This makes the results of independent work more meaningful because it is shared with a far wider audience. Often other students and classrooms will use the resources in their own curriculum, a revolutionary development in education as teachers and students begin to define exciting, new curricular resources (Leu, Karchmer, & Leu, 1999).

"How Can We Protect Students As They Begin to Explore the Wider World of the Internet?"

Part of the new literacies demanded by the Internet include the literacies of responsibility. As teachers, we need to assume new responsibilities for our students' safety. In addition, our students need to assume new responsibilities for the appropriate use of these powerful technologies. Students may travel to sites that are inappropriate for them to view, they may send out or receive an offensive e-mail message, they may be contacted by strangers, or they may interfere with the running of a computer system.

To prevent the viewing of inappropriate sites, some schools use software filters. Software filters deny students access to certain Internet sites. These filters deny access to locations where certain words appear. Teachers and parents may edit the list of words used in the blocking software. Software filters include products such as the following:

Net Nanny—http://www.netnanny.com/
SurfWatch—http://www.surfwatch.com/
Cyber Patrol—http://www.cyberpatrol.com/

Software filters, however, are not a perfect solution. They tend to block access to sites to which you might want your students to have access (e.g., Middlesex School District) and they tend to allow access to sites you might want restricted.

Whether or not your district uses a software filter, every school and district should develop an acceptable use policy as part of a comprehensive program of Internet literacy. An acceptable use policy is a written agreement signed by parents or guardians, students, and teachers defining procedures to be followed while using the Internet at school. It specifies the conditions under which students may use the Internet, defines appropriate and unacceptable use, and defines penalties for violating items in the policy. All parties involved in the education of each child need to be aware of the consequences for misusing the privilege of Internet access. Developing an acceptable use policy and then asking everyone to sign it helps to ensure that all parties understand these important issues. Acceptable use policies usually contain the following elements (Leu & Leu, 1999):

- *A description of the Internet and an explanation of how its appropriate use is important to the education of students.* Acceptable use policies explain to parents or guardians and students what the Internet is and why it is important. They also explain that students will be taught proper use of the Internet at school.

- *A definition of acceptable and unacceptable behavior that emphasizes student responsibility when using the Internet.* Acceptable use policies explain why it is important to supervise student use of the Internet. They also explain that each student must take responsibility for his or her own actions. This section defines what is appropriate and inappropriate behavior.

- *A list of penalties for each violation of the policy.* Acceptable use policies define sanctions for inappropriate behavior with Internet resources. Often they include increasing levels of penalties: a warning letter to parents or guardians for a first violation and a suspension of privileges for a repeated violation. Schools often establish a panel to review cases.

- *Space for the student, teacher, and parent or guardian to sign the agreement.* Acceptable use policies are signed by all participants. After discussing each element carefully with students, the form is usually sent home for parents and students to sign. Teachers will also sign this form before it is carefully filed in an appropriate location.

If you are interested in learning more about acceptable use policies, visit the following Internet sites:

Houston Independent School District's Acceptable Use Page
http://chico.rice.edu/armadillo/acceptable.html

Acceptable Use Policies
http://www.erehwon.com/k12aup/

Child Safety on the Information Highway
http://www.larrysworld.com/child_safety.html

Global School Network's Guidelines and Policies for Protecting Students
http://www.gsn.org/web/issues/index.htm#begin

"How Can I Keep Up With All the Changes Taking Place on the Internet?"

The Internet and other networked technologies are continually chang-ing, regularly redefining what it means to become literate (Leu, in press–a; Leu, in press–b). As a result, they require each of us to continually develop new literacies and new instructional strategies to support our students. The new literacies of the Internet and other networked technologies for infor-mation and communication have been described elsewhere (Leu, in press–b; Leu & Kinzer, in press). They build upon, rather than replace, traditional literacies and they include the following:

- Adapting to continuously changing definitions of literacy
- Developing new forms of strategic knowledge required to search for and evaluate information in extensive information resources
- Developing social learning strategies as we increasingly depend upon others for important strategies and information
- Recognizing new sources for engagement as multimedia resources allow us to motivate and engage students at many levels
- Supporting the literacies of speed, as the rate at which one can obtain and evaluate information resources becomes even more important
- Beginning to recognize the literacies of problem identification, as students learn to develop ways to identify important problems that require resolution.

Although networked technologies are responsible for these changing definitions of literacy, they also provide us with the means to keep up with the change that will be a part of all our lives. Many teachers find the use of a mailing list to be essential for professional development. This is a dis-cussion group run via e-mail. A message sent to the posting address of a mailing list is distributed to everyone who has subscribed to that list. This enables you to engage in conversations with colleagues around the world who share common interests. As you "listen" to conversations among col-leagues, you will regularly discover new ideas for instruction that can immediately be used in your classroom. Joining the right mailing list(s) will provide you with many new instructional ideas as you discover how other teachers respond to common challenges.

Depending upon the software that a mailing list uses, there are slightly different procedures for joining a list. Listserv is the most common software used for mailing lists, but other popular programs include Listproc and Majordomo. You will find directions for using the various types of software at these central sites for mailing lists:

- Liszt Select
  http://www.liszt.com
- EdWeb E-Mail Discussion Lists and Electronic Journals
  http://sunsite.unc.edu/edweb/lists.html
- Pitsco's Launch to Lists
  http://www.pitsco.com/p/listservs.html
- TileNet
  http://www.tile.net/tile/listserv/index.html

Each of these central sites contains a set of mailing lists organized by topic. Each also contains a search engine to help you find the mailing list that matches your precise interests.

To subscribe to a mailing list using Listserv software, you need to send a subscription message via e-mail to the administrative address of the mailing list. Table 10-2 indicates the administrative address for several popular mailing lists among literacy and content area educators. Type the administrative address in the "To" box of your e-mail window. Leave the "Subject" box blank. Then, type a subscription message in the first line of the "Message" box. Your subscription message should contain only the following information: subscribe [list name] [your first name] [your last name]

Be certain to disable your signature, if you use one with your e-mail software; any other information in your subscription message will confuse the mailing list software. As an example, consider how you would subscribe to RTEACHER, a mailing list for reading educators that discusses instructional practices related to both traditional and new literacies. First, type in the administrative address for this mailing list: listserv@listserv. syr.edu

Then, type your subscription message. For example, I would subscribe by typing in this message: subscribe RTEACHER Don Leu

In a few minutes, you will receive a "Welcome" message. Save this message! It gives you directions for how to post a message to the mailing list as well as how to leave the list. To "unsubscribe," or leave a list, you send an "unsubscribe" message to the administrative address. The message should read: unsubscribe [listname]

Table 10-2.
Mailing Lists Useful to Literacy and Content Area Educators

Name	Administrative Address	Message Address	Participants and Content
RTEACHER	listserv@listserv. syr.edu For subscription directions, visit: http://web.syr.edu/ ~djleu/RTEACHER/ directions.html	rteacher@listserv. syr.edu For posting directions, visit: http://web.syr.edu/ ~djleu/RTEACHER/ directions.html	A mailing list for conversations about literacy education, including the use of the Internet for literacy and learning.
TAWL	listserv@listserv. arizona.edu	tawl@listserv. arizona.edu	A discussion group on teaching from a whole-language perspective.
NCTE-talk	For subscription directions, visit http://www.ncte. org/chat	For posting directions, visit http://www.ncte. org/chat	At the NCTE Web site you can subscribe to a number of different mailing lists devoted to English education, K-12.
MULTC-ED	listserv@umdd. umd.edu	multc-ed@umdd. umd.edu	This mailing list offers a forum to discuss issues of diversity in schools.
SOCSTUD-L	mailserv@hcca. ohio.gov	socstud-l@hcca. ohio.gov	This mailing list has general conversations about the teaching of social studies.
H-NET	listserv@h-net. msu.edu	h-net@h-net. msu.edu	A mailing list for high school teachers of the humanities.
IMSE-L	listserv@uwf.cc. uwf.edu	imse-l@ uwf.cc. uwf.edu	A discussion group for math and science education.
T321-L	listserv@mizzou1. missouri.edu	t321-l@ mizzou1. missouri.edu	A discussion group on the teaching of science in elementary schools.
NMMATYC	listserv@unm.edu	nmmatyc-L@unm. edu	A wide-ranging discussion group on the teaching of mathematics.

To unsubscribe from the RTEACHER list, for example, I would again address my message to the administrative address for this mailing list: listserv@listserv.syr.edu

Then, I would send the message: unsubscribe RTEACHER

Many educators find mailing lists to be a useful way to keep up with the new literacies that will be an increasingly important part of our futures. They are a wonderful way to sustain your professional development, meet new colleagues, and make new friends. You may wish to join at least one of the mailing lists in Table 10-2 and explore its potential to support your needs.

Windows to the World: Preparing Students for Their Literacy and Learning Futures

As we begin to bring the new literacies to our students with Internet technologies, it is possible that teachers who have forged ahead and created wonderful curricular outposts will guide our way. In a world of rapidly changing technologies for teaching and learning, it is likely that the most useful source of information about effective instructional practice with these technologies will shift from university researchers to classroom teachers. Teachers who lead the way will provide all of us with new windows to the world of our futures.

Traditionally, university research has served to evaluate the efficacy of different instructional practices. However, since it often takes as long as 4–5 years between the design of a study and the publication of results, this source of information will not be able to keep up with the rapidly changing nature of Internet technologies, instructional resources, and ideas about effective practice. Teachers are able to generate powerful insights and share these insights with others much more quickly than they have been able to do with traditional epistemological approaches. It is likely that teachers who create innovative ways of using new technologies and who evaluate their efficacy in the classroom every day will become an increasingly important source of information on how best to prepare our students in content areas (Leu, Karchmer, & Leu, 1999).

Increasingly, our work in content area classrooms will be informed by the work of colleagues around the world who design effective strategies for working with their students and share their work with us on their Web pages. It is very possible that exemplary teachers such as the following have important lessons for all of us to learn:

- Anne Keller at Starline Elementary School in Lake Havasu City, Arizona
  http://www.havasu.k12.az.us/starline/akeller/home.htm

- Hazel Jobe, a Title I Reading/Language Arts teacher at Marshall Elementary School in Lewisburg, Tennessee
  http://www.marshall-es.marshall.k12.tn.us/jobe/
- Jim Cornish, a fifth-grade teacher at the ganders Academy in New-foundland
  http://www.stemnet.nf.ca/CITE/themes.html),
- Susan Silverman at Clinton Avenue Elementary School in Port Jefferson Station, New York
  http://kids-learn.org/
- Michael Hutchison at Lincoln High School in Vincennes, Indiana
  http://www.vcsc.k12.in.us/staff/mhutch/modpres/mainpage.htm
- Gary Cressman at Enumclaw Junior High School in Enumclaw, Washington
  http://www.learningspace.org/socialstudies/ejhs/
- Peter Lelong at the Fahan School in Hobart, Tasmania
  http://www.fahan.tas.edu.au//Compute/indo.html
- Maggie Hos-McGrane at the International School of Amsterdam
  http://www.xs4all.nl/~swanson/origins/intro.html)

Teachers like these will open windows to the world for all of us as we discover more effective ways to use these new technologies in our content area classrooms, preparing our students for the world that awaits them.

Some Internet Terminology

acceptable use policy
A written agreement signed by parents or guardians, students, and teachers that specifies the conditions under which students may use the Internet, defines appropriate and unacceptable use, and defines penalties for violating items in the policy.

bookmark
The feature used in Netscape Navigator to mark a location on the Internet so that you might quickly be able to return to this location at a later time.

browser
A software program on your computer allowing you to connect to locations on the Internet. There are several different browsers: Netscape Navigator, Internet Explorer, Lynx, and Mosaic. Each comes in at least two "flavors": Windows and Macintosh.

central site
A location on the Internet with extensive and well-organized links about a content area or important subject. Most are located at stable sites that will not quickly change. Examples include: History/Social Studies Web Site for K–12 Teachers (http://www.execpc.com/~dboals/boals.html), Children's Literature Web Guide (http://www.u calgary.ca/~dkbrown/index.html), or The Math Forum (http://forum.swarth more.edu/)

favorites
The feature used in Internet Explorer to mark a location on the Internet so you can quickly return to this location at a later time.

Internet Inquiry
An instructional practice using the Internet in a more student-directed fashion. Usually it consists of five phases: question, search, analyze, compose, and share.

Internet Project
A collaborative approach to instructional use of the Internet. Generally, Internet Project follows these procedures: Plan a collaborative project for an upcoming unit in your classroom and write a project description; post the project description and timeline several months in advance at one or several locations, seeking collaborative classroom partners; arrange collaboration details with teachers in other classrooms who agree to participate; complete the project, using Internet Workshop as a forum in your own class for working on the project and exchanging information with your collaborating classrooms.

Internet Workshop
A regularly scheduled time used to support students' ability to acquire information from the Internet and to think critically about the information they obtain. During Internet Workshop, students share what they have learned, ask questions about issues they do not understand, and seek information to help them in upcoming work.

search engines
Computers on the Internet that search for sites containing words or phrases you specify. These include Yahoo, InfoSeek, HotBot, and Lycos.

software filters
A means by which to deny access to locations where certain words appear. Teachers and parents may edit the list of words used in the blocking software. They include Cyber Patrol (http://www.cyberpatrol.com/), Net Nanny (http://www.netnanny.com/), and SurfWatch (http://www.surfwatch.com/)

References

Birkerts, S. (1994). *The Gutenberg elegies*. New York: Ballentine Books.

Bruce, B. C. (1997). Current issues and future directions. In J. Flood, S. B. Heath, & D. Lapp (Eds.), *Handbook of research on teaching literacy through the communicative and visual arts*. (pp. 875–884). New York: Simon & Schuster Macmillan.

Eeds, M., & Wells, D. (1989). Grand conversations: An exploration of meaning construction in literature study groups. *Research in the Teaching of English, 23*, 4–29.

Flood, J., & Lapp, D. (1995). Broadening the lens: Toward an expanded conceptualization of literacy. In K. A. Hinchman, D. J. Leu, & C. K. Kinzer (Eds.), *Perspectives on literacy research and practice* (pp. 1–16). Chicago: National Reading Conference.

Harrison, T. M., & Stephen, T. (Eds.). (1996). *Computer networking and scholarly communication in the twenty-first-century university*. Albany, NY: State University of New York Press.

Johnson, S. (1997). *Interface culture: How new technology transforms the way we create and communicate*. San Francisco: Harper Collins.

Leu, D. J., Jr. (1997). Caity's question: Literacy as deixis on the Internet. *The Reading Teacher, 51*, 62–67.

Leu, D. J., Jr. (in press–a). Literacy and technology: Deictic consequences for literacy education in an information age. In M. L. Kamil, P. Mosenthal, P. D. Pearson, & R. Barr (Eds.), *Handbook of reading research* (Vol. 3). Mahwah, NJ: Erlbaum.

Leu, D. J., Jr. (in press–b). The new literacies: Research on reading instruction with the Internet and other digital technologies. In J. Samuels & A. Farstrup (Eds.), *What research has to say about reading instruction*. Newark, DE: International Reading Association.

Leu, D. J., Jr., Karchmer, R., & Leu, D. D. (1999). The Miss Rumphius effect: Envisionments that transform literacy and learning on the Internet. *The Reading Teacher, 52*, 636–642.

Leu, D. J., Jr. & Kinzer, C. K. (1999). *Effective literacy instruction. K–8* (4th ed.). Upper Saddle River, NJ: Prentice Hall.

Leu, D. J., Jr., & Kinzer, C. K. (in press). The convergence of literacy instruction and networked technologies for information and communication. *Reading Research Quarterly.*

Leu, D. J., Jr. & Leu, D. D. (1999). *Teaching with the Internet: Lessons from the classroom* (2nd ed.). Norwood, MA: Christopher-Gordon.

Mendels, P. (1998, October 10). Schools get Internet access, but how do teachers use it? *New York Times* [On-line]. Available: http://www. nytimes. com/library/tech/98/10/cyber/education/14education.html#1

Mikulecky, L., & Kirley, J. R. (1998). Changing workplaces, changing classes: The new role of technology in workplace literacy. In D. Reinking, M. McKenna, L. D. Labbo, & R. Kieffer (Eds.), *Handbook of literacy and technology: Transformations in a post-typographic world* (pp. 303–320). Mahwah, NJ: Erlbaum.

Negroponte, N. (1995). *Being digital*. New York: Knopf.

Ogle, D. M. (1989), The know, want to know, learn strategy. In K. D. Muth (Ed.), *Students' comprehension of text* (pp. 205–223). Newark, DE: International Reading Association.

Oppenheimer, T. (1997, July). The computer delusion. *Atlantic Monthly, 280* [On-line]. Available: http://www.theatlantic.com/issues/97jul/computer.htm

Peterson, R., & Eeds, M. (1990). *Grand conversations: Literature groups in action*. Toronto, Ontario, Canada: Scholastic-TAB.

Presidents Committee of Advisors on Science and Technology: Panel on Educational Technology (1997, March). *Report to the president on the use of technology to strengthen K–12 education in the United States* [On-line]. Available: http://www.whitehouse.gov/WH/EOP/OSTP/NSTC/PCAST/K–12ed.html

Reich, R., (1992). The work of nations. New York: Vintage Books.

Reinking, D., Labbo, L., & McKenna, M. (1997). Navigating the changing landscape of literacy: Current theory and research in computer-based reading and writing. In J. Flood, S. B. Heath, D. Lapp (Ed.), *Handbook of research on teaching literacy through the communicative and visual arts* (pp. 77–92). New York: Macmillan.

Rifkin, J. (1995). *The end of work: The decline of the global labor force and the dawn of the post-market era*. New York: G. P. Putnam.

Rochlin, G. I. (1997). *Trapped in the Net: The unanticipated consequences of computerization*. Princeton, NJ: Princeton University Press.

Roszak, T. (1994). *The cult of information: A neo-Luddite treatise on high tech, artificial intelligence, and the true art of thinking*. Berkeley, CA: University of California Press.

Stoll, C. (1995). *Silicon snake oil: Second thoughts on the information highway*. New York: Doubleday.

Tompkins, G. E., & McGee, L. M. (1993). *Teaching reading with literature*. New York: Macmillan.

Part III

A Closer Look:
Teaching Ideas in Action

Chapter 11

Student-Directed Written Inquiry: Transferring Ownership to Students

Brenda A. Shearer

Molly M. Mosquito, three days old, of Shady Creek, died suddenly last Friday. Survived by her two hundred and thirty brothers and sisters, she will be missed. Molly began life as a rather small egg in the Shady Creek Park pond. She enjoyed water skipping and the taste of ankles. Her love for ankles eventually caused her death. Molly was killed by The Hand. Her sisters promise to avenge her death. A memorial service will be held on May 29 at 12:05 p.m., just after the picnic rush begins, in Shady Creek Park.

—A student from Osceola, Wisconsin, High School

Research supporting the power of writing to enhance learning, thinking, and problem solving in the content areas continues to revolutionize our ideas about how content at all grade levels "ought" to be taught. At the same time, changes such as integrated curriculum, block scheduling, and cooperative or collaborative learning provide educators with unprecedented opportunities to think about writing-to-learn in new and powerful ways. Why, then, is writing, particularly inquiry-based writing, such a daunting task for so many teachers and their students? The traditional content area writing assignment could be the cause. You remember the one: You and your teacher were engaged in what Ruddell (1997) calls "the academic dance," and it goes as follows.

The typical content area writing assignment is an essay or a report in which (a) the topic is selected by the teacher, (b) the subject is written about by the student, who records and documents learning, (c) the premise is to "show what you know," and (d) the product is graded by the teacher, who is the "audience."

In Applebee's classic national study, *Writing in the Secondary School* (1983), he discovered many troublesome aspects related to typical high school writing assignments. Collectively, these limitations create barriers that discourage the very essence of deep processing and inquiry that such assignments seek to foster. These barriers include the following:

- Assignments are on "impossible topics" (Applebee, 1983), such as, "Describe the political, social, cultural, and religious changes resulting from the Civil Rights Movement."

- Assignments require low levels of processing. They ask little more from the student than to collect information and to deliver it in much the same as its original form. I call this the *Dragnet* Model: "Just the facts, Ma'am!"

- Assignments are exercises in writing to the "expert." The teacher, who is the intended audience, is an expert in the content area and knows far more than the writer. The result is that the teacher (often unconsciously) tends to "fill in the blanks" when explanations are less than clear. Thus, the student is not pressed to write with clarity or precision.

- Information gathering becomes a primer in plagiarism. How many of us remember locating information in an encyclopedia and trying to reword it ever so slightly, knowing there was absolutely no way we could write it better?

Perhaps the biggest problem, the one that serves as the umbrella for all of the others, is the question of ownership. Who owns the writing? In Ruddell's description of the academic dance, is there any question that the writing actually belongs to the teacher? How can students be motivated to invest themselves when they have little or no choice of topic, no way to make any personal connection between the information they have gathered and their world, little prior knowledge to help them construct meaning, and no opportunity to process the information in a form or format that makes sense to them?

In this chapter, I will introduce an innovative alternative to the content area writing assignments described by Applebee (1983). By adapting a framework of inquiry called RAFT—Role, Audience, Format, Topic (Santa, 1988)—students are provided with the necessary support to reclaim ownership of their writing. You will see that RAFT writing is especially powerful at the secondary level, since it enables students to transform the increasingly technical or abstract content material into highly personal formats.

Teachers who use RAFT as a model for inquiry rarely hear the question "What does this information have to do with me?"

Teaching Idea: RAFT
Content Areas: All
Levels: All

The first step is to find ways to transfer ownership of the writing to the students. Essential to this process is the identification of the kinds of choices inherent in written inquiry. They involve all of the elements in the academic dance and include choosing a question or topic, a role or stance, an intended audience, and a format in which to present the information. Santa (1988) describes just such a transfer in the RAFT strategy. The components of RAFT reflect the following shifts in ownership:

Role: From student writes as self to student selects role: "Who will I be?"

Audience: From student writes for teacher to student chooses an audience: "To whom will I write?"

Format: From student writes essay, report, or term paper to student chooses the format: "In what form will I present my writing?"

Topic: From student is assigned a topic to student chooses the topic: "What is my topic?" "What is my question?"

RAFT reflects a philosophy of learning and critical thinking rooted in the tradition of Dewey (1938). The kind of inquiry it honors goes beyond *transmission*, transferring knowledge from one person to another (Hirsch, 1987); beyond *transaction,* individual construction of meaning (Rosenblatt, 1978); to *transformation,* the reformulation of ideas (Spivey, 1989). RAFT also recognizes that the ability to solve the problems we encounter in life is not well served by thinking of knowledge in terms of arbitrary academic "disciplines." The approach also transcends the thematic unit model in which global topics are used to teach science, social studies, mathematics, art, and music. Rather, in RAFT, the inquiry *becomes* the curriculum, and subject areas such as mathematics, music, language, and art serve as sign systems. Thus, subject areas are seen as perspectives, ways of thinking, and stances— in other words, ways to perceive the world (Short & Harste, with Burke, 1996).

The versatility of RAFT is evident in its adaptability to all content areas. Consider the examples shown in Table 11-1, from the many contained in Buehl's *Classroom Strategies for Interactive Learning* (1994, p. 88).

Table 11-1. The Versatility of RAFT			
Role	**Audience**	**Format**	**Topic**
Newspaper reporter	Readers in the 1870s	Obituary	General Ulysses S. Grant
Chemist	Chemical company	Instructions	Combinations to avoid
Plant	Sun	Thank you note	Sun's role in plant's growth
Repeating decimal	Set of rational numbers	Petition	Prove you belong to this set
Comma	Eighth-grade students	Letter of complaint	How I'm being misused
Abraham Lincoln	Dear Abby	Advice column	Problem with generals
Cook	Other cooks	Recipe	Salmonella in poultry

It's easy to see how motivating and creative these RAFTs are, especially when the above examples are compared to their more traditional forms. If you were an eighth-grade student, would you rather write an essay on the uses of the comma, or assume the role of the comma and write a letter of complaint about how you were being misused?

The Inquiry Process: Supporting Student Ownership

After using RAFT writing with students of various ages, grades, and abilities for several years, I began to notice that although students approached such assignments with unprecedented enthusiasm, they often met with frustration. They had a great deal of difficulty making the transition from having very little choice to having too much choice. And although their struggles definitely reflected developmental factors (older students were able to handle more choice than younger students), students of all grade levels needed support at each of the decision points within the RAFT. I was asking them to make choices without modeling the thinking necessary to make those choices. I began to examine with my students specific points in the inquiry-writing process that required the kind of scaffolding advocated by Vygotsky (1978), the support they needed to be successful as they tried new strategies and made meaning from new ideas.

There is considerable evidence that working in research groups enhances students' ability to access, use, and summarize information (Rekrut, 1997). In response to this, I not only placed students in collaborative inquiry groups, I also teamed with classroom teachers and reading specialists to model group decision making in minilessons at the identified points throughout the RAFT process. Support for this practice is rooted in Vygotsky's (1978) theory that language, learning, and thinking are related to the social world of the individual, suggesting that much of what students learn, they learn through social interaction.

I began to use modeling and mapping at every step of the process. I am not talking about mapping on notebook-size paper, but about teams of students huddled around large tables or working on the floor creating maps on giant sheets of chart paper. I am also talking about teachers who write with students as partners in the literacy community.

Helping Students to Ask Good Questions

> Good questions lead to good answers. In asking a question, you set up a format for learning; in looking for an answer, you learn; but when answering the question, since you have already found the answer, there is no learning—there is no expansion of your knowledge.
> (Wurman, 1989, p. 8)

If, as Wurman suggests, good questions do indeed lead to good answers, providing the modeling and allowing the time for students to create banks of questions is time well spent. Short (1993) called the process "wandering and wondering." I find that settling on a question too early tends to act as a stopper for the group, and students cease to engage in further exploration of possible topics or questions. Therefore, I urge students not to "fall in love" with a topic, but to continue to brainstorm lists of possible topics, subtopics, and questions. The rewards for doing so become apparent as groups discover that they quickly move beyond their first ideas to deeper and more creative ones. Sometimes questions change or are modified when students are well into the inquiry.

Before they develop their questions, group members create a semantic map featuring the broad topic guiding the inquiry. The mapping helps students to call forth and organize their prior knowledge. More important, since each student has constructed his or her own understanding of the topic, we are provided with shared knowledge and a window into the group's collective knowledge and understanding of the topic.

Most of us can recall being in a class where we had so little understanding of the material that we were incapable of asking a question. This is precisely the kind of position in which we place students when we choose impossible topics. Thus, student-centered inquiry writing is best used toward the end of a unit or curricular theme, so that those questions that may have arisen during the learning can be addressed in depth. A content area classroom that fosters discussion encourages children to investigate problems that are perceived as real to them.

The following steps take students through the question-writing process. It is important to carefully model them so that students know exactly what is expected.

1. Place students in research teams.
2. Start with a one-word topic and instruct students to narrow the topic by brainstorming categories or subtopics. For example, for "The Environment," one team created this list of subtopics: conservation of resources, recycling, endangered species, pollution, ecosystems.
3. Using the subtopics, have students brainstorm possible questions. For example, students generated the follow questions for the topic "Endangered Species": (a) What are some plants, animals, reptiles, or insects that are endangered? (b) How did they become endangered? (c) What is the difference between endangered and threatened?
4. How do laws affect endangered species?

Repeat the entire process for each of the subtopic headings, creating a "bank" of topics and questions. If there are many subtopics, choose five or six to develop into questions.

Students of all grade levels are capable of brainstorming lists and arriving at questions. Here is an example of the topic-subtopic-question path taken by a team of fourth graders working on the topic "The Weather:"

A Classroom Example: The Weather

Weather: Possible Subtopics

clouds	tornadoes	El Niño
precipitation	blizzards	storms
prediction/forecasting	seasons	clouds
snow	drought	rain
hurricanes	tornadoes	climate

Storms: Possible Questions for This Subtopic

1. What is a storm?
2. What kinds of storms are there?
3. What causes storms to occur?
4. Where do storms occur?
5. When do storms occur?
6. What is the most severe type of storm?
7. What happens during a thunderstorm?

One of the biggest surprises that occurred as I worked with teachers and students during question development was the degree to which the final questions varied from group to group, even though they had all started with the same overall concept. For example, in Margie Weiss's seventh-grade class, students were near the end of a social studies/language arts unit on "Freedom," and each team created a semantic map around that concept. However, after they brainstormed possible topics and subtopics and turned them into questions, they had chosen very different problems to investigate. The questions that teams developed from the central concept of "Freedom" involved such diverse subtopics as animal rights, sexual harassment in the workplace, and smoking. One of the teams moved from "Freedom" to the subtopic "rights" to a second subtopic of "women's rights and freedoms in the workplace." The group settled on the question, "What is sexual harassment and how does it affect women in the workplace?"

The day the group decided on this question I learned a great deal about my beliefs regarding choice and ownership. I had grave misgivings about the team's ability to negotiate its way around a topic so fraught with land mines, and I reminded the students of the challenges in terms of language and ideas this topic would present. Of course, the team immediately dismissed my concerns. Then I realized that although I believed in student ownership of writing as an abstract concept, I had a great deal of difficulty giving up control. I still wanted ever so subtly to steer them toward a narrower band of preconceived topics. I had secretly hoped that they would arrive at questions related to adolescent life or rights and freedoms at school. I remembered all the times I had manipulated students in this manner, making them feel as if my choices were actually theirs, and I was determined not to do that. They were so filled with enthusiasm and so eager to investigate their question that I inhaled deeply and decided to trust these students.

Creating the RAFT

The next step in creating the RAFT is to show students how to turn their questions into the Role, Audience, Format, Topic system. Again, it is important to model each step: (a) assuming a role, (b) targeting an audience,

(c) developing a format, (c) organizing information, and (d) matching the topic with a text frame.

Helping Students to Assume a Role

The ability to assume a role requires high-level processes that are difficult for many students even at the middle school and secondary levels. How can a student who has never been on a farm write from the perspective of a cow? How can a fourth grader or even a high school student assume the role of a chemist? Is it any wonder that we are so often disappointed in the results when we ask students to assume roles or write from different perspectives? At the heart of the difficulty is that we have expected students to do something that we have not taught them or modeled for them. As I worked with students over the last 5 years, I noticed that even when I allowed them to select their own roles, they were often less than successful. They would have little difficulty coming up with a creative idea, but they were unable to assume the role successfully and convincingly. I decided that I had to model how to begin with a question and then brainstorm possible roles. I also realized that students needed scaffolding, and I searched for a way to incorporate mapping into this stage.

Using a modified version of K-W-L (Ogle, 1986), I created a role map that serves as a scaffold as students assume the role. As the team investigated the sources they first listed, they invariably discovered new questions and new sources of information that they added to the role chart.

They began by examining the question and brainstormed possible roles. For example, for the question, "How, why, where, and when do earthquakes occur?" students generated these roles:

- A scientist, a seismologist, a sleeping earthquake
- The San Andreas Fault
- A tall building
- A California resident living on the fault line
- A witness to an earthquake
- A children's author

In order to develop a role, students need to consider the following:

- What do I know about this role?
- In order to assume this role, what will I need to know?
- What are some sources of information I could explore to do a good job of writing from this perspective?

A Classroom Example: "The Environment"

A sixth-grade team investigating the environment brainstormed possible roles related to the general topic, including consumer, garbage or recycling truck driver, environmentalist, animal, and rats living in the landfill. A question for their research was generated: "What kind of products can you buy that are made from recycled materials?" Students then developed the following role map (Table 11-2):

Table 11-2. Role Map: Environmentally Aware Consumer			
Know	**Resources**	**Questions**	**Learned**
What do I know that will help me to assume this role?	What resources are available to help me research my role?	What do I need to know about this role in order to do a good job?	What have I learned from my resources?
- Recycling is important. - Paper, glass, aluminum, and tin can be recycled.	-Library -Internet -Community -Polk County Recycling Center - Our parents	- What does it mean to recycle? - How are objects recycled? - What else can I do to help the environment?	- We can reuse and reduce items. - Different processes are used for various items. - What a landfill is composed of - How much Americans throw away - Americans can reduce the amount we throw away.

As students begin the RAFT process, it is sometimes tempting to overly control the process. For example, my seventh-grade team that decided to research sexual harassment came up with an idea that challenged my determination to let go of ownership. When they developed roles, they decided that they wanted to be coffeepots. "Coffeepots?" I thought to myself as my mind raced ahead to the format stage. "How will they ever be able to work that into a format?" Again, I had to resist the urge to manipulate them. Clearly, I was still wrestling with allowing them to own the writing. Even though they explained to me that the coffeepots were stored on an office shelf and had heard and seen much in the office building over several decades, I wondered how they would be able to *be* coffeepots. As they worked through their role map, I realized that this role allowed them access to all conversations, since nobody alters words or actions in the presence of inanimate objects. The students could also rely on a variety of sources to ascertain the kinds of conversations that might have been overheard. Still, I wondered what they would do when it came time to choose a format.

Helping Students to Target an Audience

Texts are shaped as much by the writers' sense of the characteristics of their readers as by the writers' actual characteristics (Goodman, 1994). Although this may seem obvious, it is given little attention in content area writing, especially in assignments where the teacher is the intended audience. Teachers who want to prepare their students to communicate ideas in real contexts must provide opportunities for these students to consider audience and to practice writing for a variety of audiences. Successful writers understand that every time they write a note to a friend, a research report, or a letter of complaint, they make fundamental assumptions about what their audience knows and needs. These assumptions have a dramatic effect on the written product. To scaffold for our students, we found it useful not only to model the brainstorming of possible audiences but also to employ a modified K-W-L map (similar to the one used to facilitate the development of a role) to target the knowledge levels and needs of different audiences. Again, we created huge maps and added to them as we discovered new ideas.

To target an audience, the team must first examine the question and role and then brainstorm possible audiences. We try not to rule out any possible audience at this point in the process.

A Classroom Example: "Earthquakes"

The following research questions were generated by the team: "The science of earthquakes: How, why, where and when do earthquakes occur?" "When will the next California earthquake occur?"

Team members then brainstormed possible audiences for various roles (Table 11-3).

Table 11-3. Brainstorming Audiences	
Role	**Possible audience**
Seismologist	A middle school or high school science class, legislators, citizens at a town meeting, *The Oprah Winfrey Show*
Children's author	Elementary and middle school students
Sleeping earthquake	Citizens of California, the seismologist, a 10-year-old girl

Deciding on an audience is much less difficult than framing a research question or selecting a role. The first two choices, question and role, usually lead in a logical manner to an appropriate audience. The team engages in a discussion of the possible prior knowledge the audience possesses and decides if there are any questions that should be added to account for this. By now, students are becoming confident in their ability to successfully complete the inquiry project with creativity and competence.

An important consideration when selecting an audience is assessing prior knowledge of that audience. The best audience is one who knows *less* than the presenter. If your audience knows less than you, you are forced to present information simply, thoroughly, and clearly. An audience who knows less than the presenter cannot fill in the blanks of incomplete or poorly presented information.

Helping Students to Develop a Format

One of the most visible signs of transformation of knowledge is in the choice of a format. It must not only be appropriate to the role, audience, and topic, it must also reflect the stance and the goals of the writer. These elements have a powerful influence on the selection of a format. Certainly, students need to be aware of the *field stance*, sometimes known as *textual stance*, within and among the various disciplines. In other words, they must have a sense of the different rhetorical strategies required to produce a scientific report versus an art critique (Bartholomae, 1985). Even a glance at some of the discourse alternatives listed below provides an appreciation for the complexity of the problem. These formats are much more than structures, they represent different ways of looking at the world.

Format or Discourse Alternatives

Hyperstudio presentations	Picture books	Lab reports
Editorials	Brochures	Graffiti
Debates	Interviews	Web pages
Recipes	Dialogues	Plays
Phone conversations	Music	Collages
Artworks	Maps	Photo essays
Travelogues	Commercials	Cartoons
TV scripts	Math story problems	Plays
Letters	Editorials	Field notes
Stories	Presentations	Science fiction
Sales pitches	Memos	Adventures
Research reports	Love Letters	Poetry
Job descriptions	Obituaries	Songs

Historical "you are there"	Biographies or sketches	Proposals
Journals or diaries	Guess who or what	Fantasy
News reports	Directions: how to	Obituary
Fact books or sheets	Campaign speeches	Poster displays
Case studies	Puzzles or riddles	Book reviews

A Classroom Example: "The Weather: Snow"

Consider the high school inquiry team whose weather-related research centered around snow, not an uncommon preoccupation in western Wisconsin. They decided to write an obituary for a snowflake. To do that, the group collected many examples of obituaries from rural and city newspapers and magazines. They interviewed, via e-mail, a journalist from a big city paper about the process of writing obituaries. Then they examined the obituaries and mapped the similarities and differences among them, noting elements common to all and unique in some. The students noticed and recorded the kinds of phrases and language used in obituaries as well as another important feature, the order in which information is presented. They even adjusted the format of the writing into a column about 3 inches wide. Imagine how powerful such discovery learning must have been for these students. All I could think of were Harste's (1994) words about inquiry as curriculum, and I understood exactly what he meant. I realized that one of the problems contributing to plagiarism is that students lack the understanding of discourse forms necessary to transform information. It is possible to show students that they can retain and use information, such as actual phrases from obituaries, and yet transform them into something that is theirs. I am convinced that the obituary that follows is a testimony to the time that the team spent investigating format and discourse.

Obituary

Sally W. Snowflake, one week old, of Winter Wonderland, died suddenly on March 2, 1998. Survived by billions of friends and family. Sally began as water vapor and was frozen into a tiny ice crystal on February 23, 1998 when temperatures dropped to 31 degrees Fahrenheit. Her life was full and beneficial. She served her life as a member of the insulation blanket that kept the Raccoon family warm for the winter. Her life was brought to an abrupt halt when temperatures rose to an excruciating 45 degrees Fahrenheit. However, her spirit will go on to travel the mountain streams. She will be sadly missed by the Raccoon family. A memorial service will be held on March 4, 1998 at 11:00 in the morning at Frosty Hillside Church.

Educators now recognize that there are many ways of knowing and many ways of showing what you know. Allowing students to choose a format that not only matches the topic but also honors the ways in which they process information is at the heart of ownership. Recall the example of the seventh-grade team investigating sexual harassment. At this stage of the RAFT process, the students became quite secretive. They had chosen to write a play and wanted to surprise me. By their deep level of engagement, their obvious enthusiasm, and the absence of any signs of struggle or frustration, I knew they had a clear vision of both the product and the means by which to accomplish it. Although they asked questions in as cryptic a manner as possible and maintained tight security on their materials and props, their pride and confidence was impossible to conceal. I could hardly wait to see the final production. I had little idea how their information would be delivered, but I had come to trust them and to relinquish control and ownership of their writing.

Helping Students to Organize Information

Today's students have access to information in both amounts and ways that are unprecedented. No longer are they limited to the resources in their libraries or communities. The use of the Internet enables students to have direct contact with primary source documents and the people who produce them. Not only can students read a research report on bovine growth hormone with the stroke of a keyboard, they can also engage in immediate conversation with the author of that research. They are able to contact farmers and special interest groups as well. One of the secondary benefits of such contact is that experts will often direct students to other resources that closely match the goals of the inquiry. These experts also help to clear up misconceptions of which the teacher may not be aware.

The search begins with the questions generated by the students. A wonderful framework for collecting, organizing, comparing, and analyzing information is the Inquiry Chart, or I-Chart. On large charts, students list their questions and resources, creating a grid on which to transfer information (Hoffman, 1992). In their investigations, students usually find much more information than they can use. We know that struggling readers have an especially difficult time recognizing important concepts and giving appropriate weight to them. Randall (1996) found that the I-Chart was particularly useful to students reading below grade level in helping them to sift through massive amounts of information while remaining focused on what they want to know.

A Classroom Example: "Animal Testing"

A group of students investigating animal testing created the following map (Figure 11-1). They also conducted an informal poll in their school and community and added that to their final project.

Figure 11-1. I-Chart

GUIDING QUESTIONS

ANIMAL TESTING	What brand of cosmetics do people use the most?	What alternatives are there for testing products?	What is the most common domestic animal used for testing?	How can we get the companies to stop testing on animals?	Other interesting facts and figures	New Questions
What We Know	We assume most people use the Cover Girl cosmetics the most.	We know they could take someone's skin cell and clone it to test their products on.	We know that rabbits, rats, mice, dogs, cats, monkeys, cows, and horses are used for testing.	- protesting - letters - persuasion	They use rabbits usually for testing eye products because they don't blink.	Is it easier to test on animals than the alternatives?
Internet	Not found Survey results from females mostly in the middle school and a few friends outside of school: #4 Clinique/Estee Lauder -13 Maybelline -7 Avon -14	They are Eyetex, skintex, Epipack, Neutral Red Bioassay Testskin, TOPKAT Ames Test, and Agarose Diffusion method.	Most think that only rats, rabbits, and mice are used for cosmetic testing - but dogs, cats, and pigs are also used.	- they started a European coalition to make people aware that their companies don't or do test on animals - inform companies of animal testing alternatives	None found	Why don't companies use the other alternatives for testing animals?
Animal Rights by Edward F. Dolan Jr.	Not Found	Single-cell testing cloning	Not in book.	Not found	Bruce Ames developed Ames testing which is an alternative.	Are the tests most accurate if you test on animals or the alternatives?
Animal Rights by Sunni Bloyd	Not Found	Not found	Primates: 49,000 - Aids vaccine development research Cats: 54,000 - vision research Dogs: 180,000 - heart surgery research Rats/mice: 12-15 million - cancer research, safety of new drugs	- We can save animals by having them as pets. - report animal cruelty - join a "Save the Animals" organization	BWC stands for Beauty Without Cruelty, which is a real cosmetic company.	
Summary	After taking our poll we found out that lots of people use Cover Girl cosmetics which test on animals. Many people cared about that when we told them, too.	We found out that there are alternatives to testing that don't involve animals, but involve humans. After all, we are the ones wearing the make up, not the animals.	After researching and looking at charts, rats and mice are the most commonly used for animal testing but that's not the only animal.	After we researched, we found out that we can protest, write letters, and use persuasion.		

Note that the I-Chart begins with a listing of what the team knows about each question. Another valuable feature is that there is a column for other interesting facts and figures, as well as one for new questions. At the bottom of each column is a cell in which to write a summary for the question listed above it. The I-Chart is ideal for a group inquiry project. It allows students to "divide and conquer," since it enables students to insert bits of information while serving to integrate all of the pieces into a coherent whole.

Spivey (1989) describes the processes of selecting, organizing, and connecting as discourse synthesis, a highly constructive act in which readers become writers. Mapping serves to reconfigure the content, not only acting as an outline but also showing what students select as most important. Mapping enables us to see how students perceive connections among ideas and how each is supported with detail. Through transmediation (Siegel, 1995), students are able to process information in one form and transform it into another. As they engage in inquiry, students gather information from various sign systems. They may find maps, charts, graphs, artwork, music, and prose that contain useful information. Siegel presents a powerful case that students can gain new perspectives through transmediation across different sign systems. Mapping is at the heart of this process.

Helping Students to Match the Research Question With a Purpose

At this point, the team must ask, "What do we want to accomplish with the information we have gathered?" Younger students find it particularly difficult to state a purpose for their work. Often they confuse the format with the purpose. Recall the classroom example with the sixth-grade teams investigating the environment. One team wanted to create a phone conversation between two friends discussing recycling. Students saw the writing of the dialogue as the end goal. It wasn't that they had no purpose, they simply had not been asked to put that purpose into words. Stating a purpose involves the use of a strong verb and matching that verb to the role, audience, format, and topic. By constructing a sentence including all elements of the RAFT and a strong verb, the team had a clear purpose and a focus for the work. They wrote, "We are an informed consumer [role] having a phone conversation [format] with a friend [audience] explaining [strong verb] recycling in Polk County [topic]."

Selecting an Appropriate Text Frame

Like effective readers, effective writers approach their work with a purpose and a mindset. They choose a stance or mindset that frames the text they produce. Text frames of mind are especially effective in helping students to analyze and organize the text according to their purpose as writers. Students can use the task descriptions shown in Table 11-4 to decide on an appropriate text frame (Jones, Palinscar, Ogle, & Carr, 1987).

Table 11-4. Task Descriptions	
Task	**Text Frame**
Do I want to solve a problem?	Problem/Solution
Do I want to show that certain outcomes result from certain conditions?	Cause and Effect
Do I want to make a concept understood?	Concept and Definition
Do I want to argue and support an idea?	Proposition and Support
Do I want to do something for a specific reason or outcome?	Goal, Action, and Outcome
Do I want to show how things are similar or different?	Compare and Contrast

Many of the earlier decisions made by the team such as role, audience, and format shape the decision about text frame, since all involve elements of stance. Still, team members may have discovered something in the information-gathering process that has altered their purpose.

An example of this involved the team investigating animal testing. They had started out to gather information and inform others about the topic, so they chose Concept and Definition as a text frame. However, as the inquiry proceeded they discovered much that evoked strong emotions, and their purpose changed from informing to arguing and supporting an idea, a Proposition and Support text frame. They created a brochure presenting a thoughtful case against animal testing for cosmetic purposes.

The RAFT: Putting It All Together

When team members have completed all the steps of the RAFT process, they are ready to put it all together. Recall the seventh-grade team investigating sexual harassment. They decided on the following RAFT:

Role: Coffeepots

Audience: Custodian or sweeper

Format: A play

Topic (+verb): To inform about sexual harassment of women
in the workplace

The big day of the team's presentation had finally arrived, and I could not wait to see how they would do it. They had managed to keep the details of the play a secret. When I walked into the room after lunch, a blue sheet was hanging in a corner. In front of it was a table on which there were four coffeepots. Directly behind each pot, a slit had been cut in the sheet through which an arm could grasp the handle. As a coffeepot "talked," the student behind it lifted it into the air. We all watched in amazement as a "custodian or sweeper" entered an office lounge at night only to hear voices. It was the coffeepots talking to each other about the things they had seen over the years involving sexual harassment. As they informed the sweeper and answered her questions, they accomplished their purpose of sharing the information they had learned through their inquiry. The performance of their RAFT was creative, entertaining, and highly informative. The team's play script is shown in Figure 11-2.

Figure 11-2. Students' Play Script

Four Little Coffeepots

Roles:

- Sweeper—Ann
- 1st Coffeepot—Kari
- 2nd Coffeepot—Molly
- 3rd Coffeepot—Dani
- 4th Coffeepot—Chris

The sweeper girl walks into the back room. She hears mumbles and walks toward the sound. She sees four coffeepots discussing an issue.

Sweeper: What's all the noise about?

1st: Well, as we've been sitting here on the shelf collecting dust, we came to find that we know a lot about the same issue.

Sweeper: What is that issue you know so much about?

cont.

2nd: That issue is sexual harassment. We've all come from different offices and realized that we have all seen a problem around those offices.

Sweeper: Sexual harassment?

3rd: Yes, sexual harassment is what we're talking about, haven't ya ever heard of it?

Sweeper: Well, sure I have, but I never knew it was a problem.

4th: The definition of sexual harassment is a form of violence used to keep people "in their place." Employers are liable for two kinds of sexual harassment. If a supervisor demands that an employee submit to sexual advances in order to keep his or her job, or get a raise or a promotion, this is called "quid pro quo" harassment or harassment by coworkers or supervisors. This can be so severe or pervasive that it creates a "hostile environment" that interferes with work.

1st: Or to sum that up, it is unwelcome sexual advances by an employer or a superior, and makes them feel uncomfortable.

2nd: An example might be a male employee telling jokes that offend you, or if the only way you can get a raise is doing what your boss tells you to do.

Sweeper: Well, how is it such a problem?

1st: In my office, Mel's law office, one guy always went around telling dirty sexist jokes, mostly against women.

2nd: In my office, which was Lunder and Lunder, one of the girls wanted to move up in her job, and her boss said that the only way she could do it is if she told everyone that they had done some sort of kissing scene in a public area.

3rd: At Don Beakman's General Computers, where I come from, I once heard that if these two people got together sometime, he could make her manager.

4th: At Wallywoo's office, I often would hear the boss say things to a young lady like he thought she was pretty and he liked the clothes she wore. Then it went too far and he told her it would help her job if they got together.

Sweeper: I'm very surprised about this. At my mom's work, something like that would never happen. I've seen their office policy, and a person would get fired on the spot if it were proven true. So how come it's such a problem?

cont.

1st: One reason may be that more women are working today. From 1985 to 1995, the number of women working grew rapidly. However, men still outnumber women in the workforce.

2nd: I think that they—men, that is—do it to feel superior. Maybe also because they think they have the right to do it.

3rd: And where is that in any job description?

4th: Then, after it happened to them, they can be further victimized by their employers.

1st: Or they could be labeled as troublemakers, or their characters or work records could be attacked.

2nd: Sometimes the alleged harasser is not investigated or reprimanded.

3rd: Yes, it's a big problem, but it doesn't happen everywhere, and it can be dealt with.

4th: It's not only part of the workplace, it can happen at schools, too.

Sweeper: Well, you guys have educated me well. In school we're starting a project that involves problems in the community. I think I'll look into this.

All: Sounds good to us!

Concluding Thoughts

When ownership of the inquiry process belongs to students, the role of the teacher changes from directive to supportive. A great deal of time is spent in discussion among the student teams. We found that students needed more time to explore ideas than the traditional middle or high school class period provided. Students were so eager to work on their inquiry projects that we spent several lunch periods meeting with groups of students who wanted to share their ideas with us and with each other. This was particularly true in the early stages of the writing, when the questions were being developed and students were deciding on possible roles and audiences.

Because of limited prior knowledge of both the topic and the research process, younger students may need more assistance and support in gathering information. It is useful to gather a variety of resources and keep them in the classroom during the research phase. Gradually, students can be shown how to extend the scope of their inquiry searches. In addition, it may be helpful to begin with inquiry writing that is more narrow in scope than a project that spans several weeks. Some teachers begin a shift of ownership through successive inquiry writing projects throughout the year. They accomplish this by limiting the number of choices in earlier writing. For example, they may choose a format but allow students to select a role and an audience.

Journals or learning logs are particularly informative to both teachers and students after each decision point in the RAFT. We set aside time at regular intervals to write about what worked well, what was difficult, and what we needed to facilitate the inquiry. Student journals reflected a great deal of uncertainty and struggle in the initial stages. Because the students were not used to owning the process, they wanted to know what the teacher wanted. Dealing with ambiguity is not always comfortable for a teacher, either, which makes it tempting to make choices for students or steer them into predetermined directions. By recognizing these reactions as part of a growth process, everyone in the writing community can work through these stages to reap the rewards that we have witnessed. One afternoon, students were discussing some of the insights they had gained through our RAFT projects. I was especially pleased to hear several of them say that they had learned much about the process of inquiry that would have a positive impact on all of their future academic writing. When students and teachers engage in the kind of inquiry writing described in this chapter, they not only transform curriculum, they transform themselves.

References

Applebee, A. (1981). *A study of writing in the secondary school* (Research Report No. 21). Urbana, IL: National Council of Teachers of English.

Applebee, A. (1983, November). *Writing in the secondary school.* Paper presented at San Diego State University Conference on New Directions in Comprehension Research, San Diego.

Bartholomae, D. (1985). Inventing the university. In M. Rose (Ed.), *When a writer can't write* (pp. 134–165). New York, NY: Guilford.

Buehl, D. (1995). *Classroom strategies for interactive learning.* Schofield, WI: Wisconsin State Reading Association.

Calkins, L. M. (1986). *The art of teaching writing.* Portsmouth, NH: Heinemann.

Dewey, J. (1938). *Experience and education.* New York: Macmillan.

Goodman, K. S. (1994). Reading, writing, and written texts: A transactional psycholinguistic view. In R. B. Ruddell, M. R. Ruddell, & H. Singer

(Eds.), *Theoretical models and processes of reading* (4th ed., pp. 1093–1130), Newark, DE: International Reading Association.

Graves, D. (1983). *Writing: Teachers and children at work.* Portsmouth, NH: Heinemann.

Harste, J. C. (1994). Literacy as curricular conversations about knowledge, inquiry, and morality. In R. B. Ruddell, M. R. Ruddell, & H. Singer (Eds.), *Theoretical models and processes of reading* (4th ed., pp. 1220–1242), Newark, DE: International Reading Association.

Hirsch, E. D. (1987). *Cultural literacy: What every American needs to know.* Boston: Houghton Mifflin.

Hoffman, J. (1992). Critical reading/thinking across the curriculum: Using I-Charts to support learning. *Language Arts, 69,* 121–127.

Jones, B., Palinscar, A., Ogle, D., & Carr, E. (1987). *Strategic teaching and learning: Cognitive instruction in the content areas.* Alexandria, VA: Association for Supervision and Curriculum Development.

Ogle, D. (1986). K-W-L: A teaching model that develops active reading of expository text. *Reading Teacher, 39,* 564–570.

Randall, S. N. (1996). Information charts: A strategy for organizing student research. *Journal of Adolescent and Adult Literacy, 39,* 536–542.

Rekrut, M. D. (1997). Collaborative research. *Journal of Adolescent and Adult Literacy, 41,* 26–34.

Rosenblatt, L. M. (1978). *The reader, the text, and the poem: The transactional theory of the literary work.* Carbondale, IL: Southern Illinois University Press.

Ruddell, M. R. (1997). *Teaching content reading and writing* (2nd ed.). Boston: Allyn & Bacon.

Santa, C. (1988). *Content reading including study systems.* Dubuque, IA: Kendall/Hunt.

Short, K. G. (1993, November). *Curriculum for the twenty-first century.* Paper presented at the annual meeting of the National Council of Teachers of English, Pittsburgh.

Short, K., & Harste, J., with Burke, C. (1996). *Creating classrooms for authors and inquirers.* Portsmouth, NH: Heinemann.

Siegel, M. (1995). More than words: The generative power of transmediations for learning. *Canadian Journal of Education, 20,* 455–475.

Spivey, N. N. (1989, November). *Composing from sources: Texts and task.* Paper presented at the annual meeting of the National Reading Conference, Austin, TX.

Vygotsky, L. (1978). *Mind in society.* Cambridge, MA: Harvard University Press.

Wurman, R. S. (1989). Hats. *Design Quarterly, 145,* 7–16.

Chapter 12

Creating Lifelong Learners: Strategies for Success

Carl A. Lisandrelli
Elaine Slivinski Lisandrelli

Lifelong learners view learning as a rich and varied experience. They make connections between learning and life, use a variety of methods to communicate effectively, respond freely, take risks, and engage in critical and creative thinking. Teachers enable students to become lifelong learners by scheduling time for them to explore subjects and interact with peers; encouraging them to make choices in selecting reading and writing topics; helping them to access and use a variety of research sources; and providing opportunities for them to integrate reading, writing, speaking, listening, and viewing in meaningful contexts.

As Maya Angelou has observed: "The teacher offers stimulation and ways in which the person can educate himself or herself. At best the teacher wakes up, shakes up that person and makes a person hungry" (Harris, 1986, p. 64). It is this hunger that encourages students to think critically and creatively, to inquire and seek meaningful responses, and to become independent learners.

This chapter focuses on classroom contexts that foster lifelong learners. Grouping practices, workshop format, information literacy, and performance tasks are discussed as characteristics of such settings. Finally, middle school classroom applications in social studies and English are presented, including project descriptions and student work.

Contexts That Foster Lifelong Learning

When students are in middle school and high school, their lives are full of promise. These are times to explore and learn, times to value working well with others, and times to discover potential. Both the student and the teacher play vital roles in this process. However, it is important to remember that the educational context also influences the outcomes. Grouping practices, workshop-based classrooms, information literacy, and student performances are among the contextual elements that influence students' achievement.

Grouping Practices

Tracking and grouping students by ability have been practiced in American schools since the early 1900s. *The Literacy Dictionary: The Vocabulary of Reading and Writing* (Harris & Hodges, 1995) defines *ability grouping* as the "placement of students according to similar levels of intelligence or achievement in some skill or subject, either within or among classes or schools; tracking; homogeneous grouping" (p. 2).

Studies concerning the effects of ability (or homogeneous) grouping have been conducted for many years. A synthesis of the research reveals an overwhelming amount of evidence showing that ability grouping fails to improve the academic achievement of students. Further, ability grouping may doom children who are not in the top tracks to second-class instruction and expectations and, ultimately, to second-class futures (Oakes, 1985; Manning & Lucking, 1990; Slavin, 1988, 1989).

Flexible grouping has emerged as a positive alternative to homogeneous grouping in many academic settings. Teachers who use flexible grouping choose a grouping pattern—such as whole class, small group, or pairs—that will function most effectively at a given time during a lesson. Flexible grouping is successful at all levels of learning, but it is especially valuable as a component of workshop classrooms during the adolescent years. Using a variety of collaborative and cooperative groupings in the context of a workshop-based classroom helps to assure the success of the heterogenous classroom (Zemelman, Daniels, & Hyde, 1998).

Through collaboration and workshop, students gain self-reliance and a talent for teamwork. These structures help to make the curriculum relevant, student centered, and integrated. Students need practice in working effectively and respectfully in large and small groups. They also need time to pair-share with classmates and conference with the teacher one-to-one. Flexible grouping facilitates these processes. (For more detailed information about grouping, see Anne Wheelock's *Crossing the Tracks*. For further information about helping diverse learners to access content, see chapter 16 of this book.)

Workshop: Working Together for Success

When you walk into a workshop-based classroom, it looks like a world in motion. Some students are writing, some are discussing, some are accessing information, some are reading, some are conferencing, and some are illustrating. The room is filled with resources and is very well organized. Every student has a goal and is using a variety of methods and materials to reach it. The teacher's role is as varied as the students'. He or she may be motivating, conferencing, observing, facilitating, formally assessing, or teaching a minilesson. One of the great benefits of the workshop format is its capacity to provide a variety of activities and resources to facilitate teaching and learning for students with a wide range of abilities.

The workshop format promotes inquiry, accommodates students' purposes, and provides a literate environment. Because it incorporates all of these characteristics, it is an ideal format for fostering lifelong learners. Further, while we may not conduct our workshop in the same manner as Nanci Atwell (1998), we are inspired by her belief that the workshop atmosphere is in the best interests of adolescent students who need independence and a chance to mature socially and intellectually.

Resources, integrated language arts, conferencing and minilessons are integral components of the workshop format. A discussion of each of these topics follows.

Resources

A workshop classroom requires many resources: Relying only upon a textbook doesn't provide optimum opportunities for learning (Kirwin cited in Lisandrelli, 1996; Savage, 1998). Content-related poetry books, picture books, short story collections, novels, biographies, articles, videos, CD-ROMs, and primary source materials, including letters and diaries, should fill workshop classrooms. Students need to be exposed to various kinds of writings by men and women from a variety of cultures. In addition, studies have shown that exposing students to quality multicultural literature reduces prejudice and that through literature students gain problem-solving skills and conflict-resolution skills (Emery, 1994).

Integrated Language Arts

Once the resources are in place, attention shifts to other components of the workshop. Integrated language arts emerge as a major focus. Students read, write, speak, listen and view daily in a workshop setting. They access myriad types of information and read, write, speak, listen, and view for a variety of purposes.

Just as students read in all classes, they need to write in every class as well. Students' writing conveys meaning and offers valuable insights about learning. In order for students to produce effective written responses, they need to understand the concepts they write about. They can also use the vocabulary of a content area in meaningful ways in their writing. By writing in many genres, students can reflect, express their thoughts, and extend their thinking. Writing helps students to deepen their understanding of the author's message. It is also a creative act, transforming an individual student's thoughts into words.

When writing in the content areas to the publication stage, students should use the same steps of the writing process—prewriting, drafting, revising, editing, and publishing—that they are accustomed to follow in their language arts classes. These steps encourage students to get feedback about their writing and engage in revision as often as necessary. If the writing is going to be evaluated, students should also be given the rubric or scoring guide that will be used before the writing process begins (for more information on rubrics, see chapter 15).

Writing helps students become better communicators and problem solvers. It is a vital skill for lifelong learners.

Conferencing

Another workshop element that helps students to become lifelong learners is the one-on-one conference. We've discovered that young adults like the social setting of conferences. They enjoy meeting one-on-one with their teacher, without their peer group watching the event.

During conference time, teachers become editors and fellow writers. The tone of the conference should be positive. We talk directly with our student-writers about their ideas, always beginning by pointing out something the student did well. The conference provides the writer with the opportunity to discuss difficulties, learn more effective strategies, and generate new ideas. Conferences provide opportunities for teachers and students to interact as reflective thinkers (Flynn & King, 1993). After the conference it is important to allow the student time to think, write, and inquire until he or she discovers a solution.

Since we have approximately 140 students each, we can't conference with students as often as we would like to, but we do schedule a minimum of two conferences per quarter. It has been our experience that these personal connections make a difference.

Minilessons

There will be occasions when you need to teach a concept to the whole class. The minilesson is an effective way for you to give this help to your students (for in-depth information see Atwell, 1998). Your decision to teach a minilesson will be based on what is happening in your students' reading and writing. The mini-lesson may last 5 to 10 minutes or as long as 20. A minilesson based on a meaningful topic helps students to gain the confidence to act independently on future assignments.

Information Literacy

The 21st century demands that learners in all content areas have the ability to access, evaluate, and use information. According to the American Association of School Librarians (1993):

> Information literate people are those who have learned how to learn. They know how to learn because they understand how knowledge is organized, how to find information, and how to use information in such a way that others can learn from them. They are people prepared for lifelong learning, because they can always find the information needed for any task or decision on hand. (p. 1)

Advances in technology have deluged the world with information. Content area students need to feel confident in their ability to access, sort, analyze, evaluate, and apply these data. To achieve this goal, courses need to be resource centered. Resources such as content-related novels, plays, poetry, short stories, trade books, magazines, encyclopedias, primary source documents, CD-ROMs, software, videotapes, music, art, and Internet access should be embedded in courses across the curriculum and available for student use.

If students are going to become effective information users, our role as teachers needs to change from prime dispensers of knowledge to facilitators of learning. We also must provide students with the time and direction to interpret, analyze, synthesize, evaluate, and communicate the information available to them. Fostering information literacy is a goal of every content area class.

The AASL (1993) provides a comprehensive list of suggestions for addressing information problem-solving skills. The following tips, useful in any content area and geared toward helping students gain confidence in information literacy, are based on some of their suggestions:

- Provide class time to brainstorm and research. Through modeling and practice, questions such as *who, what, when, where, why,* and *how* become second nature to students.
- Model paraphrasing, quotation use, documentation of sources, use of primary and secondary sources, and construction of bibliographies.
- Provide activities and experiences that facilitate students' under-

standing of the differences among fact, opinion, propaganda, point of view, and bias.
- Model the analysis, synthesis, and evaluation of information.
- Guide students in deciding whether they will use the information they access to inform, persuade, or entertain.
- Encourage students to choose a meaningful format to communicate the information (written reports, oral presentations, dramatizations, radio-broadcasts, etc).

Students are empowered when they have responsibility for selecting topics and communicating information. Furthermore, research shows that when students take more responsibility for their own learning and gather information themselves, they retain more (Hancock, 1993).

Projects, Enterprises, or Explorations: Students Showing What They Know

For students to read more frequently, write more fluently, listen more attentively, and speak more confidently, teachers need to provide opportunities for them to practice and take risks. We should encourage them to leave their comfort zone and explore new territory, and we should provide opportunities for students to express creative ideas. Creativity does not imply lack of planning and structure, but rather a chance for students to take a different perspective and think divergently. In our projects, often called *explorations* or *enterprises*, students have the freedom to self-select and explore, but we do provide a framework. When creating the projects, the students do the following:
- Include a table of contents, reference citations, and a bibliography.
- Research both primary sources and secondary sources. We present minilessons on the difference between primary (letters, interviews, journals, autobiographies, etc.) and secondary sources (textbooks, biographies).
- Practice keyboarding and word processing in a meaningful context.
- Conference with the teacher at least twice during the process. These benfit both the students and the teacher. When they are working on a project over time, students should set personal deadlines before the major deadline. Provide a checklist of items to the student that you would like to see by the midpoint conference date. Reward students for being prepared for the conference. Encourage them to see the exploration through to completion.

After the projects are complete, we ask students to reflect on their work by responding to the following:

- Describe the steps you took in completing this piece of work. What did you do first, next, and so on?
- What does the project show that you did well? Didn't do well?
- If you had an opportunity to make changes on your work, what would you do differently?
- What did you learn from this project?

In the next two sections we share some of the projects, enterprises, or explorations that have worked well for our students and for us. Although our classroom examples focus on middle school history and English, the projects are applicable in most content areas at the middle and high school levels. Since we do a lot of sharing, the projects may seem similar in structure even though we teach different content areas and grade levels. We frequently make changes to improve upon what we do, and we are always open to new ideas. We encourage you to share your ideas with trusted colleagues whenever possible. Their perspectives can be invaluable.

Carl's Perspective: Social Studies Class

Throughout the year I try to convey that history is a story about people—not just kings and leaders, but ordinary men and women who often showed extraordinary courage. Because the eighth-grade curriculum in our district consists of world history, from the Reformation to the present, the scope is tremendous. It is not a place to cram a lot of content into the year, as had been done in the past. To ensure better student understanding and foster student inquiry, the principle of covering less in more depth is followed (Zemelman et al., 1998). Presently the course centers on four areas: Rights and Revolution, Nationalism and Unification, Imperialism, and Nations at War.

Teaching Idea: Revolution Project
Content Area: Social Studies; format adaptable to all
Levels: Middle School; adaptable to High School
Sufficient time is provided to explore and incubate ideas, practice skills, and complete work with pride. Because students benefit from activities that provide time for them to work with others, they engage in both individual and group projects throughout the year. Projects often involve interviews, debates, and role-playing. These opportunities help them to develop their critical thinking skills, their oral and written communication skills, and respect for others. I encourage positive peer interaction, for as lifelong learners in the work force, students will often be required to work with others who have different strengths from their own.

At the beginning of the school year, I review "Helpful Hints for Research" (Figure 12-1). Students have a copy of this and are urged to refer to these suggestions throughout the year. These skills discourage students from plagiarizing. I also supplement the handout by offering minilessons on paraphrasing.

Figure 12.1. Helpful Hints for Research

Remember that these are just ideas to facilitate your research and get you thinking! Create your own research questions and choose the types of information that you think will best support them. Remember that I am available if there is anything you would like to discuss and that we will have mid-point and final conferences.

While you are researching:

- Raise questions about your topic that require you to think in critical, divergent, and evaluative ways.
- Use multiple resources including but not limited to books, articles, interviews, the Internet.
- Skim and scan for major ideas and keywords to identify relevant information.
- Distinguish fact, opinion, propaganda, point of view and bias.
- Classify the information into categories.
- Identify points of agreement and disagreement among sources.
- Show cause and effect.
- Reflect and draw conclusions.

Researching a Person

If you have chosen to research a person, consider including information such as the following:

1. A physical description of the person.
2. The personal history of the individual.
3. How the individual's personality affected his or her decision-making.
4. Major influences in the person's life.
5. Interesting facts about the individual.
6. A quote that the person said or that someone else said about the person you are researching. Explain the relevance of the quote and why you selected it.
7. A decision the person made. How did the decision affect others?
8. Thoughts about discrimination during the person's time. Offer an example and/or describe its impact on the individual you're researching.

cont.

9. Questions Diane Sawyer would want to ask this person in a current day interview. Predict the responses.

10. What you liked about the person and why.

11. What you didn't like and why.

12. Consider the expression "One person can make a difference." Reflect on the difference this individual made in history.

13. What advice you would give this person if you could go back in time knowing what you know now. Explain your reasoning.

14. What the person would find most fascinating if he or she came to the United States in present day.

15. What you think this person would be doing if he/she lived in present day.

16. If the individual's life would be considered a success. Justify your response.

17. What made the person a hero.

18. How the course of history would have been different if this individual had not lived.

19. A letter written by the person to someone today explaining his/her contribution to his/her country.

Researching an Event

If you are researching an event, consider including information such as the following:

1. Why the event occurred.

2. People who played significant roles in the event.

3. How history would be different if the event had not occurred or had a different outcome.

4. What role you would like to have played in the event.

If you choose to enhance your research, you may wish to include information such as the following:

1. A series of drawings or create a collage or mobile on such things as fashions, hairstyles, dances, architecture, and/or inventions of the time period or person you are exploring.

2. Information about or performances of musicians, artists, and dramatists that lived during the time period.

3. Samples of the poetry, short stories, and/or novels written in the time period. Explain your choices and offer your interpretations/reactions.

To write about a topic requires knowledge of the topic. Students make decisions about what knowledge to include in their response. They also make decisions about the appropriate words, sentence structure, and writing conventions that will make their message clear. They raise issues, identify problems, and seek solutions. They construct personal meaning by relating new experiences to past experiences.

Because I want to show students that I value writing, students frequently see me engaged in the writing process. Writing is an integral part of the history curriculum and an important part of learning in all subject areas.

My goal is for students to structure and synthesize what they know, not just regurgitate. Using a Keeping Track notebook (Rothstein & Gess, 1992), students enter key concepts and write personal responses to what they are learning. The following sentence starters are helpful in this process:

I now understand . . .

I need to know more about . . .

I would like to know why . . .

I still don't understand . . .

If I read more about . . . then I . . .

History provides an unending source of topics which students can research in depth, become "experts" in, and then share their learning with the class. Students who may have difficulty completing exams may be able to do well on a project. I've seen firsthand the success that students have with these research projects. As a result, they feel good about their learning. They feel a sense of accomplishment because they tackled a project over a period of time. This process serves a student into adulthood much better than facts learned for an objective test.

In this section I describe the Revolution Project (Figure 12-2) that my students do. It is designed to expose the students to multiple information sources and encourage critical thinking. To begin this project, I divide the room into three sections or stations and provide materials and an option sheet for the students (Figure 12-3). Students then select one packet from each station.

Figure 12-2. Revolution Project

Station 1: Early Russia to 1905

A. Read "Two Views of the Romanovs" from *Days of our Lives* by Rose Pesotta
    See Option Sheet.

B. Read "The Dead Princess and the Seven Valiant Knights" and another tale from the book *Six Russian Tales* by Alexander Pushkin.
    See Option Sheet.

C. Read available information on Peter the Great, Catherine the Great, Alexander II, Rasputin, and Nicholas II.
    See Option Sheet.

D. Additional topics to explore: Decembrist Revolt, Russo-Japanese War, and Revolution of 1905.
    See Option Sheet.

E. Select two chapters from *Nicholas and Alexandra* by Robert K. Massie, located in the back of the room.
    See Option Sheet.

Station 2: The Russian Revolution of 1917

A. View the CD-ROM on The Russian Revolution.
    See Option Sheet.

B. Work on The Russian Revolution Primary Source Kit.
    Read broadsheets, voices to remember, and "branching out." Writing historical drama is extra credit. Examine all primary documents.

C. Read available information on Lenin, Stalin, The Russian Revolution, Communism, and Karl Marx.
    See Option Sheet

Station 3: The English Revolution

A. Select either Elizabeth I or The Spanish Armada Primary Source Kit. Follow directions given for Station 2B.

B. Read two of three available biographies on William the Conqueror, Good Queen Bess, or Henry VIII.
    See Option Sheet.

C. Read available information on the English Revolution.
    See Option Sheet.

Figure 12-3. Revolution Project Option Sheet

For any of the materials you read at each station, be sure to record the title of the book, author, publisher, and copyright date. Remember to underline the title of the book.

After you have read, either select *4* of the following and respond to them or meet with me to discuss alternatives.

1. List five main points that you learned from your reading.

2. What were the most interesting parts of the book, chapter, or article you read? List and discuss each.

3. Explain specifically what you liked or disliked about the reading. List at least three examples. Quote a favorite passage of description. Remember to enclose it in quotation marks.

4. In what ways did the reading affect you? List several examples and explain each. Have they helped you to gain a new appreciation for the times and/or country in which you live?

5. Was there a major turning point in the person's life or in the event about which you read? Identify it and explain its significance.

6. Assume the point of view of the character about whom you are reading (e.g., Catherine the Great, Lenin). Defend your life and/or admit any mistakes you made. Be specific.

7. Was the person a positive or negative force on the course of history? Explain your position.

8. If you are writing about an event, pretend you are an eyewitness to that event. Who are you? What did you experience? How did you feel? Did the event end the way you expected? If you could go back in time and change the event, what would you do? How would you have improved upon what happened? What were the causes and effects of the event?

9. What qualities and achievements do you admire about the person? In an essay express your thoughts about his or her admirable qualities.

To create the stations I have acquired a large collection of materials for my classroom. In addition, I bring stacks of books to the room from our school library and the public library. Initially, the students and I take class time and carefully study the project. I give students time to process the information and then provide plenty of class time to work on the projects. The in-class project time benefits students by assuring that they have the following: a quiet, information-rich environment in which to work; opportunities to interact with peers; and me there to help them if they have questions or concerns. The in-class project time also benefits me as a teacher, because in addition to all the student benefits it provides ongoing opportunities for informal assessment (for formal assessment, see Figure 12-4).

In the Revolution Project students have the opportunity to explore at least one aspect of each of the three revolutions in depth. (Many of the primary document source packets can be purchased through JACKDAW Publications, P.O. Box 503, Amawalk, NY 10501.) Students are also provided with time to conference individually with me and also with other students who have selected the same topic. After several weeks of exploration, the class comes together to hear, view, and experience all of the presentations. Students, on the whole, are very attentive when their classmates are presenting.

Figure 12-4. Criteria for Revolution Project

The following are among the criteria we, as a class, will consider when we create a rubric for the Revolution Project:

- Focus and participation in workshop sessions
- Higher order thinking
- Multiple sources of information
- Effective writing
- Information shared in response
- Conventions of writing
- Bibliographic formatting
- Preparedness for conferences

After we agree upon the criteria, we will describe levels of performance on our 4-point rubric. For example, students who were exceptionally well prepared for conferences would earn a 4. Those who were thoroughly prepared, a 3; those adequately prepared, a 2; those who were inadequately prepared, a 1; those who were not at all prepared or did not participate, a 0.

Teaching Idea: Final Exam Alternative
Content Area: Social Studies; format adaptable to all
Level: Middle School; adaptable to High School

The projects have been very successful, so when our school was searching for alternative to final exams, my eighth-grade team decided that students should select a content area to focus on for a final project. Students received either their first or second choice. Each teacher had a heterogeneous mix of perceived high-, average-, and low-ability students. After we divided the students among the five teachers, we adjusted our class time so we would have three periods in a row several times a month. The information I shared with students who selected history as the focus for their final project appears in Figure 12-5.

Figure 12-5. Final Exam Alternative for World History

When selecting a topic for your research, please consult the extensive list of possibilities posted in the classroom. If you would like to research a topic that does not appear on the list, please discuss it with me before you begin.

Written Portion

Requirements for the written portion:

Cover Page
Table of Contents (listing your subtopics)
Report (minimum two pages, maximum seven pages double spaced)
Bibliography

You must use the word processor for all drafts. If you do not have access to a computer at home, opportunities for access will be provided during the school day.

You should include opinions, insights, and interpretations of the details you find in your research. Analyze! Synthesize!

Visual Portion
(one of the following is required)
Map, graph, collage (of images and words), painting, mural, model, time line.

Oral Portion
See Rubric.

Reminders:
You must include all of your rough drafts and your index cards.
You will receive credit for being prepared for your midpoint check and all our conferences.

When the final projects began, students were enthusiastic. They worked hard during the blocks of time provided, and the majority continued the work at home. I was impressed with the enthusiasm and work ethic of the students of all ability levels. It was clear that becoming an expert pleased them, too!

When students presented their projects, they impressed both their peers and me with the understanding of their research. I wish there were more opportunities for students during the school year to pursue subjects in depth. Student comments about the project include the following observations made by Patrick:

> I learned much from doing this report, but most of all I enjoyed doing it. This project has shown me the importance of freedom that I take for granted. It brought me great knowledge about French history that I will never forget. I hope you will continue to give projects as good as this to future classes.

Through minilessons, I explain general areas of concern, including footnotes, bibliography, quotations, and common spelling errors. Students stop and take notice when a social studies teacher presents this information. It's good for them to see that content area teachers realize the importance of the conventions of writing.

The conferences help students to improve their project by making changes that make the final product better. They learn to look at their project as a work in progress. I've seen remarkable improvement from their early drafts to their final copy. Students look forward to bringing their work to the conference and discussing their challenges or progress one-on-one. Through the conferences I also get to know my students better.

I value effective work habits and encourage students to volunteer in class, work well in their groups, be helpful and cooperative to each other, and focus on the task at hand. I also encourage students to enhance their projects in the following ways:

- Research the popular music, dances, movies, clothing, literature, art, entertainment, and modes of transportation. of the place and time they are investigating.
- Include copies of poems that were written during the period under study or contemporary poems that relate to past times.
- Write poetry related to the topics we cover (for more information on using poetry in the content areas, see chapter 8).

Figure 12-6 shows the formal assessment of the project.

Figure 12-6. Rubric for Final Exam Alternative Project

Research and Work Study
40 possible points   Your score_____

The student is focused during the research sessions.
The student is prepared for each stage of the project.
The student shows a willingness to revise.

Written Portion
25 possible points   Your score _____

The introduction captures the audience's attentions.
Substance: The writing is rich in detail and supporting information.
Organization: The information is presented clearly. The ideas flow
   well. Transitional devices are used effectively.
A bibliography is included.
The final copy is carefully proofread.

Oral Portion
25 possible points   Your score _____

Presentation
Scale: 1= weak, 2 = fair, 3 = adequate, 4 = good, 5 = excellent

Quality	1	2	3	4	5
Volume	1	2	3	4	5
Rate	1	2	3	4	5
Eye contact	1	2	3	4	5
Gestures, facial expression	1	2	3	4	5

Visual
10 possible points   Your score_____
Enhances the written portion

Possible points: 100   **Total points earned_____**

Evaluator_____

Comments:

Teaching Idea: Personal Responses to Literature
Content Area: Social Studies; format adaptable to all
Level: Middle School; adaptable to High School

During the past few years I have been building up a classroom library of historical fiction. I have multiple copies of more than 30 novels related to our themes. I also have picture books that relate to topics and themes we study. *Rose Blanche* (Innocenti, 1985), *The Wall* (Bunting, 1992), *Good Queen Bess* (Stanley & Vennema, 1990), and *Starry Messenger* (Sis, 1996) are four that students find especially meaningful. I provide time in class for students to choose, read, and respond to these works in a personal way. Novels that have received favorable responses include the following: *Night* (Wiesel, 1986), *Number the Stars* (Lowry, 1990), *Devil in Vienna* (Orgel, 1978), *The Devil's Arithmetic* (Yolen, 1990) and *The Wave* (Strasser, 1981). I provide a list of open-ended questions (Myers, 1988) that encourage students to make a personal connection with the text. Figure 12-7 presents two eighth-grade students' responses.

As I reflect upon my 25 years in the classroom, I look at the old: a lecture-heavy method in a homogeneous classroom where I attempted to "cover" the required content and relied mostly on objective tests to assess learning. I embrace the new: a workshop-based, heterogeneous classroom where students have time to explore less content in greater depth and I rely mostly on performance assessments. The new method is more rewarding for both the students and me. From the student responses I have gotten recently, I feel the number of lifelong learners is increasing.

Elaine's Perspective: English Class

As in Carl's classroom, my teaching is workshop based and my students are heterogeneously grouped. Each year when I first meet my middle school students, I tell them that we are going to concentrate on four major areas: reading, writing, speaking, and listening—skills they will need for lifelong learning.

Teaching Idea: My Favorite Poems
Content Area: English; adaptable to all
Level: Middle School; adaptable to Intermediate and High School

In September, I introduce a project that will not be due until mid-April. For the past several years it has been "My Favorite Poems" (Figure 12-8). My goal is for students to realize that poetry is a valuable part of lifelong learning.

Figure 12-7. Student Responses to Novels

What character(s) was (were) your favorite(s)? Explain your choice(s).

I feel my favorite characters were Elizer and his father. All through the story, they both stuck with each other in everlasting friendship. When odds were against them in the camps and they had no food and were starving, they were together to comfort each other and make the best of the situations.

I admire how Elizer made the right choices. When Elizer's father was dying, he showed compassion to the poor man and fed him rations despite the taunts of others to take it for himself.

Elizer, when being lashed and persecuted, had the strength to hold his tongue and withstand the most intolerable pain. Elizer had the strength and the will to fight to go on, as when they jogged 42 miles in the snow with a wounded leg. The pure punishment this person received! And still he did not crumble.

He went on when his father died. He kept going when he rode in open cattle cars for six days in freezing weather, hanging onto life with the tips of his fingers, but still he never gave up.

When Elizer was surrounded by death and it seemed to be closing in on him, he never gave in. He always fought for life, despite odds, despite challenges, and he prevailed.

> —Brian, grade 8, responding to *Night* by Elie Wiesel

How do you feel about this book? Explain your reasoning.

I like the novel *The Wave* very much. One reason is I like to read books that make me feel emotions. For me I felt many different things. I felt horror and confusion at the actions of the wave members against those who were different. I felt anger and frustration because the same kids who said that the Holocaust could never happen again did anything Mr. Ross said to do. I felt fear that the Holocaust could happen again with thinking like that.

I also thought *The Wave* was a page turner. It is the kind of book that you want to finish all at once so that you can find out what happens in the end. I also enjoy reading books on Holocaust-related subjects. My grandmother says that books like that make me depressed, but I feel it is important to read about it to prevent it from happening in the future.

I often wondered how the Holocaust could have happened. It is very hard to comprehend how one person could influence or brainwash so many people into doing so much evil. *The Wave* better helped me to understand how people can get so caught up in something that they don't see it for what it is but just blindly follow a leader.

It is easy to follow a leader, especially in difficult times. Making decisions is not always easy, but freedom to choose how to act, to think, or to feel is a gift all people everywhere should enjoy. They should never give it away.

The Wave is a book I could read again and again and still be interested in it.

> —Jessica, grade 8, responding to *The Wave* by Todd Strasser

---

Figure 12-8. My Favorite Poems Project

Enterprise 1
Select at least ten poems you like.
Copy each poem by hand or input it into the computer. If it is a longer poem, you may decide to just copy your favorite stanzas. Include the following information for each poem or excerpt you choose: title, author, title of the book in which the poem appeared, editor or "selector" of the poetry collection, publisher, and copyright date.

Enterprise 2
For each poem, find or draw pictures that illustrate some of the images in the poem. For example: "When lilacs last in the dooryard bloom'd
And the great star early droop'd in the western sky in the night, I mourn'd, and yet shall mourn with ever-returning spring."

> —stanza 1 from "When Lilacs Last in the Dooryard Bloomed" by Walt Whitman, from *Selections From Leaves of Grass* (NY: Avenel Books, 1961).

I could use pictures of lilacs, a night sky, a star, spring images, or a person who seems sad to illustrate these images.

Enterprise 3
"Word Paint"
Use a highlighter to accent some of the words, lines, or phrases that you especially liked in the poems you've selected (e.g., a special image, a figure of speech, or a vivid verb).

Enterprise 4
Pretend you are inviting one of the following poets home for the weekend. Whom would you invite and why? Poets: Robert Frost, T. S. Elliot, Langston Hughes, Emily Dickinson, Paul Laurence Dunbar, Lucille Clifton, Liz Rosenberg, Edwin Arlington Robinson, Carl Sandburg, Edgar Allan Poe, Maya Angelou, William Carlos Williams, Jack Prelutsky, Rita Dove, Gary Soto, Nancy Willard, Lee Benett Hopkins. If you have another suggestion, please present it to me. Check the board for new additions as the year goes on.
Consult two different reference books. Read the material, then give us a little background on the poet you select. (Put the information in your own words.) What were the poet's interests? Do you know when the poet first began to write poetry? How has the poet you selected made the world a better place? Include at least two stanzas from two different poems the poet has written.

cont.

Optional Enterprises

Option 1
See if you can obtain a copy of a favorite poem of a friend or relative. Interview that person. When did he or she first discover the poem? Why is it a favorite?

Option 2
Include a poem or poems that you have written.

Remember that you need to include the following in your booklet: cover page, table of contents, and page numbers.

I bring stacks of poetry books into the classroom and give students class time to select books they like. While we work on other topics and projects in the interim, every few weeks I remind students of the poetry project and provide plenty of class time for each student to create a collection of his or her favorite poems. The requirements listed in Figure 12-8 have evolved over time. For example, the "word paint" section came after I read Georgia Heard's chapter entitled "Language: The Poet's Paint" from *For the Good of the Earth and Sun: Teaching Poetry* (1989).

Students begin by reviewing numerous poetry collections, selecting 10 of their favorite poems, and creating a bibliography of the sources they used. They then hand-copy or type the poems, engaging in a technique that successful writers have practiced to improve their own writing skills by trying to feel the author's style.

Next, students illustrate the poems, using a variety of art materials, and highlight the words or phrases they especially like. They also research the lives of three poets and select one to invite home for the weekend. Robert Frost, Emily Dickinson, Langston Hughes, Carl Sandburg, Edgar Allan Poe, Jack Prelutsky, and Maya Angelou are some of the favorites. This activity encourages students to make connections with the facts they learn about the poet. For example, as a young girl growing up in Stamps, Arkansas, Maya Angelou loved Hershey's Kisses. In response, a student might report that he arranged a candy dish filled with Hershey's Kisses on the nightstand in the guest room to welcome Maya Angelou into his home. Another student, upon discovering that poet Carl Sandburg wrote a biography of Abraham Lincoln, might decide to bring Sandburg into her history class to discuss his research.

Optional activities involve creating original poetry and interviewing friends and relatives to discover what their favorite poems might be. The students organize all this work into an attractive booklet with a table of contents. Some students purchase blank books from bookstores, some use binders, others create their own with construction paper and notebook paper. The majority of students' collections far exceed the criteria. We have midpoint conferences so I can check their progress.

As students present their booklets to the class, they have an opportunity to share a favorite poem. The sharer uses our poet's chair, and we relax and enjoy snacks during the readings.

In the fall of a new school year, I ask former students to bring in their poetry collections so I can show samples to the new seventh-grader students. They are happy to do so. A few years ago, I noticed that one student had included 15 additional poems that she hand-copied and illustrated during the summer, long after the project had been evaluated. I now share that piece of good news with my students and many view their booklets as works in progress.

Teaching Idea: Poetry Showcase
Content Areas: English; format adaptable to all
Levels: Middle School; adaptable to Intermediate and High School

In conjunction with the Favorite Poems project, students select a favorite stanza from a poem we have read in class and copy it on a 5 x 7 index card. They then give a brief summary of the poem and a reason that the stanza appealed to them. Maura, one of our middle school students, wrote the following:

> My favorite stanza is stanza number two from "The Children's Hour" by Henry Wadsworth Longfellow.
>
> > "I hear in the chamber above me
> > > The patter of little feet.
> > The sound of a door that is opened,
> > > And voices soft and sweet."
>
> The poem is about a father with three daughters. Father is sitting in his study when suddenly he hears the girls and sees the lamplight in the hall. He sees by their eyes that the girls are plotting against him to take him by surprise. Then the girls run in and hug him and they seem to be everywhere. They almost devour him with kisses and then he says how they will stay in his heart until he dies.
>
> I like these lines because they are so heartwarming and it is just like when I sneak up on my dad. I think that is the greatest poem in the book.

Students read their favorite stanzas, decorate the cards, and place them on a large bulletin board entitled "Poetry Showcase."

Teaching Idea: Picture Book Response
Content Areas: Middle School; adaptable to all
Levels: Middle School; adaptable to Intermediate and High School

Another project that students enjoy is responding to picture books. I keep an extensive collection in my classroom as resources. They include the following: Nanci Willard's (1990) *The High Rise Glorious Skittle Skat Roarious Sky Pie Angel Food Cake,* Julius Lester's (1997) *From Slave Ship to Freedom Road*, Susan Bartoletti's (1997) *Dancing with Dziadziu*, Rosemary Wells's (1997) *McDuff Moves In*, Dyanne DiSalvo-Ryan's (1991) *Uncle Willie and the Soup Kitchen*, William Miller's (1997) *Richard Wright and the Library Card*, Patricia Polacco's (1992) *Mrs. Katz and Tush*, Candice Ransom's (1995) *The Big Green Pocketbook,* Cynthia Rylant's (1985) *When I Was Young in the Mountains*, Jane Yolen's (1987) *Owl Moon*, and Barbara Cooney's (1985) *Miss Rumphius*. I remind students of the craft involved in writing and illustrating these books. Picture book manuscripts tell a story within 32 pages, which is not an easy task. They are excellent examples of complete action—a story that has a beginning, a middle, and an end. Students enjoy reading and learning from these books. They learn organizational skills and the need to credit sources by keeping track of publication information. Students then select a book they would like to use for their picture book response. Figure 12-9 illustrates the components of the project (for other ways to use picture books in the content areas, see chapters 3 and 7).

Once again, midpoint conferences are essential. Not all students have developed the self-discipline to work on a project over time. Checkups ensure that students are completing certain stages of the project. Conferences are also necessary to discuss rough drafts. As noted in Figure 12-10, when I evaluate this project I give credit for all stages.

During the year we also read stories together, share a novel, make time to choose and read other novels, and give oral presentations. A dictionary remains on every desk and students come to view it as a source of new words and a necessary editing tool. We also have plenty of classroom thesauruses that are used frequently.

Figure 12-9. Picture Book Response Project

Name of student:

Title of picture book:

Author:

Illustrator:

Publisher:

Copyright date:

- Write a summary of the story (maximum 5 sentences).

- Tell specifically what you liked or disliked about the picture book. List at least three examples.

- Comment on the art work. Was it appropriate and varied for the text? Did you have a favorite illustration? Why did you like it?

- If there was dialogue, copy an excerpt that you liked. If there was no dialogue or very little, copy a passage that you found especially well written. Please use quotation marks.

- Which character was most memorable? Explain why.

- What did you think of the ending? Explain. Can you suggest an alternative way to end the book?

- List a few of the words, phrases, or sentences that made the book special for you. (Please use quotation marks.) Explain why you chose them.

Figure 12-10. Picture Book Response Evaluation Form

---

1. Cover page and organizational strategy (10 points)

2. Final copy (30 points)

3. Rough draft and writing conference (30 points)

4. Record of picture books read (25 points)
    (Contains title, author, illustrator, publisher, copyright, and
    brief summary and/or reaction)

5. Index card listing three books under consideration for your
    final project and your explanation of your choices (5 points)

6. Any extra information (optional)

Total points earned:

In this project my strength was:

One area I need to work harder on is:

We no longer spend week after week completing grammar exercises. I know the "grammar debate" continues. I often hear comments like the following: "All that writing and project work is nice, but where do you find the time when you have all that grammar to cover?" I believe that explicit teaching of grammar is useful, but we need to decrease isolated lessons and help students to learn grammar and mechanics in context during the editing stage of their writing (Zemelman et al., 1998).

Students are excited about learning when they have the opportunity to explore language in a context that is meaningful to them. Students' comments about their projects have included the following: "Thank you for helping to discover my talent for writing." "Thank you for being so supportive this year with writing." "I really appreciate you helping me with my writing." "Your projects and ideas were great. I never met an English teacher who smiled so much."

Creating a workshop-based classroom is challenging, but it is easy to smile when I see the results: students reading and writing, communicating openly, working cooperatively, and taking risks. These students are well on their way to becoming lifelong learners.

Concluding Thoughts

Students need to see us as readers and writers, as adults who still get excited about learning, who may not know all the answers but are willing to take the time to try to find out. Students also need to see us as colearners. We need to create an environment where we learn and grow together.

If we want our students to be lifelong learners, we must be lifelong learners. We must constantly examine new practices and be willing to embrace principles of learning that research and our own classroom experiences tell us are in the best interests of our students.

In the spirit of Maya Angelou, we, as teachers, should always be willing to embrace creative and innovative techniques to help our students become "hungry to learn." A rich and varied curriculum is the right of every student.

References

American Association of School Librarians. (1993). *Information literacy: A position paper on information problem solving*. Chicago, IL: American Library Association.

Atwell, N. (1998). *In the middle: New understandings about writing, reading, and learning* (2nd ed.). Portsmouth, NH: Boynton/Cook.

Emery, F. (1994, October 22). *The world in small hands: Exploring multicultural issues in children's literature*. Paper presented at the Fall Philadelphia Conference, Northeastern Region Society of Children's Book Writers and Illustrators, Exton, PA.

Flynn, T., & King, M. (1993). *Dynamics of the writing conference: Social and cognitive interaction*. Urbana, IL: National Council of Teachers of English.

Hancock, V. (1993, May). *Information literacy for lifelong learning*. Syracuse, New York: ERIC.

Harris, R., (1986, Fall). Zelo interviews Maya Angelou. *Zelo*. p. 64.

Harris, T. L., & Hodges, R. E. (1995). *The literacy dictionary: The vocabulary of reading and writing*. Newark, DE: International Reading Association.

Heard, G. (1989). *For the good of the earth and sun*. Portsmouth, NH: Heinemann.

Hopkins, L. B. (1994, September/October). Before English class. *Teaching and Learning Literature*, pp. 26–27.

Lisandrelli, E. (1996). *Maya Angelou: More than a poet*. Springfield, NJ: Enslow.

Manning, R. L., & Lucking, R. (1990). Ability grouping: Realities and alternatives. *Childhood Education, 66,* 254–258.

Myers, K. L. (1988). Twenty (better) questions. *English Journal, 77* (1), 64–65.

Oakes, J. (1985). Keeping track.. In R. E. Slavin (Ed.), *School and classroom organization*. Hillsdale, NJ: Erlbaum.

Rief, L. (1992). *Seeking diversity: Language arts with adolescents*. *Portsmouth*, NH: Heinemann.

Rothstein, E., & Gess, D. (1992). *Teaching writing: A developmental, systematic, cooperative approach for learning to write and writing to learn*. (5th ed.). Nyack, NY: ERA/CCR.

Savage, J. (1998). *Teaching reading and writing: Combing skills, strategies, and literature* (2nd ed.). Boston: McGraw-Hill.

Slavin, R. E. (1988). Synthesis of research on grouping in elementary and secondary schools. *Educational Leadership, 46,* 67–77.

Slavin, R. E. (1989). Grouping for instruction in the elementary school. In *School and classroom organization*. Hillsdale, NJ: Erlbaum.

Wheelock, A. (1992). *Crossing the tracks: How "untracking" can save America's schools*. Hillsdale, NJ: Erlbaum.

Zemelman, S., Daniels, H., & Hyde, A. (1998). *Best practice: New standards for teaching and learning in America's schools* (2nd ed.). Portsmouth, NH: Heinemann.

Trade Books

Bartoletti, Susan. *Dancing with Dziadziu.* (1997). San Diego: Harcourt Brace.

Bunting, Eve. (1992). *The wall.* Boston: Houghton Mifflin.

Cooney, Barbara. (1985). *Miss Rumphius.* New York: Viking Penguin.

DiSalvo-Ryan, Diane. (1991). *Uncle Willie and the soup kitchen.* New York: Morrow.

Innocenti, Roberto. (1985). *Rose Blanche.* Mankato, MN: Creative Education.

Lester, Julius. (1997). *From slave ship to freedom road.* New York: Penguin Books.

Lowry, Lois. (1990). *Number the stars.* New York: Bantam Doubleday Dell.

Miller, William. (1997). *Richard Wright and the library card.* New York: Lee and Low.

Orgel, Doris. (1978). *Devil in Vienna.* New York: Puffin Books.

Polacco, Patricia. (1992). *Mrs. Katz and Tush.* New York: Bantam.

Ransom, Candice. (1995). *The big green pocketbook.* New York: Harper Collins.

Rylant, Cynthia. (1985). *When I was young in the mountains.* NY: Dutton.

Sis, Peter. (1996). *Starry messenger: Galileo Galilei.* New York: Farrar Straus Giroux.

Stanley, Diane & Vennema, Peter. (1990). *Good Queen Bess: The story of Elizabeth I of England.* New York: Four Winds Press.

Strasser, Todd. (1981). *The Wave.* New York: Dell.

Wells, Rosemary. (1997). *McDuff moves in.* New York: Hyperion.

Wiesel, Elie. (1986). *Night.* New York: Bantam.

Willard, Nancy. (1990). *The high rise glorious skittle skat roarious sky pie angel food cake.* San Diego: Harcourt Brace Jovanovich.

Yolen, Jane. (1987). *Owl moon.* New York: Philomel.

Yolen, Jane. (1990). *The devil's arithmetic.* New York: Puffin Books.

Chapter 13

Middle School Students Learning to Research: An Inquiry-Based Approach

Linda Poorman
Mary Wright

Jose shouted, "I've found the answer to the question about *The Mikado* on the Internet!" Katrin exclaimed, "I found the value of the dollar in Germany today!" Sam asserted, "I know which French king and queen were executed during the French Revolution!" Kameron said, "I've got a picture of the $500 bill! Guess who's on it?" Kyndal yelled, "I found Estonia on a map of Eastern Europe!"

When such comments occur during a "treasure hunt" we smile, acknowledging that students can locate information by applying what they've learned about researching in the content areas. Our challenge has been to engineer teaching and learning events that will entice students to become actively and productively engaged in the pursuit of content-based information. With our help, they have assumed ownership of this process.

Once engaged, students pursue their research by using various activities including dialectical journals. Their learning experiences occur in thematically structured contexts that feature social interaction, reflection, and multiple assessment opportunities.

In this chapter, we present a close up look at students learning research skills in our unit, *A Century of Kids*. We begin by offering a brief foundation for our teaching methods. Then we describe our assessment plan and book selection process. This is followed by techniques for activating prior knowledge and creating a community of readers. The next section describes the research process from the treasure hunt to the use of dialectical journals to the creation of circle books. Various prompts, criteria, and examples of student work complete the chapter.

Background

The unit we present in this chapter is grounded in principles of constructivism as illuminated by Brooks and Brooks (1993). (For more information about constructivism, see chapter 3 of this book.) The unit provides focus and depth for learning, integrates the language arts, offers authentic learning experiences, utilizes multiple resources, provides opportunities for interaction, and encourages reflectivity (Burns, Roe, and Ross, 1999; Cooper, 2000; Pike, Compain & Mumper, 1994; Vogt, 1996; Willis, 1995).

Specifically, this unit has been designed to reflect classrooms where student-generated questions, reflection, flexible grouping, and ongoing assessment inform instruction. *A Century of Kids* uses the works of Russell Freedman (1980, 1983, 1995) to offer a close-up look at how students use inquiry to learn about research skills and American history. In the process, it also motivates students and makes learning more enjoyable.

Teaching Idea: A Century of Kids
Content Areas: Language Arts, Social Studies
Levels: Intermediate, Middle School

A Century of Kids is a thematic unit that integrates the nonfiction works of Russell Freedman and the study of American history. The focus of our close-up is students' use of inquiry to learn research skills. This section of the unit framework features a reading strand, which generates a research strand, which in turn drives a writing strand (Figure 13-1). While this unit concentrates on a particular period of American history, the processes, strategies, and instructional methodology presented can be used in any content area. The following is a close-up look at *A Century of Kids*.

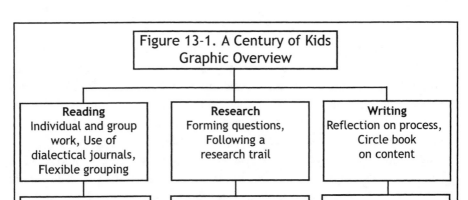

Figure 13-1. A Century of Kids Graphic Overview

Reading	**Research**	**Writing**
Individual and group work, Use of dialectical journals, Flexible grouping	Forming questions, Following a research trail	Reflection on process, Circle book on content

Reading the Major Texts
Part 1 grade will be based on individual and group work as well as dialectical journal.
Your Jobs:
1. Read your book and keep a dialectical journal while you read.
2. Organize your focus chapter information.
3. Discuss your focus chapter with your other group members.
4. Listen carefully when others report because you will be representing your whole book to your subgroup.
5. Meet with one person from each of the other groups and report on your book to them. Use your dialectical journal and any information that you got from other group members.
6. Listen carefully when others report, and write down any questions that you may have about their books.

The Research Trail
Part 2 grade will be based on questioning and work in the library.
Your Jobs:
1. Prioritize your questions about the topics that you read or heard about.
2. Decide on several general topics that might provide information about your question.
3. Choose at least three different kinds of reference materials that might have information related to your general topic (e.g., encyclopedia, nonfiction book, fiction book, magazine article, Internet).
4. Read in the reference books and keep a dialectical journal entry for everything that your read. *Be sure to include your heading, as it will have valuable information about your resource that you will need later.*
5. You will only have four days in the library to do research, so it is important for you to be in school and stay on task while in the library.
6. *Think*—To learn, you must be an active thinker.

Writing
Part 3 grade will be based on two final written products.
Your Jobs:
1. You will be asked to write a paragraph that reflects on how well you gathered information.
2. Your paragraph will follow the paragraph-writing format that we have gone over and will include a topic sentence and a minimum of three examples, which are each supported by at least two details.
3. A complete writing packet will be turned in.
4. You will make a circle book or other project that shows the important information that you found.

Assessment Plan

Throughout this unit, assessment is standards-based, interwoven with instruction, and designed to be both formal and informal in nature. The standards of our unit are twofold, encompassing process and content. For process, each of our students is expected to develop questioning strategies for reading nonfiction and to create individual research plans to locate, connect, and extend information. The content standards focus on gaining information about the 100 years of American history between 1830 and 1930 as framed by western expansion, immigration, and the Industrial Revolution. To accomplish these goals, students integrate the use of the library and media center with guided response strategies and create a book or other project based on information drawn from nonfiction texts. Students also generate a reflection paper that evaluates how the research process has worked for them as individual learners and how new information has expanded previous knowledge. The reflection paper addresses such questions as "What did I need to learn?" "Did I learn everything I needed to learn?" "Is there anything I did not learn?" "Why didn't I learn it?" "Where did my learning break down?" and "What fix-up strategies can I use to help myself?"

On an informal level, students monitor their own progress through self-reflection and interaction as they complete each strand of the unit. On a more formal level, three different teacher-created guides are used for evaluation. These scoring guides are shared prior to each task, thus allowing students to know the criteria upon which their evaluation will be based. One assesses reading, journals, and cooperative group participation (Figure 13-2). Another assesses use of the library and the research process (Figure 13-3). The third is used to evaluate the written products (Figure 13-4).

Figure 13-2. Reading, Journal, and Cooperative Group Criteria

Name_____ Date_____

As a cooperative group member, I had a productive day (10 pts. each):
1. I read my assigned book alone or with a partner each day and remained on task for the designated reading time.
2. I kept an appropriate dialectical journal.
3. I wrote in my dialectical journal each day, making connections to what I read.
4. I conferenced with my teacher about my focus chapter.
5. I studied the main ideas of my focus chapter.
6. I discussed my section of the book with my other group members.
7. I listened carefully to all parts of the book as they were reported to the group.

cont.

8. I met with my subgroup for discussion.
9. I have a list of questions about my book and the other books presented.
10. I have thought about general topics that might include information about my questions.

Some deficiencies in cooperation, so that each day was not a totally productive day (8 pts. each):
1. My attention strayed from our task several times, requiring redirection by Mrs. Poorman.
2. My dialectical journal could include more information.
3. The response side of my dialectical journal does not connect to my reading.
4. I was not ready to conference with my teacher.
5. Some of my main ideas are vague.
6. Sometimes my information was incorrect when I discussed my part of the book.
7. My attention strayed from other people's reporting of their parts of their books.
8. I was not ready to meet with my subgroup.
9. My list of questions is too short.
10. I do not have enough general topics to cover my questions.

Serious problems with reading, journal, and group work (4 pts. each):
1. I did not focus on the daily task.
2. The text side of my dialectical journal does not reflect my reading of the text.
3. The response side of my dialectical journal does not reflect my reading of the text.
4. I did not conference with the teacher about my focus chapter.
5. Most of my main ideas do not reflect the important main ideas in my part of the book.
6. I talked about other things and/or my information was factually incorrect.
7. I didn't pay attention to the reporting of others in my group.
8. I met with my subgroup but didn't have much to offer them and/or didn't listen to them.
9. I have few or no questions on my list.
10. I have no general topics to cover my questions.

Figure 13-3. Research Criteria

Name_____ Date_____

As a cooperative and successful library researcher (10 pts. each):
1. I had a list of questions from which to start my research.
2. I narrowed my questions to an interesting few.
3. I checked key words in two different encyclopedias for information.
4. I chose two other kinds of references to search for information about my question.
5. I read the references that I found.
6. I kept dialectical journal entries for my findings.
7. I wrote down the names and page numbers of the references that I used.
8. My journal responses were thoughtful, reflected my questions, and/or stirred up other questions.
9. I stayed on task in the library.
10. I looked for things on my own first before I asked for help.

Research with some deficiencies in library expectations (8 pts. each):
1. My list of questions is very short.
2. My list of questions needs to be narrowed further.
3. I checked in only one encyclopedia.
4. I chose only one other type of reference besides an encyclopedia.
5. I read few of the references that I found.
6. My dialectical journal was incomplete.
7. I wrote down some of the book titles and/or page numbers that I used.
8. My journal responses reflected my questions, but were missing some elements.
9. I was confused in the library and lost valuable time.
10. I asked for help before trying to find information on my own first.

Research with serious problems (0 pts. each):
1. I did not develop a list of questions.
2. I did not narrow my list to an interesting few.
3. I did not check the encyclopedias.
4. I did not check references other than the encyclopedia.
5. I did not read my references.
6. I did not keep a dialectical journal.
7. I did not write down the names and page numbers of the references that I used.
8. My journal responses did not address my questions.
9. I wasted time in the library and did not complete my research.
10. I looked at things and for things that were not related to this assignment and/or used my time unwisely.

Figure 13-4. Writing Criteria

Name_____ Date_____

A complete paragraph, correctly organized and well written (10 pts. each):
1. Turned-in packet includes graphic organizer, first draft, second draft with student edit sheet, final draft, and scoring sheet with name, date, and group number correctly placed on the scoring sheet.
2. Final draft is written on every other line, one side of the paper, and is *very* neat.
3. All words are spelled correctly.
4. All sentences express a complete thought.
5. All sentences begin with a capital letter and end with the proper punctuation.
6. Paragraph has a topic sentence that states the main idea.
7. Paragraph has a 6-day sequence with statements that show research trail.
8. Each day includes evaluation of research details.
9. Transition words are used to ease the flow of the paragraph.
10. Packet has research papers included (scoring guide, dialectical journals, etc.).

Paragraph has some deficiencies in organization and correctness (8 pts. each):
1. Turned-in packet is missing one of its components or the heading is incorrect.
2. Final draft is written on every line or on both sides of the paper or is not neat.
3. One or two words are spelled incorrectly.
4. One or two sentences are run-ons or fragments.
5. One or two sentences do not begin with a capital letter or some do not have punctuation.
6. Topic sentence is confusing.
7. The research trail covers 6 days but is confusing.
8. One or 2 days do not include an evaluation of research details.
9. Use of transition was attempted but could be better with a little more thought.
10. A required research paper is missing.

Paragraph with serious problems (4 pts. each):
1. Turned-in packet is missing two or more of its components or a proper heading.
2. Final draft is written on every line and both sides of the paper or appears to be messy.
3. Too many words are spelled incorrectly.
4. Too many run-on sentences or fragments.

cont.

5. Most sentences do not begin with a capital or end with the proper punctuation.
6. Topic sentence is missing or does not cover what the examples show.
7. Major parts of the research trail are missing (i.e., only encyclopedias were checked).
8. More than 2 days are missing evaluation of research details.
9. No transition words were used.
10. Few research papers are included.

The criteria are used by students for self-evaluation. Teachers use them to evaluate students and gain insights for future teaching.

Book Selection

Nonfiction literature can be a rich and motivating source for content learning. Three nonfiction books by Newbery Award winner Russell Freedman are used as the major texts for this unit: *Kids at Work* (1995), *Children of the Wild West* (1983), and *Immigrant Kids* (1980). Because the subjects of these books are school-age children, many parallels can be drawn between the present and the historical time periods studied. Social studies content related to western expansion, immigration and the Industrial Revolution is powerfully presented by Freedman. All of the books contain attractive photographs that enhance interest and learning, and all of the books are organized into subsections that can stand alone and be evaluated by a smaller group in a jigsaw fashion. Three related picture books—*The Ledgerbook of Thomas Blue Eagle* (Grutman & Matthaei, 1994), *When Jessie Came Across the Sea* (Hest, 1997), and *Bobbin Girl* (McCully, 1996)—are also used because of their strong links with the themes, time periods, and/or topics of the unit. (For more information about using trade books in the content areas, see chapters 7 and 12.)

Activating Prior Knowledge

Shared Reading

Our students are introduced to the major texts through the shared reading of the picture books. These are paired with Freedman's works by theme, time period, and/or topic: *The Ledgerbook of Thomas Blue Eagle* (Grutman & Matthaei, 1994) with *Children of the Wild West* (Freedman, 1983); *When Jessie Came Across the Sea* (Hest, 1997) with *Immigrant Kids* (Freedman, 1980); *Bobbin Girl* (McCully, 1996) with *Kids at Work* (Freedman, 1995). The teacher shares each picture book with the entire class. Each shared reading is followed by literature circle discussions that focus on the content and issues of the picture book.

Literature Circles

After the shared reading experience, our students form four-member literature circles to discuss the shared picture book, record the key points of the discussion, and report the consensus of the group to the whole class. Each group member has a specific role to play in the literature circle. The *recorder* is responsible for writing the group's responses on chart paper so that they can be used as a guide by the *spokesperson,* whose job it is to report the group responses to the entire class at the end of the discussion. The *keeper of the questions* has a list that can be referred to as needed to get the discussion rolling or move it to a new place (see Figure 13-5 for sample questions). The *encourager* monitors the group's flow, keeps members focused on the discussion, and invites reluctant participants to offer contributions. Within the social context of the discussions, our students activate and share prior knowledge and experiences that relate to each particular picture book, theme, and topic in preparation for reading one of the nonfiction Freedman books. As teachers, we move among the groups, listening to assess, mediate, and question as needed. We are looking for dialogue that includes questioning words such as *why, how, I wonder,* and *did they.* This provides evidence that students are reaching beyond the text.

After the discussions, each literature circle presents its main points to the entire class and responds to any questions or comments from the class. The entire process, including shared reading, literature circle discussion, and reporting takes about 90 minutes for each picture book and builds a solid background for all three of the nonfiction major texts. All of our students are, in one way or another, exposed to and asked to respond to all three of the nonfiction books and their content.

Figure 13-5. Sample Questions for Literature Circles

Talk with the people in your group and find out how they feel about some of the issues in the book *The Ledgerbook of Thomas Blue Eagle.*
- Why do you think the White settlers wanted the Indian children to attend schools like the Carlisle School?
- What do you think was good about the Carlisle School?
- What do you think was bad about it?
- What things in Thomas Blue Eagle's culture were the same as or similar to things in your culture?
- What do you think about Blue Eagle's ideas about bravery? How are Blue Eagle's ideas about bravery the same or different from yours?
- What stood out for you and for each member of your group about this book?
- If you had the opportunity, what questions would you ask Blue Eagle? What do you think he would answer?

The Major Texts: A Community of Readers

As participants in literature circles, our students identify curiosities, express opinions, and begin to formulate questions that will direct and frame future research. This process is greatly influenced by each student's interaction with Russell Freedman's books. To maximize the number and types of opportunities for students to reflect on and share ideas about this information, a variety of grouping arrangements are used.

Initially students work alone and in pairs. Choosing one of the Freedman texts, they read, reflect, and respond through a dialectical journal. We explain that, for our purposes, a dialectical journal is a two-part journal in which the writer converses with him- or herself about what is read. The goals are to explore the concepts that are presented in the text; to question, generalize, compare, and personally connect; and, in general, to reflect on and respond to what was read.

For our purposes, we want students to use the dialectical journal to digest the content and provide a record of questions as they occur. Each journal page is divided into two columns. On the left side students refer to the text or a portion of the text in some way, and on the right side they personally respond to the text (see Figure 13-6 for a dialectical journal format). Students focus on questions such as "What does the author want me to know after I have read?" and "What does this mean to me?" We model the strategy of forming questions while reading, using passages from each of the books in a "think-aloud" to show students' comprehension in action. We also stress that generating a list of questions for the research component of the unit is critical. Ideas such as "What questions does this raise for me?" and "How can I find more information?" are important to the foundation of the research. Questions of this nature drive the research component of the unit.

In addition to the dialectical journal, which the students maintain throughout the entire book, we work with each student to identify a particular chapter that will require more intense scrutiny of content. For this chapter, the student is asked to become an *expert*. The focus chapter is shared with others reading the same book, thus requiring all students to organize and discuss specific information. These book discussion groups allow our students one more opportunity to extend their knowledge about a particular topic.

After discussing a single book in depth, our students are rearranged to form "jigsaw" groups of three, with each member of the new group having read a different book. It is now the job of each individual to present his book for the other two members of the group who have not read it. The *reviewer* has the job of presenting his book. The other two group members have the job of listening and recording any questions that arise for them, adding to the growing list. These questions, along with the previous student-generated questions, expand the options for the research component. Figure 13-7 shows this grouping within the community of readers.

Figure 13-6. Sample Dialectical Journal

Student Directions: Dialectical Journal Entries, A Century of Kids

Use the following format to set up your Dialectical Journal page entries as you work through this nonfiction unit. Each page of your journal should have this information at the top:

Journal entry no. _____

Your name and group no. _____

Book title and author _____

Page numbers to which the journal entry refers _____

TEXT: On the left side of your page you should include information about what you've read. These may include but are not limited to the following:	RESPONSE: On the right side of the page you should include your personal reactions to what you have read. These may include but are not limited to the following:
• Your comments on events or certain information • Brief summaries • Questions • Interesting words or phrases • Unfamiliar words or phrases • Brief quotes, descriptions, or passages or confusing passages • Key information, references to certain events	• Your comments on events or certain information • Your thoughts on the writing • Possible answers to questions raised • Connections to familiar things • Questions raised from confusion • Personal reflections or connections to information and/or events • Thoughts on why the author organized the information in the way that he or she did • Comparisons and contrasts to your life • Connections to people and places that you know • Questions you still have • Final thoughts

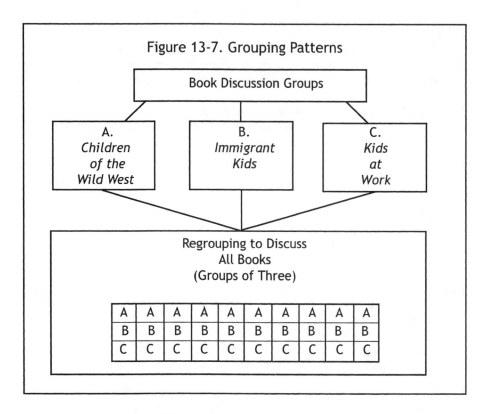

The following figure appears:

Figure 13-7. Grouping Patterns

Book Discussion Groups

A. Children of the Wild West • B. Immigrant Kids • C. Kids at Work

Regrouping to Discuss All Books (Groups of Three)

A	A	A	A	A	A	A	A	A	A
B	B	B	B	B	B	B	B	B	B
C	C	C	C	C	C	C	C	C	C

The Research Begins

Once our students finish reading, questioning, and reporting, the focus of the unit shifts from reading and responding to research and information gathering. At this point students narrow the focus of their research by asking, "About which three questions on my list am I the most curious?" For example, one student narrowed her research to these three questions during her reading of *Immigrant Kids*:

- What is trachoma and why did it make people get sent away from America?
- How often did people get sick and die from spoiled food when they didn't have refrigeration?
- Where did the iceman get his ice in the summer? Why didn't it melt?

In order to complete their research successfully, students need some key skills, including how to develop a researchable question and access appropriate sources. "How do I know what I need?" and "Where do I go to find it?" are initial questions that students need to answer as they begin working in the media center. To facilitate this process, we model how to move from the specific to the general as a starting point for locating information. Through quick conferences we help the students get to general topics where specific information might be found.

Teaching Idea: Treasure Hunt
Content Areas: All
Levels: Intermediate, Middle School

The first day that we go to the library is a workday masked by the fun of a Treasure Hunt. With the assistance of our librarian and fortified by our research goals, students engage in a Treasure Hunt to locate various types of information from multiple sources. Figures 13-8 and 13-9 provide a list of the library goals and sample Treasure Hunt prompts. This activity is designed to help the students locate and use different types of references and to help teachers diagnose general and particular student needs. Based on this information, we generate minilessons on topics such as choosing key words, using an index to locate information, searching the card catalog for information sources, and using the Internet. Using skimming, scanning, previewing, and text patterns to locate information relevant to a topic is also stressed.

Figure 13-8. Seventh-Grade Library Goals

1. Students will use the electronic card catalog (Boolean Search using "and/or").
   a. Students will demonstrate understanding of the call-number sequence.
   b. Students will locate specific materials using call-number sequence.
   c. Students will recognize the importance of correct spelling for accurate searches.
2. Students will use the Ebsco Middle Magazine Search (Boolean Search using "and/or").
   a. Students will understand the tracking code.
   b. Students will apply the tracking code to our library.
   c. Students will recognize the importance of correct spelling for accurate searches.
3. Students will refine the use of the encyclopedia index to locate information.
   a. Students will refine the use of key words as a referencing starting point.
   b. Students will accurately interpret the index code.
4. Students will discriminate between generalized encyclopedias and specialized encyclopedias.
5. Wild Card: Students will develop an awareness of other specialized references as needed (Customized to specific project and teacher assignments).

Created by P. Dillner, L. Poorman and P. Wells

Figure 13-9. Treasure Hunt Prompts

1. Who wrote the music of *The Mikado*?
2. What kind of boat was manned by slaves in the days of the Romans?
3. For what is J. J. Audubon famous?
4. What is the mascot of Princeton University?
5. What do the stars in the American flag represent?
6. What is the colored circle of the eye called?
7. Who was the king of England at the time of our country's Revolutionary War?
8. What is a nosegay?
9. Who invented wireless telegraphy?
10. What is the Big Apple?
11. Who made the first solo nonstop flight across the Atlantic Ocean?
12. What is a vendetta?
13. Who invented the character Robinson Crusoe?
14. What is the essential principle of the Golden Rule?
15. What is the oldest form of traditional drama in Japan?
16. The game of quoits is similar to what other game?
17. What is the dollar exchange value in Germany today?
18. What French king and queen were executed during the French Revolution?
19. What is perhaps the most famous statement made by writer Gertrude Stein?
20. Who was Aristotle's teacher?
21. What are the three main parts of an insect's body?
22. Name three sections in the back of the dictionary that have nothing to do with the definitions of words.
23. What is the exact temperature today in Rome, Italy?
24. What gothic novel did Mary W. Shelley, wife of English poet Percy Bysse Shelley, write?
25. What is Boxing Day in England?
26. Name a commonly used analgesic.
27. In what art form does Leontyne Price excel?
28. Who organized migrant labor groups during the 1960s into what is now known as the United Farm Workers of America?
29. If you were going to buy Bell Atlantic stock today, how much would it cost you?
30. In U.S. money, what portrait appears on the $500 bill?
31. What is Mrs. Dillner's maiden name?
32. Who invented the first practical phonograph?

Created by P. Dillner, L. Poorman, and P. Wells

As students discover sources that might have relevant information, they use their research skills to locate the information and select passages that accommodate their needs. Once the information is found, students read and respond in their dialectical journals, including full citation of the source of the information. Students are encouraged to read for information as opposed to reading to find the answer to their question.

After 3 or 4 days of individual treasure hunting, reading, and making journal entries, writing about findings, students use a sequencing graphic organizer to retrace their research process and reflect on the usefulness of each step of their individual journey. At this point the research leads into the formal writing phase of the unit.

Writing: Understanding and Creating

Graphic Organizers

Although some of the student-generated questions may have remained unanswered, all of our students arrived at the final phase of this unit with much to write about. The writing process begins with a personal review of the sequence organizer created to trace the research process. Each block of the organizer represents a day in the library and holds a brief account of the work completed. Outside the block, each student has self-evaluated the usefulness of the day's activity. Basically three questions are addressed: "What steps did I go through in the library?" "Did this help me or not?" "Are there any gaps in my research process that I need to address?"

Through this type of self-assessment, students create their own prescriptions for success. It gives them an opportunity to map out a fix-up strategy and make the most of a short amount of make-up time in the library. On a follow-up "fix-up day," students who initially were not successful follow their own prescriptions by retracing the research steps that need improvement. They attach their make-up plan to their reflective writing packets and are able to add on to the evaluation they received on the library portion of the project.

Evaluating the Experience

Once the organizer is complete, our students write a summary and evaluation of their completed research activity. We emphasize that this writing should reflect a true picture of exactly what was done in the library as well as how it has or has not helped. Our students are not shy about telling us that on the first day they spent some of their time talking with their friends, but before they left the library some serious steps were taken to locate the information they needed. Their responses to whether it helped tend to be more obscure, although everyone understands which behaviors were productive and which were not. The following is an example of a student evaluation:

> Our class went to the library to check references for information on questions related to the particular nonfiction book we were each reading, which for me was *Kids at Work*. The first day didn't start off to [*sic*] good. Even though I got a chance to read, this did not help me at all. On the second day I made two mistakes: I grabbed Volume L of the *Encyclopedia Americana* without looking at the index. I tried to look up (child) *labor* but all I got was a section on labor in childbirth. Second, I let myself be slightly distracted by my friends, who were acting like goofballs. However on the third day, I got the index on the *Encyclopedia Americana* and looked up *labor* for *child labor*. It was under C for *child*. I quickly snatched up that one volume, sat down, and started to read. I was about half finished when time was up, so I quickly wrote down the source and page number. It was very helpful because I found some useful information. Since I wrote the page number down, I'd know just where to start the next day. The next day I quickly found the place where I left off and finished reading the article in the first 10 minutes of our fourth day in the library. Then I thought about how I could use this information to answer my questions in the dialectical journal. Finally, I started to write my dialectical journal entries and stirred up an extra question while doing it. This day in the library was extremely helpful to my research. I got more than the maximum amount of work done. I was about half done at this point. On the fifth day in the library, I got a spot on the computer, entered *Compton's Interactive Encyclopedia* and typed *child labor*. I received a printout on basically what child labor is, early regulations, and compulsory school attendance. Afterwards, I wrote my other two dialectical journals. This was very helpful to my research. The sixth day in the following week was a day on which I had nothing to do. I had already completed my research and received a great evaluation, so I did not need to change it. I spent my time in the library reading part of a new book.

With the completion of the reflective piece, our students have recorded unique perspectives on the information they have gathered. This helps them to make personal connections when creating a piece of content-based writing.

Teaching Idea: Circle Books
Content Areas: Social Studies, adaptable to Science and Math
Levels: Middle School

Because the unit is constructivist in nature, students can choose from a number of options to report what they have learned. One particularly popular format is the circle book (see Figure 13-10). When creating a circle book, each student plans 15 pages of text and illustrations based on what they found most interesting about and representative of their Russell Freedman book and related research. Students readily enjoy the creative features of circle books. As they move beyond cutting the circles, taping them together, and watching the pages roll into one another, students review what they have planned to put on each page. For the next several days they create their narrative and their illustrations. The resulting books are wonderful. Whether done by gifted writers and artists or those who write simply and draw stick figures, these books clearly show the hearts of their creators. Figure 13-11 provides criteria for the circle books.

Figure 13-10. Directions for Making Circle Books

1. Trace a circle of 6" diameter onto a four-color stack of paper.

2. Cutting through all four papers at the same time, cut the circle out so that you have four circles of the same size, each a different color.

3. Holding all four circles together, fold them like a taco, open them up, and refold them like a taco so that the circle is now quartered by two perpendicular diameters.

4. Still holding all four circles together, cut one radius from the edge of the circle to the center, through all four layers.

5. Lay the circles on a flat surface with the cut radius at the top (pointing north).

6. Take the top right quadrant of the top circle on the pile and fold it toward you. You are now looking at 3/4s of the top circle and 1/4 of the circle below it. Tape the top circle to the second circle along the cut line. (This is the trickiest part.)

7. Fold the top left quadrant of the top circle and the top right quadrant of the second circle (which are taped to each other) toward you. Now you are looking at the top left of the 2nd circle and the top right of the 3rd circle. Tape them together along the cut line. Fold them forward. Repeat the taping to the end.

Example of a Student's Circle Book

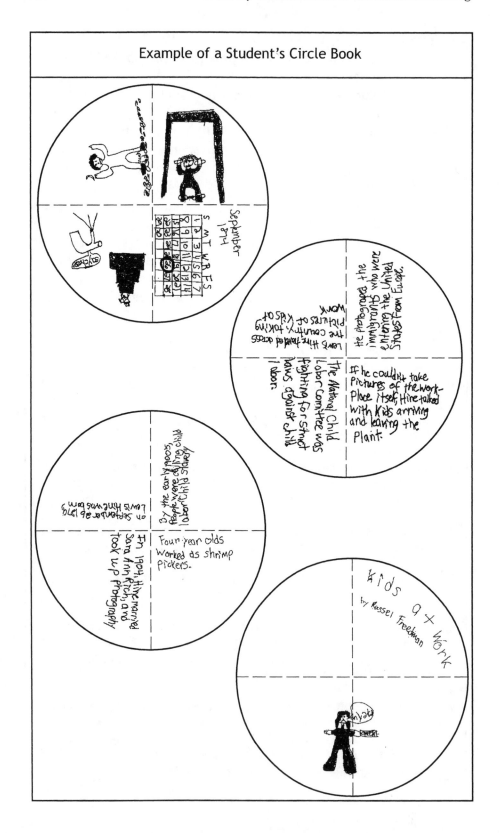

Example of a Student's Circle Book

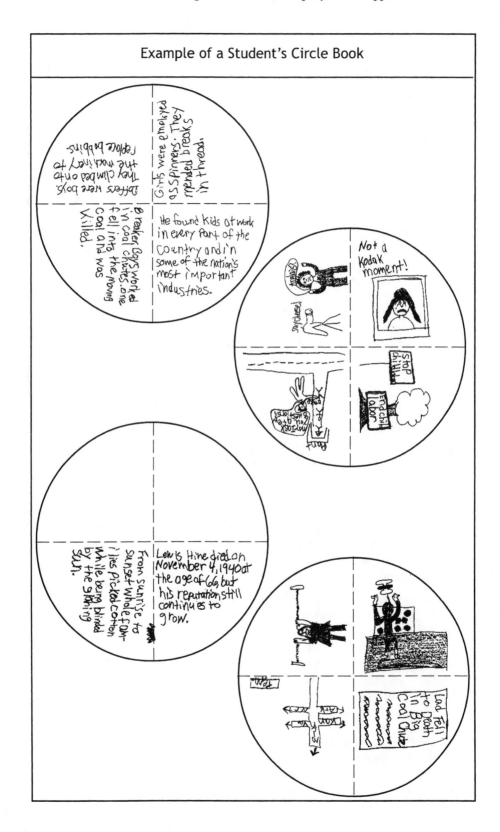

Figure 13-11. Circle Book Criteria

Name_____ Date_____

A complete circle book, correctly constructed, organized, and written (10 pts. each):
1. Turned-in packet includes graphic organizer, circle book, and scoring sheet with name, date, and group number correctly placed on the scoring sheet.
2. Circle book is constructed according to directions and rolls properly.
3. *All* words are spelled correctly.
4. *All* sentences express a complete thought.
5. *All* sentences begin with a capital letter and end with the proper punctuation.
6. Circle book has a logical beginning and ending.
7. Information contained in the circle book is connected and makes sense.
8. Information is factually correct.
9. Each page of text has a corresponding illustration.
10. Circle book has an overall appeal and makes sense.

Circle book has some deficiencies in organization and correctness (8 pts. each):
1. Turned-in packet is missing one of its components or the heading is incorrect.
2. Circle book has flaws in construction.
3. One or two words are spelled incorrectly.
4. One or two sentences are run-ons or fragments.
5. One or two sentences do not begin with a capital letter or some do not have the proper punctuation.
6. Beginning or ending is confusing.
7. Information contained in the book does not seem connected.
8. Some factual problems exist.
9. Some illustrations are missing.
10. Circle book is messy or uninviting.

Circle book with serious problems (4 pts. each):
1. Turned-in packet is missing two or more of its components or a proper heading.
2. Circle book doesn't work.
3. Many words are spelled incorrectly.
4. Many sentences are run-ons or fragments.
5. Many sentences do not begin with a capital letter or end with the proper punctuation.
6. Beginning or ending is missing.
7. Some pages of information are missing.
8. Many factual problems exist.
9. Many illustrations are missing.
10. Circle book does not flow or make sense.

By the time this segment of the unit is completed, students have taken ownership of the research process. They view themselves as capable of locating, evaluating, and using information effectively. Further, they understand the applicability of these skills across the curriculum.

Concluding Thoughts

Thematic instruction offers myriad benefits to both students and teachers. Its ability to coalesce cross-curricular information helps students understand that subject areas are interrelated and learning is not a fragmented process. It also provides meaningful opportunities for students to learn research skills and strategies.

Watching students emerge as researchers is a rewarding experience. They raise questions, use multiple resources, integrate technology, work cooperatively, engage in reflection and use multiple types of assessment. All of these processes nurture students' abilities to become critical thinkers.

References

Brooks, J. G., & Brooks, M. (1993). *The case for constructivist classrooms*. Alexandria, VA: Association for Supervision and Curriculum Development.

Burns, P. C., Roe, B. D., & Ross, E. P. (1999). *Teaching reading in today's elementary schools* (7th ed.). Boston: Houghton Mifflin.

Cooper, J. D. (2000). *Literacy: Helping children construct meaning* (4th ed.). Boston: Houghton Mifflin.

Freedman, R. (1980). *Immigrant kids*. New York: Penguin.

Freedman, R. (1983). *Children of the wild west*. Boston: Houghton Mifflin.

Freedman, R. (1995). *Kids at work*. New York: Scholastic.

Grutman, J., & Matthaei, G. (1994). *The ledgerbook of Thomas Blue Eagle*. Charlottesville, VA: Thomasson-Grant.

Heibert, E. H. (1994). Becoming literate through authentic tasks: Evidence and adaptations. In R. Ruddell & M. R. Ruddell (Eds.), *Theoretical models and processes of reading* (4th ed.). Newark, DE: International Reading Association.

Hest, A. (1997). *When Jessie came across the sea*. Cambridge, MA: Candlewick Press.

Lapp, D., & Flood, J. (1994). Integrating the curriculum: First steps. *Reading Teacher, 47* (5), 416–419.

Martin, M. & Poorman, L. (1996). *Russell Freedman: A classroom unit*. Unpublished manuscript.

McCully, E. A. (1996). *Bobbin girl.* New York: Dial Books.

Pike, K., Compain, R., & Mumper, J. (1994). *New connections: An integrated approach to literacy.* New York: Harper Collins.

Robertson, S. L. (1998). Using dialectical journals to build beginning literary response. In K. Beers & B. G. Samuels (Eds.), *Into focus: Understanding and creating middle school readers* (pp. 199–221). Norwood, MA: Christopher-Gordon.

3500 color clip art images™. CD-ROM. (1995). Coral Gables, FL: Expert Software.

Vogt, M. E. (1996). *Cross-curricular thematic instruction.* Boston: Houghton Mifflin.

Willis, S. (1995). Refocusing the curriculum: Making interdisciplinary efforts work. *ASCD Education Update, 37* (1), 1–8.

Chapter 14

Dancing as Fast as We Can: Developing Literacy, Content, and Curriculum

Martha Rapp Ruddell

Many upper-grade teachers today perceive that in all the flurry of activity and discussion about literacy across the nation, very little has been directed toward students, teachers, and classrooms above third grade, and they feel more than a little bit neglected—left out of the conversation and ignored. Even a moment's reflection reveals how true this perception is: Upper-grade literacy issues have been neglected because, by far, the recent focus of national, statewide, and local discussion about literacy has been on issues of *learning* to read and write, and upper-grade students, teachers, and classrooms are not part of that discussion. Witness President Clinton's call, and the echoing calls by politicians at all levels, for "every child to be reading on grade level by the end of third grade" and the legislation passed or pending directed toward that goal. One of the reasons for this is the Great Fourth-Grade Shift.

Fourth grade is the point at which we dramatically reduce our attention to children learning to read and write and begin focusing on children using their reading and writing abilities in the course of learning the content of the upper-grade-school curriculum. This does not mean that we are no longer interested in their continued general literacy development. Quite the contrary; we want students in the upper grades to become even more independent and interested in recreational reading and writing as well as to develop their literacy abilities in subject areas. Nor does it mean that upper-grade teachers' jobs are any easier than primary-grade teachers' jobs. Again, quite the contrary; upper-grade teachers face an almost overwhelming job of doing all the necessary things to increase students' literacy abilities, teach content, and cover the curriculum.

Upper-grade teachers therefore have a "fast dance," indeed. Literacy, subject matter learning, and the school curriculum are inextricably intertwined in the upper grades. Teachers must have a deep understanding of each of these areas in combination with the ability to orchestrate classroom events to promote students' continued literacy development, learning in subject areas, and continuing enjoyment of independent reading and writing. It is a unique and important role that upper grade teachers have, and I propose that the only possible way to fulfill this role is to rethink our traditional conceptualization of the relationship between literacy development and subject area learning in the upper grades.

The tradition in intermediate and middle school education for some time has been to consider literacy development and content learning as two parallel yet complementary processes. That is, within the curriculum of the upper grades, we teach reading and writing on the one hand and social studies, math, science, art, music, and physical education on the other, with some crossover instruction in literacy skills as they apply to content learning. To understand this segmentation, one need only to consider that, by far, the bulk of what we term "literacy instruction" in the upper grades focuses on fiction reading and creative writing, while content instruction utilizes predominantly informational text and formal report (or other) writing. Reading and writing have thus been taught as separate general subjects with, at about fourth grade, increasing amounts of study skills instruction for learning in the subject areas. This tradition is rooted in the belief that literacy and subject area learning are separate entities, and that certain literacy behaviors—such as identifying main ideas, separating main ideas from significant details, writing summaries and reports, using graphs and charts—contribute significantly to learning the content of the curriculum. These literacy behaviors—study skills, if you will—are then taught as subskills within the context of general literacy instruction. This study skills perspective assumes that a causal relationship exists between the acquisition of specific reading and writing study skills and successful learning in the subject areas (Ruddell & Ruddell, 1995).

This separation of literacy development and subject area learning and the study skills perspective, however, does not in and of itself account for the full complexity of learning transactions, nor does it provide adequately for students' continued literacy development. Certainly students continue to develop general literacy abilities throughout the upper grades. Having the right "tools" or "skills" for reading in subject areas is also important, but current theories of reading and learning suggest that an integrative view of these processes is more valuable in guiding instruction than is a segmented view (Goodman, 1994; Rosenblatt, 1994; Ruddell, 1997). Learners do far more than apply reading skills, study or otherwise, to text. Rather, readers construct (or create) meaning in the very act of reading—extending their prior knowledge base, arriving at insights, integrating new information, and constructing new knowledge. These constructions of meaning, both during and after reading, are influenced not only by application of reading study skills, but more importantly by the myriad interactions and transactions that occur in reading events: transactions involving the reader's prior knowledge base, reader intent or stance, social interactions, reading and learning goals, instructional decisions, and so forth (Ruddell, 1997).

The same holds true for writing. Writing in subject areas has always focused on recording information and documenting what one has learned rather than being a means for extending and refining one's thinking. Hence, the dominant and continuing presence in classrooms of written book and informational reports, essay tests, and term papers; the separation of these from the more personal writing of reminiscences, stories, and journal entries; and the virtual nonexistence of curriculum-based writing to work through a problem or an idea (e.g., reflections on what one has learned, lists of ideas about a topic, articulation of problem areas, or predictions for problem solution).

Students have long understood that the purpose of writing in subject area learning is to "show what you know," and they have dutifully copied from encyclopedias, textbooks, biographies, and each other (and now they download from cyberspace) whatever is necessary to produce informational reports, lab reports, research papers, essays, and term papers. Writing study skills traditionally have emphasized various forms of report writing and mechanics—paragraph construction, punctuation, spelling, and outlining, with a parallel emphasis on the written product rather than the process itself.

This is changing. Our most recent understanding of the writing-learning relationship suggests that writing is considerably more than a way to record and demonstrate knowledge. Writing is, most importantly, a *way of knowing,* a way of working through confusion and fuzzy ideas and moving toward clarification and articulation of knowledge. Writers literally achieve insight *in the act of writing*; new ideas come as we write and from what we write (Ruddell, 1997). Consider the times that you have written something and realized during or after writing, "I didn't know I knew that." Such experiences illustrate how we achieve insight and create new thoughts as we write. When we understand the impact of this experience, we understand the power of classroom writing intended to guide students as they work through new ideas and construct new knowledge (Langer & Applebee, 1987; Ruddell, 1997).

So it is that literacy, content, and curriculum are inextricably interrelated in the upper grades, not separate entities that can be taught and practiced in a parallel manner. Thus, we must reexamine what we do in classrooms to promote students' literacy development and content learning in the upper grades. It simply is not enough for us to teach reading and writing "study skills," important as these may be, because such skills do not begin to address the full extent of the relationships between reading, writing, and learning. Nor is it enough for us to assume that students' general reading and writing abilities will transfer automatically to subject area learning; they will not. Rather, what we should understand is that the upper-grade curriculum must promote students' reading and writing development *in combination with* subject area learning to produce the kind of classroom interactions and transactions that engage students completely. Such instruction not only assists students in learning the content itself, it also teaches them how to become increasingly independent, fluent readers and writers in general *and* in subject areas.

That is what this chapter is about: developing ways to orchestrate literacy instruction to (a) guide students' literacy development well beyond the learning-to-read-and-write level, and (b) guide students' reading and writing in subject area learning so that they become increasingly independent subject area readers and writers. A basic assumption here is that *telling* students to engage in literacy events (e.g., "Read the next chapter" or "Write a summary of our trip to the city") does not stimulate rich reader-text or other learning transactions, nor does it teach students how to extend their thinking and learning in the act of reading or writing (Ruddell, 1997). For students to become effective learners, they must repeatedly experience learning events that are themselves robustly engaging, literate, and content rich.

A further assumption here is that subject area literacy is not something separate from general reading and writing instruction or subject area learning itself; rather, it is a natural extension of both. Thus, what goes on in the writing workshop or during "reading instruction" becomes part and parcel of subject area literacy learning, and vice versa. For purposes of discussion here, however, we need to look for a moment at each of these literacy processes separately; we will then bring them back together in the discussion that follows.

Reading in the Upper Grades

Let's begin with a look at what good readers do as they negotiate text. In a summary of research conducted during the decade of the 1980s, Pearson, Roehler, Dole, and Duffy (1990) provide a profile of the reading comprehension strategies that highly effective readers use. Pearson and his associates label such readers "expert" or "thoughtful" readers—I like the term "strategic" readers—and draw from many different research studies to arrive at the following expert reader characteristics. Thoughtful readers do the following:

- Constantly search for connections between what they know and what they encounter as new information in the text being read
- Constantly monitor the adequacy of the models of text meaning they build
- Take steps to repair faulty comprehension once they realize that they have failed to understand something
- Learn very early on to distinguish important from less important ideas in the text they read
- Are especially adept at synthesizing information within and across texts and reading experiences
- Make inferences during and after reading to achieve a full, integrated understanding of what they read
- Sometimes consciously, almost always unconsciously, ask questions of themselves, the authors they encounter, and the texts they read.

Compare that list with what Jimenez, Garcia, and Pearson (1996) discovered about successful Latina/o readers. Successful Latina/o readers do the following:

- Understand the unitary nature of reading, whether the process is Spanish or English
- Use a variety of techniques to identify unknown vocabulary, including context, prior knowledge, inferencing, searching for cognates, and translating
- Monitor their comprehension by checking to make sure that their constructions of meaning make sense
- Make large numbers of inferences during reading that serve as temporary meaning units to be confirmed or disconfirmed by further reading and/or additional information
- Occasionally ask questions to assist in meaning construction.

Notice how similar these lists are and how clearly they highlight metacognitive thought: Good readers, whether reading English as a first or second language, search for connections, monitor their reading, repair faulty comprehension, make inferences, and ask questions. Pearson et al. (1990) further suggest that these complex reader characteristics, "can be the goals that constitute the infrastructure of what we teach in the name of comprehension instruction" (p. 13). I agree, and I also recommend that these same reader characteristics be the goal of content reading instruction. The teachers' instructional approach should be to guide students' reading of science, mathematics, and social studies texts with the explicit intent of promoting their ability to (a) develop connections between what they already know and the new information in texts, (b) monitor the adequacy of the meanings they construct, (c) repair faulty comprehension when it does occur, (d) distinguish important from less important information in text, (e) synthesize information within and across texts, (f) draw inferences during and after reading, and (g) ask questions of themselves and the texts they read.

Let me emphasize that Round Robin Oral Reading, in which students take turns reading text aloud up and down the rows or around a circle, does not count as a useful way to guide students' reading of *any* kind of text. I know that this is common practice in schools. I also know that teachers often use Round Robin Oral Reading because the good readers clamor for it (there are better ways to give readers oral reading opportunities in class) and because teachers believe that it helps the less able readers to "read along" silently as someone else reads fluently aloud. Round Robin Oral Reading is not good practice. In fact, Singer (1970) reports a study almost 60 years ago that found that trying to follow along while another person reads disrupts the eye movement of poor readers. Thus, they aren't "reading along" with the uninterrupted flow of fluent reading; rather, their visual focus lags behind the text being read or strays to the window. Round Robin Oral Reading does *not* help the poorer readers or English language learners to understand and learn content or become better readers. It terrifies those who do not read well orally, and it does nothing to challenge or engage the thinking of better readers. It certainly doesn't promote any of the characteristics of "thoughtful readers" that we discussed earlier, and it is a dreadfully boring, sometimes agonizing, experience to endure the tortured performances of students who do not read well.

Nor can we assume that if we teach students to be good readers, this general reading ability will transfer somewhat automatically to subject area reading. Unfortunately, that assumption doesn't hold. Students who can read well can usually read well in some subject areas (generally those for which they have a high interest or aptitude) but need instruction and guidance in others. Students who can't read well need instruction and guidance in all subject area reading.

Consider for a moment your own reading ability. Then think about the academic subject areas in which you were or are least able. You can be very general in your categories (e.g., mathematics, science, social studies) or very specific (e.g., algebra, chemistry, English, history, general mathematics, geometry, physics, foreign language, biology, literature, geography, philosophy, anthropology, psychology, calculus). How would you assess your reading ability in those areas? Now do the same rating for the subject areas in which you were or are most able. Finally, think back on the subject area instruction you experienced in school: Do you remember teachers guiding your reading in mathematics books, poetry books, or science and social studies texts, or was reading simply assigned? Do you remember exciting, exuberant discussions about subject area text, doing class and small-group projects, and really getting "into" a topic or project? How often do you remember doing Round Robin Oral Reading in school?

I suspect that most of us get about the same results in reflecting on our own literacy history. Some degree of discrepancy (maybe even a great difference) exists between general reading ability and the subject areas in which we're least able. Considerable congruence exists between general reading ability and reading ability in the subject areas in which we're most able. Little or no guidance was given in reading mathematics books, poetry books, or science and social studies texts. Instruction consisted mostly of question-and-answer "discussions" instead of class and small-group projects, and there was a *lot* of Round Robin Oral Reading. This profile is fairly common and is a clear reflection of the tradition of literacy instruction in the upper grades.

Writing in the Upper Grades

Much of what we've just said about expert reading, reading instruction, and students' experiences with content area reading is also true about writing; only the details differ. In fact, you can rate your writing abilities in much the same way you rated your reading abilities. Research examining the uses of writing in the content areas has traditionally focused on secondary rather than elementary classrooms (Applebee, 1981; Martin, D'Arcy, Newton, & Parker, 1976), in all likelihood because the subject areas are so clearly distinct in secondary schools. However, there can be little doubt that in the upper grades, subject area writing has always been dominated by the informational report—the traditional "staple" of elementary classrooms, as Beach (1983) suggests. (She also comments that the headaches that accompany informational reports, for students and teachers alike, are just as traditional as the assignment itself!)

The informational report is, in my mind, clearly parallel to Round Robin Oral Reading: a ritualistic classroom event that students learn to do that only touches the surface of the text or of whatever is to be learned, and in which students' real attention and interest are not engaged. Most of us remember well the information reports in school with all their accompanying rituals—the search for "copyable" text, the paragraph and page count, the tracing or copying of illustrative maps, scenes, and people. The essential fact remains that informational reports, long a tradition in upper-grade classrooms, are exercises in plagiarism, tracing, and tedium. Some students become very, very good at both Round Robin Oral Reading and informational report writing, whereas others do not. Whatever the case, there is little inherent in either task that invites engagement, avid attention, or learning.

Guiding Students' Reading and Writing in the Upper Grades

The goal of reading and writing instruction in the upper grades is to guide students toward progressively independent reading and writing in all subject areas. In essence, it is to lead students toward avid reading and writing in the subject areas (just as we have always promoted avid reading and writing of recreational text) and to engage them avidly in the curriculum. When that happens, learning satisfies—it becomes exciting, exhilarating, and fun. Think for a moment about a time in your life when you *really learned*. Do you remember how you felt and what you did during that learning time—how easy everything seemed, how you read everything you could get your hands on, how time flew when you worked, and how you couldn't stop talking about what you were doing? That's what we want students to feel. Lucy Calkins (1991) opens her beautiful book, *Living Between the Lines,* with a poignant reflection on her own childhood and childhood today:

> As a child, I draped plaid blankets between the sofa and chair, and when the sunlight streamed in, my shadowy forts became castles with stained glass windowpanes. I lashed birch logs together to make walls for forest forts and turned tree stumps into tables and chairs. My forts were a lot of work, but childhood was a time of industriousness, of projects. It was a time of secret chemistry experiments in the attic, of carefully fashioned yarn dolls, of elaborate dams along the Eighteen Mile Creek.
>
> When I moved into my present house several years ago and saw that there was a swamp across the street, I couldn't wait to see children poling their homemade rafts through the tall reeds, searching for muskrats and jellied strings of frog eggs to incubate in the bathtub

and for their own magical Terabithia. But the neighborhood children aren't there.

I wonder if they are sitting glassy-eyed in front of the VCR, the television, the Nintendo game. I wonder if they are being driven from soccer to computer camp, from gymnastics to aerobics, or if they are drifting around the shopping mall. James Howe, author of *Bunnicula*, recently said, "My greatest worry for children today is that they are losing their capacity to play, to create a city out of blocks, to find a world in a backyard, to dream an adventure on a rainy afternoon. My greatest fear for children today is they are losing their capacity to play" (1987).

When I think of the long afternoons I spent building forts, I cannot help but wonder whether I was playing or working. Perhaps our fear should be not that children are losing their capacity to play so much as they are losing the recognition that there can be a thin line between work and play. (p. 1)

In school we have been loath to recognize this same truth: hearty, robust, fully engaged learning feels like play. It is the kind of learning that Johnstone and Allington (1991) refer to as "task involving," which immerses learners thoroughly in the curriculum and, by so doing, increases literacy development as well. Thus, we must be willing to look honestly at traditional instructional practices and eliminate those that are not rich, complex, and full; we simply cannot tolerate classroom events and assignments that are exercises in tedium. Furthermore, we must guide students' reading and writing generally and in subject area learning so that avid reading and writing become a natural part of all that goes on in the classroom.

There are many, many ways that teachers can organize instruction to do all of the things I've talked about so far (Ruddell, 1997). I'm going to suggest one here. It's a big idea, not a little one, and you'll probably want and need to think about it a little while before you apply it to what you're doing in school. I wish I could say the idea is mine, but it's not, it belongs to Lucy Calkins (1991). In *Living Between the Lines,* Calkins tells another story—one about building principals from 20 New York City elementary schools who spent a day aboard an 80-foot schooner working together toward the dual purposes of crewing the boat and organizing effective writing workshops. She describes how barriers dropped and intimacy developed as everyone worked together to set sail, steer a course, and carry out all of the crew responsibilities. From this shared experience, discussion of curriculum was heartfelt, energetic, and vibrant in a way that simply could not, and would not, have been possible in the confines of the district-headquarters box, and the power of that sailing day stayed with the principals throughout the school year. Then she says the most important thing of all. In her reflection on the power of the shared experience to touch individuals deeply and change the way they interacted with each other, the way they thought about things, and the way they worked together to carry out a complex task, she asks why it is that we plan special events in school—weeklong outdoor education trips, overnight "read-ins," museum and art gallery and Exploratorium trips—for the *end* of the school year. Why don't we do them at the beginning of the school year so that they become the foundation for everything we do in the name of curriculum throughout the rest of the year? And I thought, "Of course. Why didn't I think of that?"

Then last summer while on vacation in Oregon, I took a jet-boat trip up the Rogue River. It was a full-day trip—we boarded at noon and arrived back at the dock at 8:15 p.m. Figure 14-1 is a map of just a few of the things I remember and learned from that river trip. These boats run several trips a day everyday, from May 15 through October 15, carefully regulated by the Wild and Scenic Rivers Protection Act. On the trip down the river, I said to

Figure 14-1. The River Map

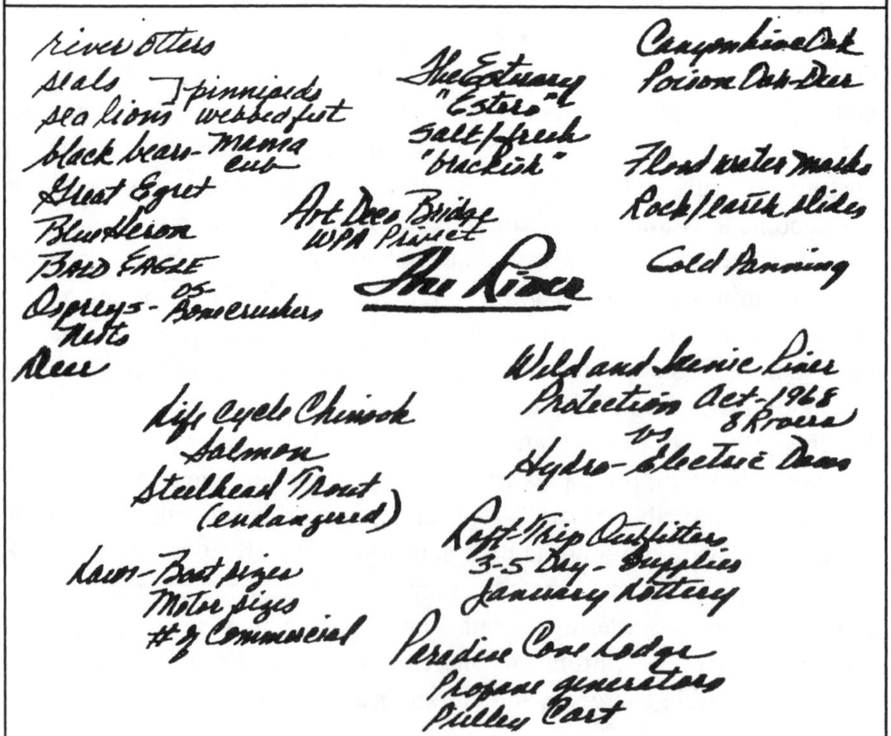

my companion (now my husband), "If I taught school anywhere within a 60-mile radius of Gold Beach, Oregon, I'd be making the arrangements to take my class next May 16." Then I remembered Lucy Calkins, and I turned back to him and said, "No I wouldn't. I'd do it in September. I'd *start* school with a trip up the Rogue River."

Consider all the possible content we could cover from such a trip. Think of the projects students could plan, the research they could do: endangered species, the Wild and Scenic River Protection Act, the rafting and powerboat regulations on protected rivers, hydroelectric dams, the Depression and the WPA, freshwater and saltwater habitats and the convergence of the two in the brackish water of the estuary where river current meets ocean tide, or the study and construction of simple machines. It is not difficult at all to find ways to center the social studies and science curriculum around a river or water theme—the mighty Mississippi or the Amazon, the Nile or the Missouri, the Ohio or the Rio Grande come immediately to mind; the explorations of Lewis and Clark do as well. Nor is it hard to find literature and informative primary sources, art, and music that have a water theme or setting: *Jacob Have I Loved, Wind in the Willows, Witch of Blackbird Pond, Island of the Blue Dolphins,* and *Life on the Mississippi*; "Old Man River" and "The Blue Danube"; the works of Claude Monet, Mary Cassatt, Alfred Sisley, Pierre-Auguste Renoir, and Thomas Hart Benton. Furthermore, studying the environment, the flora and fauna of a river plain; hopping onto the World Wide Web for information about river habitats in general or the life and times of a particular river; or figuring out all the necessary arrangements (doing the math) for a weeklong trip to and down a river covers just about all the curriculum, content, and literacy skills that upper-grade students need to have in one year. Four guiding principles and a number of specific instructional approaches are useful to support this curriculum.

Principle No. 1:
Begin With What Students Already Know

One of the simplest, least difficult ways to initiate learning events is to give students a few moments to think about what they already know about any topic. One way to do this is with the Content Directed Reading-Thinking Activity (Ruddell, 1997), often referred to as the Content DR-TA.

Teaching Idea: The Content DR-TA
Content Areas: All
Levels: Intermediate, Middle, High School

The Content DR-TA requires students to be in partnerships or small-group teams (generally consisting of no more than three people per team).

Each team is to have paper, pencils, and textbooks. Instruction begins when the teacher directs the teams to work together to jot down everything they know about the general topic within which the lesson topic fits. So, for example, in preparation for our Rogue River trip and river curriculum, we might begin by asking teams to list everything they know about rivers. Students should be given about 6 to 8 minutes to work while the teacher observes and listens in from a distance and/or assists any teams that appear to be having trouble. It is not unusual for the noise level in the room to reduce at some point well before the end of the 6 to 8 minutes, signaling that students have exhausted their immediate, top-of-the-head ideas and are searching their memories for more ideas. Generally, it's best to allow time for those additional ideas to surface; after about 8 minutes, teams should be ready to move on.

The teacher then announces the specific topic of the reading and focuses student attention. For example: "In preparation for our trip, we're going to read an account of someone else's trip down the Rogue River. Go back to your list and put a check mark beside anything you listed that you think might be in our reading. Add any new ideas that occur to you." Students review their lists for 2 to 3 minutes, checking and adding ideas. Then, to initiate the reading, the teacher directs, "As you read, put an asterisk beside any item on your list that appears in the text."

Students read the assignment individually; however, even though they are reading individually, the room is by no means silent. You can expect to hear a low buzz of conversation as students read—partners and teams will talk to each other and comment about information found in the text. (I once heard someone call this "mumble reading"—an apt description.) Students will read to each other to support a point they made ("Listen, it says right here…"), exclaim over words or ideas in the text ("Here it is—seals are 'pinnipeds'"), and respond to text ("I didn't know that!"). The teacher observes, "tuning in" to different groups' discussions to monitor how well students are doing; when the reading is completed, the teacher leads a short discussion of content. This simple activity then launches the class into the curriculum. It may be used over and over—before reading or project development or planning any of the many activities that such a unit might include.

Principle No. 2:
Encourage Multiple Responses to Learning Events

A very easy way to encourage multiple responses to classroom events is to have students create visual maps to record experiences, learning events, and information gained from reading. Students can construct their own individual visual representations, or maps, that serve both to organize information and prepare for writing or other idea development. I've taken my notion of mapping from Jane Davidson's (1982) group mapping activity.

Teaching Idea: The Group Mapping Activity
Content Areas: All
Levels: Intermediate, Middle, High School
The Group Mapping begins after a learning event (often reading); instructions for the initial mapping activity should be something like the following: "Without looking back at the book and without talking to anyone, map your interpretation of the reading you just did on rafting down the Rogue River." The first time you do this, add, "A map is a diagram of what you think the reading was about; there is no right or wrong way to map. You may use lines, words, picture, forms—anything you want to use to create your map." Show a couple of mapping examples. Then add, "You are going to use this map to record important information as we go through our river unit. Our maps will change and grow as we learn. Be sure to include on your map all the information you consider to be important at this time."

After completing the maps, students are directed to share their maps with partners by telling them what they considered important, how they chose to organize the information, and why they made the choices they did. Partners are to respond by eliciting elaboration about important information (e.g., "What made you choose that point?") and by looking to see what relationships are shown on the map.

Emphasis is placed on the value of the maps as the basis for further study or as starting points for individual and group projects throughout the unit. Students are reminded that their and their partner's maps do not have to look alike, but whatever information and organization schemes used, the map should be complete. After one map is discussed, partners then exchange roles. During this discussion, the original text is consulted repeatedly to verify information and add details and ideas missed in the original mapping.

Principle No. 3:
Allow Students to Help Shape the Curriculum

I can think of any number of ways, small and large, to achieve this principle, but here I will address only one. An area of acute need in content learning is learning the language of the curriculum—vocabulary study. I think it is safe to say that we have not been wildly successful in bringing vocabulary learning into the realm of learning in a way that feels like fun. However, it can be done—I've done it using the vocabulary self-collection strategy (VSS) (Haggard, 1982, 1985; Ruddell, 1997). I created VSS and have used it successfully with many students and varied age and grade levels; I can attest to its efficacy and appeal to students, as can other teachers who have tried it.

Teaching Idea: The Vocabulary Self-Collection Strategy
Content Areas: All
Levels: Intermediate, Middle, High School

VSS begins after the reading and discussion of text (or any learning event) and is initiated by the teacher asking students to nominate one word or term that they would like to learn or know more about and that they think should appear on a class vocabulary list. The teacher also gets to nominate one word. Students are encouraged to find words that are important to the topic at hand and are required to tell the following:

1. Where they found the word (read the sentence if in text or recall the context if from a discussion or other learning event).
2. What they think the word means in this context.
3. Why they think the class should learn it (e.g., identify the word's importance to the content topic).

In most classrooms, this part of VSS is most efficiently done with students in nominating teams of two to five people, depending on the number of words the teacher wishes to have in the nominated pool. (A good basic rule is 8 to 10 words, with a target of 5 to 6 words for the final class list.) Don't forget that the teacher nominates one of the original pool words as well. Generally, 3 to 5 minutes is sufficient time for groups to reexamine a text or review an event and find words, prepare their definitions, and develop a rationale for learning each word. It is often useful to rush students a bit, keeping them on task and leaving little time for extraneous discussion, and then extending the time if it is really needed. The teacher is also wise to predetermine his or her selection (and, in fact, have two or three words on deck in the event of duplication with student choices) in order to be free to monitor group functioning and answer any questions that might arise.

As soon as groups are ready, a spokesperson from each group presents a nominated word, tells where it was found, what the group believes it means, and why it was chosen. The teacher writes the words on the board and leads the discussion to define each one—first from the context, as the nominators tell what they think their word means, and then, if necessary, from any references available in the room. Discussion should include contributions from other class members as well, so that definitions are extended and personalized.

The focus is always on the meaning of the word in the specific context of the immediate content topic or text; however, conversation is likely to range across other meanings or contexts that are part of students' prior knowledge and experience. These other meanings serve as useful comparisons and contrasts to the topic-specific meaning under discussion. After all words have been nominated, a final class list is established by eliminating duplicates, any words or terms the class feels it already knows, and any that do not appear to be appropriate.

During this process, words chosen for the class list are circled (or identified in some way), and eliminated words are simply left alone, so nothing is erased from the board. Chosen words are then redefined and written with definitions in vocabulary journals or any ongoing unit or lesson documents (e.g., entered in appropriate places on study maps). Students who wish to include them on their own personal vocabulary lists may record words not chosen for class study. The power of allowing students to construct their own vocabulary lists of words that they want to learn or know more about simply has to be experienced to be believed.

Principle No. 4: Monitor Collaborative Work and Develop Students' Ability to Monitor Their Own Work

When students are working in collaborative groups, and especially when the work they are doing is project based, one of the most important things you can do to make the experience successful is maintain an organizing system that assists students in focusing their attention and energy on the work at hand. A very simple way to do this is to provide time at the beginning and end of class each day for stating the work to be done today and later reflecting on the day's accomplishments and planning for the next day's work. I recommend a "status of the group" roll call at the beginning of class (Ruddell, 1997) that asks each group in turn, "What are you doing today?", "What do you plan to accomplish?" and "How may I or anyone else help you?" At the end of class, guide students similarly in reflecting on the completed work. This gives groups and individuals the opportunity to monitor their own progress ("What did we accomplish today?" and "What are our plans for tomorrow?") and share with other students and the teacher what they've found in their research and any problems they're encountering. Analytical discussion of this kind increases students' ability to self-monitor their working progress and develops their planning and strategic inquiry skills. It also keeps you informed of the progress they're making and provides information for your record keeping and evaluation procedures.

A Project Work Management Sheet (see Figure 14-2) is one way to maintain records of group planning and progress. To make a Project Work Management Sheet for each working group, put the group's name or project topic at the top and list all group members in the space allotted. Each day at the status-of-the-group roll call, record (in abbreviated form) each group's outline of its plan for the day. Later, during reflection time ("What did you accomplish today?" and "What do you need for continued progress?"), record group accomplishments. Make note of any other pertinent information. This becomes your working record of project development for each group.

Figure 14-2. Project Work Management Sheet
Group: _____
Members: _____
_____
_____
_____
_____
Date   Work Planned   Work Accomplished

Concluding Thoughts

Our complex goal of developing literacy, content, and curriculum is most likely to be achieved by bringing to bear students' natural tendency toward industriousness—to engage them in lots of talking with others about learning topics, in many opportunities to connect prior knowledge with new learning, and in reading and writing activities that are natural and integral parts of the learning process. An experience like the Rogue River trip provides a great deal of substance for creating a rich curriculum. Our job is to establish and maintain learning environments and conditions that make time "fly" and encourage student excitement, exhilaration, intense interest, and curiosity in learning.

Let us recall the premise of my discussion and its logical conclusion. If upper-grade teachers are to accomplish all that is necessary to develop successful readers, writers, and learners in their classrooms and teach the stipulated curriculum, then we must rearrange our view of literacy development, content learning, and the curriculum into an integrative whole for which *all* instruction benefits each one. By so doing, we do a different dance: Rather than fragmenting instruction into the traditional pigeonholes of story reading and writing, study skills, and curriculum and attempting to teach them in parallel universes, we engage students in activities that simultaneously teach, reinforce, and increase all three. Then our classrooms vibrate with students' energetic engagement in learning, then students use and increase literacy abilities on a daily basis in the service of developing content knowledge, and then we are doing our dance very well indeed.

References

Applebee, A. N. (1981). *Writing in the secondary school*. Urbana, IL: National Council of Teachers of English.

Beach, J. D. (1983). Teaching students to write informational reports. *Elementary School Journal, 84*, 213–220.

Calkins, L. M. (1991). *Living between the lines*. Portsmouth, NH: Heinemann.

Davidson, J. L. (1982). The group mapping activity for instruction in reading and thinking. *Journal of Reading, 26*, 52–56.

Goodman, K. (1994). Reading, writing, and written texts: A transactional sociopsycholinguistic view. In R. B. Ruddell, M. R. Ruddell, & H. Singer (Eds.), *Theoretical models and processes of reading* (4th ed., pp. 1093–1130). Newark, DE: International Reading Association.

Haggard, M. R. (1982). The vocabulary self-collection strategy: An active approach to word learning. *Journal of Reading, 26*, 203–207.

Haggard, M. R. (1985). An interactive strategies approach to content learning. *Journal of Reading, 29,* 204–210.

Howe, J. (1987, Spring). Reflections. *Writing Project Quarterly Newsletter 1* (3), 12.

Jimenez, R. T., Garcia, G. E., & Pearson, P. D. (1996). The reading strategies of bilingual Latina/o students who are successful English readers: Opportunities and obstacles. *Reading Research Quarterly, 31,* 90–112.

Johnstone, P., & Allington, R. (1991). Remediation. In R. Barr, M. L. Kamil, P. B. Mosenthal, & P. D. Pearson (Eds.), *Handbook of reading research* (Vol. 2, pp. 984–1012). New York: Longman.

Langer, J. A., & Applebee, A. N. (1987). *How writing shapes thinking* (Research Report No. 22). Urbana, IL: National Council of Teachers of English.

Martin, N., D'Arcy, P., Newton, B., & Parker, R. (1976). *Writing and learning across the curriculum.* London: Ward Lock.

Pearson, P. D., Roehler, L. R., Dole, J. A., & Duffy, G. G. (1990). *Developing expertise in reading comprehension: What should be taught? How should it be taught?* (Technical Report No. 512). Champaign, IL: University of Illinois at Urbana-Champaign, Center for the Study of Reading.

Rosenblatt, L. M. (1994). The transactional theory of reading and writing. In R. B. Ruddell, M. R. Ruddell, & H. Singer (Eds.), *Theoretical models and processes of reading* (4th ed., pp. 1057-1092). Newark, DE: International Reading Association.

Ruddell, M. R. (1997). *Teaching content reading and writing* (2nd ed.). Boston: Allyn & Bacon.

Ruddell, R. B., & Ruddell, M. R. (1995). *Teaching children to read and write: Becoming an influential teacher.* Boston: Allyn & Bacon.

Singer. H. (1970). Research that should have made a difference. *Elementary English, 47,* 27–34.

Part IV

Making the Transition to Creative Teaching

Chapter 15

Assessment for the 21st Century: Performance, Portfolios, and Profiles

Maureen McLaughlin

When I opened the classroom door, I saw clustered desks, walls covered with posters and student writing, and tables displaying projects. Students were talking and the teacher was invisible among them. The sounds were distinctive: a single voice reporting some late-breaking news from the National Institutes of Health, multiple voices discussing a just-completed dissection, a group singing a rap tune about DNA, low whispers from pairs engaging in a computerized experiment, and keyboards tapping out e-mail responses to European peers. The perspectives were diverse. The atmosphere was an air of exploration. The feelings it exuded were engaging, confident, inquisitive, and discovery oriented. Mutual respect and trust permeated the experience. I stood on the edge of possibility, knowing that I had opened the door to a content area classroom of the 21st century.

How has content area instruction become so diversified and so inviting? The response is multifaceted. Principally, the paradigm has shifted from a more traditional focus to student-centered learning. Consequently, learning has become more inquiry-based; the physical setup of the room has been restructured to accommodate diverse, multidimensional learning experiences; student interaction and student-teacher interaction have increased dramatically; critical and creative thinking have become the standard rather than the exception; and access to information beyond the classroom walls has experienced a technological explosion. The curriculum has been updated, the texts reflect best practice, and numerous creative and innovative ideas and resources have become integral facets of teaching and learning.

The students are motivated, highly engaged, and enthusiastic. The teachers are energized, involved, and fervent. These classrooms are amazingly different from the "read the chapter and answer the question" contexts traditionally associated with content area instruction. The assessments also differ dramatically from the "your grade is the average of your test scores" practices of the past.

Eisner (1999) attributes the change to "the demise of behaviorism and the rise of constructivism" (p. 658). He further notes, "We have come to realize that meaning matters and that it is not something that can be imparted from teacher to student.... Meanings are not given, they are made." His thinking supports the theme of this volume: using creative and innovative teaching ideas to foster the personal construction of meaning.

Zemelman, Daniels, and Hyde (1998) concur, noting that best practice can be described as providing authentic, reflective, collaborative, cognitive, and challenging teaching and learning experiences. Rasmussen (1999) agrees, adding that "instruction should be relevant and meaningful to students, help them become reflective and critical thinkers who can identify and demonstrate different points of view, and provide them with the knowledge and skills they need to function in a democratic society" (p. 3). Darling-Hammond (1993) believes that we can accomplish these goals if we "focus students' energies on challenging performance-oriented tasks that require analysis, integration of knowledge, and invention as well as highly developed written and oral expression rather than merely recall and recognition of facts" (p. 19).

This chapter explores the use of these innovative assessment tasks in the content areas. It begins by offering a theoretical framework that is followed by a brief glossary. Next, informal assessments such as observation, reflection, and informal writing are described. Then examples of more formal performance assessments, including exhibitions, group projects, research, and debate are presented. Following this, portfolios and performance profiles, two ways to illustrate student growth over time, are discussed. Next, rubrics and innovations in reporting student progress are presented. Finally, considerations for implementing innovative assessment practices are introduced.

Rationale for Innovative Assessment

Theoretical Framework

The theoretical underpinnings for innovative assessment practices can be found in constructivism, schema-based learning development, social negotiation and the zone of proximal development, and reflective practice (McLaughlin & Vogt, 1996). This framework provides a sound foundation for both informal and formal assessments.

Constructivists believe that learning is a self-regulated process that involves experience, discourse, and reflection (Brooks & Brooks, 1993). Schema-based learning development purports that learning takes place when new information is integrated with what is already known (Anderson, 1994). Vygotsky's (1987) work serves as the foundation for social negotiation and the zone of proximal development. This supports student learning that is scaffolded by more experienced people, and it promotes social interaction. The zone of proximal development represents the difference between what the student can do alone and what the student can do with the assistance and support of others. Through reflective practice teachers develop understandings and insights that can lead to better ways of teaching (Schon, 1987). Students develop similar insights about their learning through ongoing reflection.

Recent Developments

Assessment has undergone a major reformation in recent years (McLaughlin & Vogt, 1996; Valencia, 1998). What has emerged is assessment that is multidimensional, dynamic, authentic, collaborative, reflective, and standards based. The performance assessments, portfolios, and performance profiles discussed in this chapter embody all of these characteristics.

Multidimensional

Multidimensionality is an essential characteristic of assessment because it enables students' use of strength modalities. For some students, that strength may best be exhibited through writing; for others, it may be through oral discourse, dramatization, or projects. It is therefore important to offer a variety of assessment choices to accommodate students' individual needs. The activities presented throughout this text provide ways to assess student progress through a variety of modalities.

Dynamic

Because assessment has a dynamic nature, it is viewed not as an event but rather as a natural, purposeful component of teaching and learning. As Brooks and Brooks (1993) note, "In a constructivist setting, assessment of student learning is done naturally within the context of lessons and activities. Teachers analyze student products and exhibitions as benchmarks and garner information for use in developing future activities and informing ongoing practice" (p. 122).

Authentic

Authenticity is another critical characteristic of innovative assessments. Authentic tasks are those that are grounded in instruction, personally meaningful, and situated in real-world experiences (Clinchy, 1995; Hiebert, 1994; McLaughlin & Kennedy, 1993). Linking tasks to life experiences helps students to understand the applicability of their learning beyond the classroom.

Collaborative

Innovative assessments can also be collaborative in nature. This characteristic, which is supported by the work of Vygotsky (1987), encourages learners to develop understanding within a social context. Collaborative problem solving enables students to complete tasks that most would not be able to complete alone.

Reflective

The assessment process is reflective for both teachers and students. The reflection in which both engage can serve as an informal assessment of teaching and learning. It offers insight into students' thinking and leads to personal goal setting, a valuable life skill.

Standards-Based

Because a majority of academic disciplines and virtually all states have developed standards, current assessments are often standards based. This is a positive development because, as Schmoker and Marzano (1999) observe, "The success of any organization is contingent upon clear, commonly defined goals" (p. 17).

In any discussion of standards, three categories appear to emerge: *content standards*, which delineate what students should learn; *performance standards,* which describe what students should demonstrate to show proficiency; and *delivery standards,* which define the quality of educational opportunities and resources that must be provided to students (Mabry, 1999).

Robin Fogarty (cited in Mann, 1998) believes that "teachers should use the standards movement to help make decisions about what to teach, what to spend time on, what to assess and what to eliminate from the curriculum" (p. 4). A major challenge is to decide which content to teach and which to eliminate (Schmoker & Marzano, 1999; Strong, Silver, & Perini, 1999; Wiggins & McTighe, 1998; Zemelman et al., 1998). Bob Jervis (cited in Mann, 1998) suggests using "backward mapping" (p. 4) to facilitate this process. He proposes that teachers turn the standards into questions and allow those queries to serve as the focus of teaching and learning. After the questions have been developed, he suggests that teachers should design performance assessments. Finally, in the third step, teachers should develop their lessons. This process aligns standards, performance assessments, and teaching.

Designing down from state standards is a common way for districts to accommodate standards. In this process, school districts use state standards to create benchmarks or grade-level indicators of expected student performance. Reviewing K–12 benchmarks demonstrates how students begin to achieve the standards in kindergarten and progress throughout their academic careers to graduation. This gives direction to teaching and learning at all levels. Figures 15-1 and 15-2 feature excerpts from Pennsylvania's Berks County Intermediate Unit's K–12 Grade Level Benchmarks which trace student performance expectations for geometry and research from the start of their school experiences until their graduation. The committee that created the benchmarks describes them as a work in progress and notes the benchmarks can be downloaded at berksiu.K12.pa.us.

Curriculum-Based Reform

Curriculum-based reform, which aligns curriculum with content and performance standards, is a topic of research for the Mid-Continent Regional Educational Laboratory (1999). Although the alignment of curriculum, instruction, and assessment has been an ongoing focus of innovative assessment practices, McREL's study has identified four state-level components that facilitate successful curriculum-based reform: ongoing review of standards, professional development plans, an assessment program, and an accountability system.

Assessment Terminology

As with most educational developments, there are numerous terms associated with innovative assessment practices (for detailed glossaries, see Arter, 1996; McLaughlin, 1995). The following terms are critical to understanding the concepts in this chapter.

Assessment is the gathering and synthesizing of information concerning students' learning (Ferrara & McTighe, 1992).

Authentic assessment involves engaging students in tasks that are grounded in instruction, are personally meaningful, and take place in real-life contexts (McLaughlin & Kennedy, 1993).

Benchmarks are grade-level indicators of students' progress toward achieving the standards.

Evaluation is making judgments about students' learning (Ferrara & McTighe, 1992).

Performance assessment requires students to demonstrate what they know.

Figure 15-1.
Excerpts from K-12 Grade-Level Geometry Benchmarks
(Pennsylvania's Berks County Intermediate Unit)

Kindergarten	Draw two-dimensional geometric shapes
Grade 1	Construct a triangle, rectangle, and square using the geoboard and reproduce the figure on grid paper.
Grade 2	Draw and compare common geometric shapes
Grade 3	Draw two- and three-dimensional geometric shapes and construct rectangles, squares, and triangles on the geoboard and on graph paper, satisfying specific criteria
Grade 4	Create a reflection of a given drawing
Grade 5	Identify and measure circles, their diameters and radii
Grade 6	Identify and locate triangles, quadrilaterals, circles, prisms, pyramids, cylinders and cones
Grade 7	Define, describe, classify, and sketch triangles, quadrilaterals, circles, prisms, cylinders, and cones
Grade 8	Classify familiar polygons as regular or irregular up to a decagon.
Grade 9	Construct deductive proofs involving segments and angles
Grade 10	Apply angle measures of polygons to solve problems
Grade 11	Identify and prove the properties of quadrilaterals involving opposite sides and angles, consecutive sides and angles, and diagonals using deductive proofs
Grade 12	Demonstrate appropriate use of vectors and vector operations to solve real world applications

Figure 15-2.
Excerpts from K-12 Grade-Level Research Benchmarks
(Pennsylvania's Berks County Intermediate Unit)

Kindergarten Think about topic, look at pictures, gather materials, discuss topic.

Grade 1 Think about topics, discuss prior knowledge in groups, select and survey texts to determine purpose, preview illustrations to construct meaning, discuss topic.

Grade 2 In addition to Grade 1: Use picture dictionaries, newspapers, magazines and texts and preview charts, diagrams, tables.

Grade 3 Locate resources for a particular task, select sources (dictionaries, encyclopedias, family interviews, observations and electronic media), use table of contents, key words, and guide words, use traditional and electronic search tools.

Grade 4 In addition to Grade 3: Survey sources (those listed for grade 3 and nonfiction trade books), select appropriate sources, use appendixes.

Grade 5 In addition to Grade 4: Evaluate the usefulness and quality of sources, select sources (those previously listed and computer data bases), use cross references and appendixes.

Grade 6 In addition to Grade 5: Use traditional and electronic search tools.

Grade 7 In addition to Grade 6: Evaluate the effectiveness of qualities in the sources.

Grades 8 & 9 In addition to Grade 7: Determine valid resources for researching the topic, including primary and secondary sources, evaluate the importance and quality of sources, select essential sources.

Grades 10 & 11 In addition to Grades 8 & 9: Select sources appropriate to the breadth and depth of the research.

cont.

Grade 12	Use a variety of reliable primary and secondary sources to research topic, evaluate the importance and quality of the sources, select sources appropriate to the breadth and depth of the research, use table of contents, indexes, key words, cross references, and appendixes, use traditional and electronic search tools.

Portfolio assessment is a standards-based, multidimensional collection of student performances over time.

Performance profiles are standards-based documents used at the high school level that feature a student-selected performance from each major subject area for each year the subject is studied. The profiles, which include students' self-reflections on the standards, offer an overview of individual students' progress toward achieving standards and provide performance documentation often required for university admissions.

Rubrics are scoring criteria designed to describe progressive levels of performance.

Performance Assessment

Background

Performance assessments incorporate motivation, content knowledge, thinking processes, and authentic tasks. This type of assessment has quite a long history in education (Madaus & O'Dwyer, 1999). Its latest renaissance can be traced to a number of factors.

First, and perhaps most important, is the depth and variety of information that performances offer. Traditional measures such as multiple choice questions simply do not provide the types of information necessary to understand student learning (Haertel, 1999). Performances invite students to demonstrate what they know. This offers insight into students' thinking.

The second factor is performance assessment's connection to life experiences. A vast majority of professions are assessed through performance. Using similar assessments in our schools prepares the students for experiences beyond the classroom. According to Eisner (1999), this reflects our desire for concurrent or predictive validity. We want assessments to tell us how students will use their knowledge beyond the classroom.

Third, performance assessments are multidimensional. They can accommodate individual needs, including learning styles, because performances provide opportunities for students to make choices to accommodate their strengths.

Finally, context is a factor when using performance assessment. These assessments are situated in response-centered classrooms that foster motivation, hold high expectations for all learners, value self-selection, encourage student ownership of learning, nurture risk taking, and support cooperative and collaborative learning.

Informal Assessments

Informal assessments are less structured and occur naturally in everyday teaching and learning experiences. A number of informal assessment techniques facilitate the use of more formal performance assessments. Examples of informal assessments include observation, reflection, and informal writing. The following informal assessments can be used in all content areas at all levels.

Observation

Observations are informal assessments that allow teachers to capture the essence of a live performance by watching students as they engage in a task. These informal assessments offer evidence of student motivation, communication, interaction, risk taking, critical and creative thinking, and collaboration.

One way to organize and manage observations is to use a clipboard. One sticky note or mailing label is attached to the clipboard for each student in the class. When a student is observed, the teacher's notes are recorded on the sticky note or mailing label, dated, removed from the clipboard, and placed on a sheet of paper either in the student's portfolio or in an observation folder. The names of students who have not yet been observed remain on the clipboard. When all students have been observed, the sticky notes or mailing labels are replenished. As students are observed multiple times, the sticky notes or mailing labels are placed chronologically on the designated sheet in either the portfolio or observation folder. This offers a running history of observations throughout a marking period and, eventually, throughout the year. Observations help teachers to remember specific attributes of student performance, and they provide informal assessment information for student evaluation.

There is no magic number of observations that should be done. Observing just one student, using the clipboard approach is a good way to begin. After everyone has been observed once, teachers generally find a comfort level with this process.

It is important to remember that every observation should have a pur-

pose. The following prompts will help in observing students who are working independently:

- Does the student demonstrate an interest in learning?
- How does he or she interact with the course materials?
- How does the student use new information?
- Does the student appear to be a risk taker?
- Does he or she readily share ideas?
- Does he or she relate new concepts to previously learned informa-
  tion?
- Does the student link learning to life experiences?
- Does the student engage in critical and creative thinking?

The following prompts will help in observing students who are working
in cooperative groups:

- Does the student focus on the group task?
- Does he or she participate in group discussions?
- Does the student take an active role in the group activity?
- Does he or she respect the ideas of others in the group?
- Does the student demonstrate curiosity?
- Does he or she apply content area concepts to the group activity?
- Does the student communicate ideas effectively?
- Does he or she engage in critical and creative thinking?

Reflection

Reflection engenders student ownership of learning and affirms that students' thinking is valued (McLaughlin & Vogt, 1998). Reflection is also a
component of constructivism. Brooks and Brooks (1993) note that from a
constructivist perspective, learning is understood as a process that incorporates concrete experience, collaborative discourse, and reflection. The results
of reflection lead us to "ask better questions, break out of fruitless routines,
make unexpected connections, and experiment with fresh ideas" (Brandt,
1991). Students, peers, and teachers can all engage in the reflection.

Self-Reflection. Self-reflection encourages students to examine their
learning process by contemplating what they are doing, why they are doing
it, how they are doing it, what contributed to its success, and what they
would do to improve it next time. Topics of student self-reflection include
progress in meeting a standard, connections between academic work and
other life experiences, their view of learning as a process, and what they do
and do not understand.

Peer Reflections. Peer reflections demonstrate that the work in which
students are engaging is valued and that all students have ownership of the

process. Suggestions from peers can affirm students' ideas and raise questions that guide revision.

Teacher Reflections. Teacher reflections on student performance can assess students' progress, question process and understanding, discover strengths and needs, and support revision and personal goal setting. For teachers this is just one dimension of their role as reflective practitioners. In support of this, Fran Zimmerman (cited in Mann, 1998) observes, "Reflective practice requires an environment where teachers can ask good questions, collect data, and draw conclusions from critical thinking. All of this goes hand-in-hand with assessment for understanding" (p. 4).

Informal Writing

Informal writing encourages reflection, provides a means of documenting students' reasoning, and promotes inquiry. Examples of informal writing are content histories, journals, and quickwrites.

Content Histories. A content history details a person's development in a particular content area from earliest memory to the present (adapted from McLaughlin in McLaughlin & Vogt, 1996). It may take a variety of forms, including a written account, a scrapbook, an illustrated book, or a poem. Having students contemplate their previous experiences in a content area has numerous benefits. For the student, it promotes reflectivity, helps to make connections between past and present experiences, and cultivates self-understanding. For the teacher, it provides insights into students' previous learning experiences that can be used to foster motivation and inform planning. Prompts to facilitate this process in mathematics can be found in chapter 9. These are easily adapted to all content areas.

Journals. In addition to providing background information about students, informal writing can be used for many other purposes. A primary example of this is journals, which can be maintained in all content areas either traditionally or electronically. Three types of journals frequently used in the content areas are dialogue, investigative, and dual entry.

Gordon and MacInnis (1993) describe the use of *dialogue journals* in mathematics. Their students use the journals for both prompted and unprompted responses. When using prompts, the teachers ask a direct question about learning, such as "What are decimals?" When using unprompted responses, students write their reactions to and queries about learning. Journal entries offer teachers insights into students' thinking. Teacher responses may validate students' ideas, offer new information, and pose new questions. Example math journal prompts, which can be adapted for other content areas, can be found in chapter 9.

Investigative journals (see chapter 3) document student thinking about topics of special interest. Students record " I wonder" statements in their journals, which are later used to guide their development of research questions. Investigative journals are often also used as the basis for student-teacher and peer discussion. When students maintain investigative journals, they have immediate access to research topics of personal interest.

Dual entry journals are also frequently used in the content areas. These journals help to monitor students' reading outside of class, promote reflectivity, and provide solid foundations for student interaction, class discussion, and conferencing. There are several ways to format dual entry journals. One method is to have the students draw a line down the center to divide each notebook page in half. To the left of the line, students write summary statements or note important ideas from a chapter they have read. To the right of the line, students write their reflections or questions about the information they recorded on the left.

Dual entry journals can also be maintained by having students read a chapter or an informational article and write a brief summary of it. For the second half of the journal entry, students write their reaction to what they have read.

Quickwrites. Another type of informal writing, quickwrites, can also be used in any content area. These require very little time and provide an effective way to informally assess student thinking. Depending on when the quickwrites take place, they can provide insight into students' prior knowledge, monitor students' understanding, or delineate what students have learned. To use this technique in class, teachers should first communicate the purpose of the quickwrite. This is important because students need to know if they are writing for themselves or if their teacher or peers will be reading their work. The purpose will also determine if students need to put their names on their work. Once the purpose has been set, simply offer the students a specified period of time (generally, 3 to 5 minutes), provide them with a topic or prompt, and ask them to write in response to it.

If students are creating content histories, maintaining journals, or using quickwrites, it's important that teachers model each of these types of informal writing. Because these activities involve writing at the draft stage and communication of ideas is the ultimate goal, the writing should not be evaluated for spelling or grammar. Teachers can, however, model conventional spelling and grammar in their written responses and/or conduct minilessons on these topics after the writing has been returned to the students. From an assessment perspective, informal writing helps teachers to monitor student understanding and gives direction to future planning.

Formal Assessments

Formal assessments are generally more involved than informal assessments and occur over a longer period of time. Formal assessments are usually evaluated through the use of rubrics. Examples of formal performance assessments include exhibitions, group investigations projects, research, and debate.

Exhibitions

Exhibitions usually embody multiple performance requirements that extend over a period of time. These are typically multimedia in nature and may involve writing a paper, making an oral presentation, building a model, creating computer graphics, and responding spontaneously to questions. Exhibitions may be individual or collaborative in nature and are often used as culminating activities (Willis, 1996).

Exhibitions generally begin with students' self-selected topics and a project plan that includes the standards that will be used to evaluate student performance. Student-teacher conferencing and cooperative learning play integral roles as students progress with their investigations. To complete the exhibition, its creators present it to an audience. The final step involves reflection by the students creating the exhibition, their peers, and their teacher.

Maria Ramirez has used collaborative exhibitions in her seventh-grade science classes for several years. At the outset, Ms. Ramirez provided students with a description of the exhibition and a rubric delineating the evaluation criteria. Students self-selected their topics, and cooperative groups were structured based on topic interest. A group that selected noise pollution researched its topic by using multiple resources including the Internet. The students also based their research on primary and secondary sources. One of their primary source evidences was an interview the students conducted at the local airport with a pilot from U.S. Airways. They also used multimedia to present their exhibition, including film, transparencies, compact discs, and audiotapes. At the conclusion of their presentation, the students conducted a question-and-answer session with their audience. Afterwards, the students self-evaluated their project by completing the rubric provided at the start of their work. In addition, they received rubric feedback from their teacher and their peers.

Group Investigations or Projects

When engaging in group investigations or projects, students "work together on a complex problem that requires planning, research, internal discussion, and group presentation" (Arter, 1996). Projects offer students opportunities to demonstrate their knowledge while engaging in risk taking, creativity, and authentic experiences. As with all performances, evaluative criteria are shared with the students before the investigations or projects begin.

Debi Stinner and her colleagues created an interdisciplinary group investigation entitled "Mystery in Room 3." This culminating project for a unit integrating science and literature focuses on forensic chemistry, the mystery genre, and descriptive writing. Students experience the roles of detective, pathologist, and crime scene reporter. In addition, they analyze and synthesize clues to develop a theory to solve the mystery.

Assessment is based on students' participation, collaboration, lab reports, and writing. A rubric, created by teachers with student input, includes criteria for evaluating the accuracy of the information presented, the logical order of events, the mechanics of writing, creativity, and the solution. It is shared with all participants prior to the start of the project.

Research

Research can also be used as a performance assessment. It may be completed individually or by a group of students. In Amy Sou's biology class, students complete an individual research project. They self-select their topics, often using their investigative journals as an aid in developing their research questions (see chapter 3). Again, students are provided with a rubric prior to the start of the research. The rubric focuses on criteria such as the research question, resources, primary and secondary sources, technology, and presentation. The research occurs over a period of 2 months, and includes techniques such as interviewing and surveying. Student-teacher conferences are held periodically.

When the research is completed, students self-select the methods they will use to share the results with the class. Dramatizations, demonstrations, computer software programs, and written reports are the formats most commonly selected. Although Mrs. Sou evaluates the research according to the rubric, students also engage in self-evaluation and receive peer evaluations after they have presented their work.

Debates

Because standards place great emphasis on developing critical thinking and students' abilities to speak and listen for a variety of purposes, debates appear to be regaining popularity. These performances provide the opportunity for students to take positions and express, challenge, and defend ideas orally (for more information about debates, see chapter 3).

I recently observed debates at three different levels: intermediate, middle school, and high school. At the intermediate level, students were just beginning to learn the debating process. They began by focusing on a class-selected topic familiar to everyone. Not surprisingly, it was fast food. Students used the discussion web strategy to focus their thinking and then debated fast food's merits and faults. At the middle school level, social studies students debated whether the United States should intervene when conflicts develop in foreign countries. At the high school level, biology students debated the practice of cloning. In all three situations, students were very well prepared and their critical thinking abilities were highly evident. The teachers acknowledged that in addition to its other positive attributes, debate motivates students and offers an alternative method for student performance.

Performance assessments can be used in all content areas. Students may create them independently or in cooperative groups. The performance tasks discussed in this section illustrate the dynamic, multidimensional nature of such assessments. Suggested steps for creating performance assessments are described in Figure 15-3. For examples of performances and accompanying rubrics, see Lewin and Shoemaker (1998).

Figure 15-3. Creating A Performance Assessment

Performance assessments incorporate motivation, content knowledge, a variety of thinking processes, and meaningful life applications. The following guidelines articulate the development of performance assessments.

1. You may wish to work with colleagues when creating performance assessments. This will offer additional perspectives that may enhance the authenticity and reliability of the task.

2. Contemplate the purpose of the performance assessment. What will it tell you about your students? Use your response to this question to develop standards, goals, or expectations for the assessment. These should be shared with the students through the development of a rubric.

3. What will the assessment task be? Can multiple approaches to the assessment be used successfully? Does it engage students' reasoning and thinking skills? Students' interest? Students' communication abilities? Does it support its goals?

4. Let your teaching serve as the foundation for the assessment. Have you taught the necessary content? Have you modeled and taught the strategies required to complete the task? Are the necessary resources available?

cont.

5. Consider the audience for the assessment. Students will engage in the performance. Design the task so it can be related to their prior knowledge. Incorporate strategies they are accustomed to using. Think about how the assessment will accommodate individual needs. Are there other audiences for the performance? Think about the roles that parents or other stakeholders may play in this assessment.

6. Think about how you will motivate students to engage in the performance.

7. Design the assessment, considering processes and products.

8. Will the assessment be evaluated? What are the evaluation criteria? Will students engage in self-evaluation? Peer evaluation? Will others be invited to comment on the performance?

9. How will students receive feedback on their performance? How will you use this information to inform teaching and learning?

Rubrics

Rubrics are scoring guides that provide criteria for evaluating performances (Arter, 1996; Goodrich 1996-1997, McLaughlin, 1995). Rubrics are designed to accommodate a range of levels; 4- and 6-point are the most common. They also provide gradations of quality for each criterion. For example, on a 4-point rubric, gradations might include *exceptional, thorough, adequate,* and *inadequate* when describing levels of understanding or *consistently, frequently, occasionally,* and *rarely* when describing levels of proficiency.

The process of creating rubrics for performance assessments is delineated in Figure 15-4. Student involvement is an important consideration in rubric design. Students may have input into the process from the beginning or after the teacher has created a draft of the rubric. Students should also have the chance to use the rubric for self- and peer-evaluation and to revise their work based on the results. This opportunity for revision gives students additional confidence in the assessment process as well as an opportunity to improve their work before it is submitted for teacher evaluation. This also benefits the teacher because the performance that is ultimately submitted has already undergone two evaluations and revisions.

Figure 15-4. Creating A Rubric for a Performance Assessment

A rubric is a scoring guide that offers a description of student performance. It is used to evaluate a performance and to offer students specific feedback. The following guidelines delineate rubric design.

1. Begin with the standards the performance task is addressing. Then review several rubric models and consider working with peers to develop the rubric.

2. Think about each standard in terms of performance levels. Decide how many levels of performance the rubric will have. Generally, 4- and 6-point are the most commonly used. Decide which criteria should be in the rubric. Next, describe each level of performance for each criterion. You may wish to begin by detailing what an exemplary performance is and then moving on to how an unacceptable performance would be described. This often makes it easier to describe the middle level or acceptable performance. Make sure that there are clear distinctions between levels for each standard. Make the descriptors as detailed as possible.

3. Having a model of the performance at each level facilitates the use of rubrics. For this reason, you may wish to designate "anchor performances" that you feel are truly representative of each level of the rubric.

4. The rubrics should be shared with the students before they begin the performance. This enables the students to focus on the criteria they are working to achieve.

5. When the performance is complete, students can use the rubric for self- and peer evaluation. After this has occurred, be sure to provide the opportunity for students to revise their work before submitting it to you.

6. You use the same rubric to evaluate students' performances. When first beginning to use rubrics, you may wish to invite the peers with whom you designed the performance task and rubric to join you in evaluating the performances. This may offer greater reliability to the evaluation process.

7. Return the completed rubrics to the students. They can use the information to set new personal goals, and you can use the results to inform future planning.

Teachers who are just beginning to use rubrics may wish to develop one that addresses a nonacademic area with colleagues and/or students. I often recommend creating a restaurant rubric. Suggestions for criteria include quality of food, service, atmosphere, and cost. Gradations of quality must then be discussed. For example, on a 4-point rubric, food might be described as *delicious, tasty, adequate,* or *unpalatable.* Service might be described as *exceptional, thorough, adequate,* or *inadequate.* Actually visiting a restaurant allows participants to use the rubric in an appropriate context. As an alternative, participants can use the rubric to evaluate a restaurant with which they are very familiar. Beginning with a nonacademic topic helps participants to focus on the structure of the rubric and often makes the initial reasoning experience more enjoyable.

Rubrics clearly delineate the criteria on which the performance will be evaluated. They offer direction to student work, facilitate teacher and student evaluation of performances, provide information for future goal setting, and guide student revision. The completed rubrics also influence instructional planning.

Portfolio Assessment

From kindergarten to university admissions to graduate classes, portfolios are the focus of dynamic assessment. Portfolios come in many shapes and sizes and are constructed for a variety of purposes. In this section of the chapter, I focus on portfolios that are standards-based, multidimensional collections of student performance over time. They demonstrate students' efforts, progress, and achievement and are both descriptive and evaluative in nature. They afford insight into the student's engagement in learning and are created through the collaborative efforts of students and teachers.

To facilitate the development of portfolios in the content areas, consider the following guidelines (for more details, see McLaughlin, 1995):

- Decide upon which standards the portfolios will be based.
- Align curriculum, instruction, assessment, and reporting.
- Develop a list of possible performance indicators to support the standards.
- Develop criteria to evaluate the performances.
- Incorporate both student and teacher reflection.
- Develop an efficient plan to manage the system.
- Use the results of portfolio assessment to document student progress and give direction to teaching and learning.

The benefits derived from using portfolios in the content areas include the following:

- Students, parents, teachers, and administrators are aware from the outset of the standards the students are striving to achieve.
- Students, parents, and teachers can see evidence of student growth over time.
- As a collaborative process, portfolios often reinvent the student-teacher relationship.
- Students engage in self-reflection and set personal goals within the framework of course standards.
- Portfolios accommodate students' learning styles.
- Portfolios provide a focus of student-teacher conferencing (Figure 15-5) and student-parent-teacher conferencing (Figure 15-6).
- Portfolios can be directly linked to standards-based reporting systems.

The challenges encountered when using portfolios include the following:

- With traditionally structured scheduling, finding the time to develop and implement portfolios can be difficult.
- Organizing and managing portfolios when teaching 150 or more students a day can be complex.
- Having the school district continue to use traditional standardized tests to evaluate student progress while using portfolios for classroom assessment can create tensions.
- When portfolios are implemented, reporting procedures also need to be updated.

Performance Profiles

Although portfolios are frequently used at the elementary and middle school levels, their integration in high schools has been slower in developing. This means that many high school students and teachers are not benefiting from portfolio use, and many prospective college students are lacking performance documentation to submit as part of their university admissions requirements. Performance Profiles, which provide an overview of high school students' performance in the major academic areas, offer an alternative method of documenting student achievement over time.

Performance Profiles are standards based and can be maintained either traditionally or electronically. Profiles are not course portfolios, but rather a type of academic program performance review. A profile contains one performance from each course the student takes in the major academic areas. The profiles also include student reflections on process and content, provide evidence of student achievement of standards, and accommodate university admissions requirements.

Figure 15-5. Student-Teacher Portfolio Conferencing Guidelines

When conferencing with students, remember that they are sharing their work with you. The conference is a collaborative effort. Ask questions that will give the discussion direction and access the students' thinking about their progress. If the primary purpose of the conference is to examine the student's progress toward the standards, most questions will reinforce the curriculum-instruction-assessment/evaluation link.

You may wish to share your conferencing prompts with students a few days ahead of scheduled meetings. This eliminates anxiety and contributes to the efficiency of the conferencing process.

Sample Conferencing Prompts

1. Examine your baseline measure for standard _____. Compare and contrast it with your latest piece of evidence for this standard. How would you evaluate your progress? What new personal goal can you set to promote your continued progress?

2. Examine the evidence you have included to support the standards. List what you consider to be your areas of strength. Then list what you feel may be some areas in which you need improvement.

3. Is there an evidence in your portfolio that you are especially proud? Is there an evidence that you wish you could do over? How would you change it?

4. Do you think the portfolio process allows you to demonstrate what you know about our course goals? How do you think it compares to assessment practices of the past?

5. What are some things you think you've learned this marking period? How does your portfolio support your response?

6. What is your favorite piece of evidence in your portfolio? Why do you value it?

7. Our conference with your parents will be held shortly. What would you like them to know about your portfolio? Is there any particular question we addressed that you think we should share in the parent conference?

Figure 15-6. Student-Teacher-Parent Conferencing Guidelines

1. Share the format of the conference with parents before the actual conferencing date. They should know that their child will be sharing his or her portfolio with them and that it will be followed by a three-way discussion involving them, their child, and you. Naturally, parents should feel comfortable asking questions or expressing concerns during and after the conference.

2. Use input from your conference with the student to give direction to this meeting. The student's response to prompt 7 in Figure 15-5 will be particularly helpful.

3. At the student-teacher conference, the two of you may wish to designate pieces of evidence that you would like to emphasize at the three-way conference. These should address areas of strength as well as need. The portfolio evidences can be marked with paper clips, sticky notes, or tabs.

4. You and the student may decide that part of the discussion should focus on the piece that he or she values the most. If so, you may wish to ask the student to write why he or she feels that way. You may then wish to write why you value that particular piece. When sharing this with the parents, you may also wish to ask them to write why they value it. This acknowledges the quality of the student's work and affirms that the student, the teacher, and the parents are all active participants in the assessment process.

5. Be sure to offer parents ideas about what they can do at home to encourage their child's positive attitude and progress.

6. At the conclusion of the three-way conference, you may wish to request a written record of the parents' reaction to the meeting. This can be returned to you via the student the next day. The commentary then becomes a part of the student's portfolio.

Parent Reactions to Portfolio Conferences

Thank you for taking an active role in your child's portfolio conference. Please respond to the following questions so we can continue to improve our assessment and evaluation processes.

1. What is your overall reaction to the portfolio process?

2. Do you feel the conference was beneficial?

3. Is there anything that wasn't included in this conference that you would like to see included in future meetings?

4. Additional comments:

Name_____ Date_____

Profiles are most often maintained electronically, but they can also be constructed in a more traditional format. For this purpose, the most common construct has been a 1-inch three-ring binder. As the binder opens, the reader sees the student's name, the subject areas, and the academic year(s) that the performance profile describes. This is followed by a contents page. Next, the student's in-depth reflection on the achievement of the standards and his or her future goals appears. After this, there is a series of dividers, one for each area of study. The standards for each academic area appear on the appropriate divider. In most performance profiles, for example, state standards for English, foreign language, mathematics, science, and social studies appear on five different dividers. Once the initial divider is turned, one sees the student's performances from that academic area. There is a performance included for each year the student studied the subject. Interdisciplinary performances are listed on the contents page as evidences for all appropriate content areas. Each performance is accompanied by the student's reflection, noting what he or she learned and how the student's work connected to the standards. Examples of science and foreign language segments of performance profiles follow.

Among the evidences in Diane Lane's Performance Profile are those from her high school science courses. They include a model she made for ninth-grade general science showing that light is a form of energy and an audiotape of her explaining how it works. Diane's tenth-grade performance is her research for her biology course on cystic fibrosis, a genetically transmitted disease. It incorporates the history of the disease and its treatment as well as a discussion of chromosomes. To represent chemistry, Diane selected her project contrasting kinetic, potential, and activation energy; this features slides of her presentation. For environmental science, Diane included a research and reaction paper on the use of antibiotics in animal feed.

Foreign language examples can be found in Kevin Gress' Performance Profile: Evidences begin with an exhibition about French culture that he created during his first year of studying French. A copy of his written report as well as photos of his presentation are included. Subsequent performances in the foreign language section of Kevin's profile are a group project focusing on everyday use of the French language from his second year of study and a group exhibition about Versailles, which was presented entirely in French, including an audiotaped tour, from his third year. The final evidence was an audiotape that contained three recordings of Kevin speaking French, one at the end of each year of study. Kevin's written reflections appeared prior to each evidence.

With recent technological developments, maintaining profiles electronically is remarkably easy. Students can use the computers to input their reflections; they can scan in their performances or transfer them from a disk; performances that incorporate software programs can easily be included; and a number of graphics programs provide the necessary formatting as well as additional enhancements. Of course, the great extra benefit of maintaining a profile on disk is the minimal amount of space required for storage.

Performance Profiles provide a dynamic overview of student performance, integrate student self-reflection, and relate student learning to state and district standards. In a time when standardized measures such as the Scholastic Achievement Test are still highly valued, Performance Profiles offer a performance-based view of student learning.

Reporting

Reports of student progress should also be standards based, directly correlating with the curriculum and course assessments. The reporting process is greatly facilitated and much more meaningful when curriculum, instruction, assessment, and reporting are aligned. The ultimate goal is to provide accurate, meaningful information about student progress.

If the reporting process is standards based, it should follow the same levels of performance as the course rubrics. For example, if the rubrics are based on a 4-point scale, then the reporting system should be as well. Students are then evaluated for multiple standards, with the final number representing a composite of the scores.

Once the standards and the scale are in place, levels of quality need to be developed. Marzano (1998) suggests that the 4 points should indicate "novice (1), basic (2), proficient (3) and advanced (4)" (p. 4). As shown in Figure 15-7, I often use *emerging* (1), *developing* (2), *proficient* (3), and *advanced* (4). Campbell-Hill and Ruptic (1994) offer a wider range of terms to accommodate students' development from the primary grades.

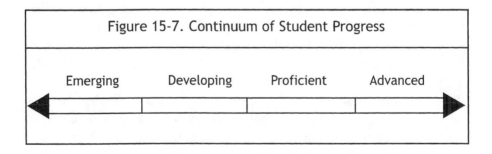

Figure 15-7. Continuum of Student Progress

Emerging   Developing   Proficient   Advanced

Using a continuum to record student progress accommodates tensions concerning accurate evaluation. When a student seems to be more than "developing" (2), but not quite "proficient" (3), the teacher can indicate this by marking the continuum in the "developing" section, but appropriately closer to "proficient." Further, the criteria that underpin each level of gradation are clearly defined for students, parents, and teachers. These innovations in reporting can also be managed electronically.

Both students and parents should be informed of reporting procedures at the start of the school year. This can be accomplished by sending a letter or newsletter home or by holding an open house at the school to share information and address parents' and students' questions and concerns. This facilitates students' and parents' understanding of the process, demonstrates consistency across grade levels, and helps to create a learning community.

Implementation Considerations

In the numerous districts in which I've assisted with the implementation of performance assessments, portfolios, and performance profiles, faculty members have consistently identified five topics that they believed facilitated the process. They are the following:

Administrative support. Teachers have found it essential to have administrators who support, understand, and enable the development of innovative assessments. This has often involved administrators' full participation in professional development programs.

Ongoing professional development. Teachers have deemed *communication with experts* as essential to their knowledge and understanding of contemporary practice. They have also identified *colleague interaction* as a frequently overlooked professional development resource that is essential to learning and contextualizing educational innovations. Professional conferences, professional publications, colleague observation, and innovation sampling are learning *opportunities* that the teachers believe provide connections between what they know and up-to-the-minute educational developments.

Time. Teachers need time to learn about innovative practices, share knowledge with colleagues and students, integrate innovations, conference with students and explore resulting outcomes. In addition, teachers need time to analyze and synthesize data provided by school or state mandated assessments (Angaran, 1999).

Communication with parents. Inviting parents to join the conversation has been recognized as a critical component of successful implementation. Developing newsletters and sponsoring community meetings are two effective ways to encourage parents to participate.

Transitioning students. Plans for transitioning students to the next grade, the next school building, or the university must be in place before the innovative assessment practice begins. This provides continuity for the students and allows teachers to view standards-based assessment as a progressive process.

Openly addressing these issues in the early stages of planning greatly facilitates implementation of innovative assessments. Discussions based on these topics also help to establish a sense of trust and confidence among participants.

Concluding Thoughts

Innovative assessment practices such as performances, portfolios, and performance profiles accommodate individual learning styles, relate learning to life experiences, incorporate educational standards, and value students' thinking. They offer windows into students' minds and insights into students' cognitive processes. Further, in student-centered learning contexts, these assessments support students' engagement in inquiry-based learning that is richly characterized by critical and creative thinking.

Integrating innovative assessments is a challenging, time-consuming task, but the rewards are plentiful. Some will ask if it's worth all the effort. Eisner (1999) offers a simple but eloquent affirmative response: "What's at stake is not only the quality of life our children might enjoy but also the quality of the culture that they will inhabit". (p. 660)

References

Anderson, R. C. (1994). Role of reader's schema in comprehension, learning, and memory. In R. B. Ruddell, M. R. Ruddell, & H. Singer (Eds.), *Theoretical models and processes of reading* (4th ed., pp. 469–482). Newark, DE: International Reading Association.

Angaran, J. (1999). Reflection in an age of assessment. *Educational Leadership, 56* (6), 71–72.

Arter, J. (1996). *Assessing student performance: A professional inquiry kit.* Alexandria, VA: Association for Supervision and Curriculum Development.

Brandt, R. (1991). Time for reflection. *Educational Leadership, 48* (6), 3.

Brooks, J. G., & Brooks, M. G. (1993). *In search of understanding: The case for constructivist classrooms.* Alexandria, VA: Association for Supervision and Curriculum Development.

Campbell-Hill, B. C., & Ruptic, C. (1994). *Practical aspects of authentic assessment: Putting the pieces together.* Norwood, MA: Christopher-Gordon.

Clinchy, E. (1995). Learning in and about the real world: Recontextualizing public schooling. *Phi Delta Kappan, 76* (5), 400–404.

Darling-Hammond, L. (1993, November). *National Association of Secondary School Principals Bulletin*, pp. 18–26.

Eisner, E. (1999). The uses and limits of performance assessment. *Phi Delta Kappan, 80* (9), 658–660.

Ferrara, S., & McTighe, J. (1992). A process for planning: More thoughtful classroom assessment. In A. Costa, J. Bellanca, & R. Fogarty (Eds.), *If minds matter: A forward to the future* (Vol. 2). Palantine, IL: Skylight.

Goodrich, H. (1996–1997). Understanding rubrics. *Educational Leadership, 54* (4), 14–17.

Gordon, C. J., & MacInnis, D. (1993). Using journals as a window on students' thinking in mathematics. *Language Arts, 70*, 37–43.

Haertel, E. H. (1999). Performance assessment and educational reform. *Phi Delta Kappan, 80* (9), 662–666.

Hiebert, E. (1994). Becoming literate through authentic tasks: Evidence and adaptations. In R. B. Ruddell, M. R. Ruddell, & H. Singer (Eds.), *Theoretical models and processes of reading* (4th ed.). Newark, DE: International Reading Association.

Lewin, L., & Shoemaker, B. J. (1998). *Great performances: Creating classroom-based assessment tasks*. Alexandria, VA: Association for Supervision and Curriculum Development.

Mabry, L. (1999). Writing to the rubric: Lingering effects of traditional standardized testing on direct writing assessment. *Phi Delta Kappan, 80* (9), 673–679.

Madaus, G. F., & O'Dwyer, L. M. (1999). A short history of performance assessment. *Phi Delta Kappan, 80* (9), 688–695.

Mann, L. (1998). Matching assessment with curriculum. *Association for Supervision and Curriculum Education Update, 40*, (4), 1, 4–5.

Marzano, R. (1998). Advances in grading. *Association for Supervision and Curriculum Education Update, 40* (8), 4.

McLaughlin, M. (1995). *Performance assessment: A practical guide to implementation*. Boston: Houghton Mifflin.

McLaughlin, M., & Kennedy, A. (1993). A classroom guide to performance-based assessment. Princeton, NJ: Houghton Mifflin.

McLaughlin, M., & Vogt, M. E. (1996). *Portfolios in teacher education*. Newark, DE: International Reading Association.

McLaughlin, M., & Vogt, M. E. (1998). Portfolio assessment for inservice teachers: A collaborative model. In M. McLaughlin, M. E. Vogt, J. Anderson, J. DuMez, M. G. Peter, & A. Hunter, *Professional portfolio models: Applications across the profession*. Norwood, MA: Christopher-Gordon.

Mid-Continent Regional Educational Laboratory. (1999). *Taking stock of states' curriculum-based reform efforts*. Aurora, CO: Author.

Rasmussen, K. (1999, Fall). Social studies: A laboratory for democracy. *Curriculum Update*. Alexandria, VA: Association for Supervision and Curriculum Development.

Schmoker, M., & Marzano, R. J. (1999). Realizing the promise of standards-based education. *Educational Leadership, 56* (6), 17–21.

Schon, D. (1987). *Educating the reflective practitioner*. San Francisco: Jossey-Bass.

Strong, R., Silver, H., & Perini, M. (1999). Keeping it simple and deep. *Educational Leadership, 56* (6), 22–24.

Valencia, S. W. (1998). *Literacy portfolios in action*. Fort Worth, TX: Harcourt Brace.

Vygotsky, L. S. (1987). The development of scientific concepts in childhood. In R. W. Rieber & A. S. Carton (Eds.), *The collected works of L. S. Vygotsky* (Vol.1) New York: Plenum.

Wiggins, G., & McTighe, J. (1998). *Understanding by design*. Alexandria, VA: Association for Supervision and Curriculum Development.

Willis, S. (1996). Student exhibitions put higher-order skills to the test. Association for Supervision and Curriculum *Education Update, 38* (2), 1, 3.

Zemelman, S., Daniels, H., & Hyde, A. (1998). *Best practice: New standards for teaching and learning in America's schools* (2nd ed.). Portsmouth, NH: Heinemann.

Chapter 16

Content Learning for Students Needing Modifications: An Issue of Access

MaryEllen Vogt

"Mrs. Vogt, I read the papers for homework. I really did. I just don't know what they said…" George, one of my favorite middle school students, stood in front of me with his copy of the Constitution homework pages in his hand. His head bowed, I thought he was going to start crying, but there were too many students in plain sight for him to break down in front of them. He swallowed, handed me his uncompleted homework assignment, and returned to his seat. I can still picture him standing there. It's a painful memory. Here was a student who was highly motivated, very bright, conscientious, and basically a nonreader. A homeschooled student until seventh grade, he had wonderfully supportive parents and a rich background of learning experiences, including museums, travel, real-world learning, and hundreds of books. Still, he hadn't learned to read and write and he had to pass a test on the U.S. Constitution.

My job, as the school reading specialist, special education teacher, and social studies teacher for the lowest performing eighth graders, was to make sure that all of them passed the required eighth-grade test on the Constitution. If they didn't pass, they couldn't graduate and go on to high school. It was as simple as that.

Throughout that year and several following years, I was faced with the issue of accessibility to content. Access was by no means equitable for all students in the middle school. For the proficient readers in the eighth grade, this test was a snap. For my group, however, which included English language learners (ELLs) as well as students with reading difficulties and learning disabilities, this exam represented an insurmountable hurdle. Frankly, the first year that I taught these students and was faced with ensuring their graduation from middle school, I was no more confident than they were that any of us was going to be successful. Here I was, trying to teach difficult and complex content concepts to students who lacked the reading, study, and language skills required to successfully pass a rigorous, required written examination on the U.S. Constitution. What could I do to make this work?

In this chapter, I will explore content instruction and its accessibility for students needing modifications, including those who are low achievers and those who are ELLs. I begin by describing how we have traditionally (and mostly unsuccessfully) tried to meet the academic needs of low achievers and ELLs. I then offer specific methods and approaches for modifying content instruction, including sheltered instruction, text adaptation, SQP2RS (an instructional framework for teaching content), alternative reading options, suggestions for implementing flexible grouping, and Jumpstarting, an approach to preparing students for content learning prior to a whole-class or small-group lesson. Equity, and how to attain it for all students, is a central focus of this chapter.

Background on Students Traditionally Labeled as "Low-Achieving"

For many teachers and students, the issue of accessibility to content information and to instructional materials is of prime concern. After World War II, the concept of *readability* was widely promoted in an attempt to provide students with content texts they could read comfortably. Readability formulas were developed, and over the years textbooks were written in various content areas, particularly language arts and social studies, with carefully controlled vocabulary intended to provide students with access. Most readability formulas were created to measure sentence length and word length to determine the difficulty level of the text. It was generally believed that the longer the sentences and words, the more difficult the text. In an attempt to reduce the reading demands of texts, shorter sentences were written and longer words (more than five letters, usually) were eliminated. Although the texts were indeed easier to read, the content information was also considerably reduced; thus students who had difficulty reading were denied access to the same content as their more proficient-reader peers.

Readability formulas (for a complete discussion see Ruddell, 1997; Tompkins, 1997; Vacca & Vacca, 1999) are still helpful for content area teachers in that they provide a quick assessment of a text's difficulty. However, they should be used only with caution. Frequent repetition of key vocabulary (e.g. *photosynthesis*) may artificially inflate a readability score for a particular text. Also, readability measures do not consider issues such as students' background knowledge or the complexity of ideas and concepts within a given text. Therefore, the notion of text difficulty depends on other factors than just sentence and word length.

In addition to the use of controlled content text, over the years students with reading problems were also tracked, especially in middle and secondary schools, into "special" content area classes with students of similar ability. The belief was that tracking would benefit the students, because the content materials (such as textbooks) would all be easier to read and the teacher could better meet students' needs by teaching to their "own levels." Most often this resulted in watered-down content, reduced to a commensurate level of the students' reading ability. Once again, as with the controlled text, the gap in content knowledge between the high-achieving and low-achieving students increased exponentially (Stanovich, 1986). The tracked students' interest in school waned, and ability grouping ultimately denied them access, intellectually, academically, and emotionally (Allington & Walmsley, 1995; Vogt, 1989).

Clearly, instructional materials and class placements have impacted students' access to content. However, teaching approaches for high-achieving and low-achieving students have also been found to differ substantially. With the higher achieving students we tend to do the following (Vogt, 1989):

- Talk less and encourage more interactions between the students themselves
- Use less structured teaching
- Frequently include creative and generative approaches to teaching
- Ask higher level questions and allow more wait time after questioning
- Cover more material and spend more time on instruction
- Provide more opportunities for leadership and independent research
- Have warmer and more personal relationships with the students
- Hold higher expectations for students' success
- Praise students for "good thinking" with frequent elaboration of their responses
- Use a greater variety of instructional materials
- Spend little time on behavior and classroom management

The list goes on. Just state each of these as opposites and you'll quickly see how inequitable instruction has been for low-achieving students. While teaching low-achieving students, teachers have been found to do the following:

- Talk more, with fewer opportunities for students to interact with each other
- Use more structured teaching with fewer creative and generative methods
- Ask primarily literal questions
- Allow less wait time after questioning with little elaboration of student responses
- Cover less material and content
- Spend more time on behavior and management concerns
- Provide few or no opportunities for leadership and independent research
- Have less congenial relationships with the students, primarily because of behavior and management issues
- Hold lower expectations for students' success
- Praise students for "trying hard" rather than for "good thinking" and successful endeavors
- Use fewer and lower levels of instructional materials
- Spend twice as much time on behavior and management issues

It is obvious from years of research on the harmful effects of tracked instruction in content areas that the practice has had deleterious effects on students, both socially and academically. The practice of tracking has also clearly differentiated students across socioeconomic and ethnic lines and has promoted differentiated expectations for students' success in the minds of teachers, parents, and even in the students themselves.

At present, in many schools throughout the United States, students identified as "low achieving" have been integrated into heterogeneous content classes as tracking practices have been recognized as ineffective. These students include low performers, special education students (e.g., learning disabled), Title I students, and often ELLs. However, this move to inclusion has brought the problem of access to the forefront once again. Teachers must contend with such a wide range of student abilities and reading proficiencies that content teaching becomes very problematic. If grade-level text is used, how do students with poor reading abilities cope with it? If grade-level standards for content knowledge are implemented, how do students with huge gaps in their background knowledge and experiences succeed? How do teachers meet the academic needs of gifted and talented students who need (and deserve) appropriate, challenging instruction in content areas when there are many students in the same class who need substantial support and assistance?

Background on Students Identified as Limited English Proficient

As mentioned above, ELLs are also frequently grouped with low-achieving native English speakers for content instruction. During the 1980s–1990s, an influx of immigrant children and adolescents entered the public schools in the United States, with more than 90% of recent immigrants coming from non-English-speaking countries. From 1986–1995, the number of limited English proficient (LEP) students in schools grew 109%, and in 1994–1995, more than 3.1 million school-age children were identified as LEP, approximately 7.3% of the K–12 public school population in the United States (Echevarria, Vogt, & Short, 2000). By the year 2050, it is estimated that Hispanics will represent 30% of the country's total pre-K–12 school population (Waggoner, 1999).

While the number of students with limited English proficiency continues to grow, the academic achievement of these students consistently and significantly lags behind their native English-speaking peers. Moss & Puma (1995) reported in a congressionally mandated study that ELLs with limited proficiency receive lower grades, score below their peers on standardized tests, and are perceived by their teachers as having lower academic abilities. Furthermore, LEP students have higher school dropout rates, they are placed more frequently in low-track (lower ability) groups for content instruction (Bennici & Strang, 1995; Cummins, 1994), and it is more likely that their content teachers will be teaching subjects for which they hold inadequate or no certification (Vogt, 1989).

As stated previously in this book, there is a growing demand in the United States for the implementation of content standards that all students are expected to meet, at each grade level and for graduation from high school. At the same time, there is serious and at times contentious debate among educators, researchers, and politicians about the benefits of bilingual education, in which ELLs receive content instruction in their native language while they are learning English. In at least one state (California), voters overturned legislation providing for bilingual education for LEP students. Thousands of ELLs are now receiving little or no primary-language (L1) instruction in the content areas. It remains to be seen how well these students will do. Many educators are greatly concerned that learning English at the same time that one is trying to learn history, math, and science (all taught in English) may further increase the gap in achievement for students with limited English proficiency (Short, 1999).

Another concern is that there seems to be a misconception that all ELLs are alike and that their educational needs are similar (Echevarria & Graves, 1998). However, students come to U.S. schools with a wide range of language proficiencies (in English as well as in approximately 180 native languages), reading proficiencies (again in L1 and L2), age of arrival, socio-economic levels, backgrounds, and life experiences. All of these impact the kind of educational and instructional decisions that educators need to make in order to ensure these students succeed in school (Echevarria, Vogt, & Short, 2000; Gunderson, 1991; Jimenez, Garcia, & Pearson, 1996; Peregoy & Boyle, 1997).

For example, some students arrive in U.S. schools with strong academic backgrounds and highly proficient language skills in their native language and perhaps in other languages as well. These students need intensive English language development so they can transfer their content knowledge, well-developed study skills and habits, and background knowledge to the content classes they are taking in the United States. At the other end of the continuum are students who have poor or nonexistent literacy skills in their native language, little or no academic schooling, and background experiences that may be irrelevant to "doing school" in the United States. Obviously, these students must learn not only English but also significant amounts of content information if they are going to be successful. Other students have grown up in the United States and are fluent in a language other than English, but they are illiterate in both their L1 and in English (Echevarria & Graves, 1998). In urban areas of California, for example, there are many students who have in been in school for years, but they have not learned to read and write well in either of their spoken languages (Echevarria, Vogt, & Short, 2000).

Again we find great variation in these students' needs. How can these ELLs be expected to master content from grade-level textbooks written in English? How do we measure an ELL's content knowledge when it is at or above grade-level if the student is tested in his or her native language? Does the student meet the content standard, or fail it because of her limited English proficiency? How does a content area teacher meet the needs of these deserving students while trying to provide appropriate content instruction for all the other students in the class?

Improving Instruction for Students Needing Modifications

Before I begin to recommend some ways that we can provide meaningful and appropriate content instruction for students needing instructional modifications, I must make an important distinction. These are not "special needs" students; most have no learning disabilities, nor are they "slow" learners (Allington & Walmsley, 1995). I'm using the phrase "students needing modifications" because most of these students can be successful in content classes if they receive modified instruction.

For example, think for a moment about a time when you learned a new language. If you were expected to succeed in content area classrooms where the spoken language was the new one you were learning, would you have had difficulty? What would have made the content more accessible to you? Would you have needed information "watered down," or would you have needed for someone to make it understandable and accessible for you? I suspect that the latter is true for most of us.

In the section that follows, you will find some suggestions for providing better access to content for struggling readers and ELLs. Each of these is congruent with the creative activities and innovative approaches recommended in this book; that is, these wonderfully creative ideas can be used successfully with all kinds of students. But, you may find that in order to provide them with access to the content, some modifications in your teaching, such as those suggested below, are necessary in order for the creative activities to provide successful learning experiences.

Sheltered Instruction

Sheltered instruction (SI) is an approach to teaching ELLs that is also appropriate for students who have difficulty learning content (Echevarria & Graves, 1998). The approach, also referred to as Specially Designed Academic Instruction in English (SDAIE), has been developed over the years by English as a Second Language teachers, content area teachers, and bilingual specialists. It provides additional language support for ELLs while they are learning content information. This approach is not just an "add-on" or a list of techniques; rather, SI utilizes and complements sound instructional methods and strategies widely recommended for both L2 and mainstream classrooms (for a full discussion of an SI model, see Echevarria, Vogt, & Short, 2000).

SI most often occurs in content classrooms where native English speakers and ELLs are heterogeneously mixed with ELLs who have an intermediate level of English fluency. All content instruction is delivered in English but the teacher incorporates methods of teaching that have been found to be highly effective in supporting ELLs' development at the same time that the content is being learned.

As an example, for ELLs to become successful in learning content, they need to learn not only English grammar and vocabulary but also the "language of school." Some classroom routines that are familiar to native English speakers may be confusing to ELLs. Therefore, you may find it helpful to clearly and simply describe any instructions you expect to give to students, such as "discuss," "share with a partner," "exchange papers," "read with a buddy," "take turns," and "debate." Effective SI teachers anticipate before a lesson occurs which terms and procedures may need additional explanation and modeling for students acquiring English.

How these processes are used in relation to the content requires another level of knowledge—key content concepts and vocabulary also need to be carefully explained, repeated, and modeled for ELL. What we have learned from these students is that they need assistance with all three knowledge bases: knowledge of English, knowledge of the content topic, and knowledge of how tasks are to be completed. Together, these are the key components of academic literacy. Note that this type of teaching is also effective for low-performing students and is consistent with effective mainstream instruction in which teachers provide authentic opportunities for students to practice their academic skills (Adamson, 1990; Chamot & O'Malley, 1994; O'Malley & Pierce, 1996; Short, 1994).

Within a constructivist perspective, SI incorporates a wide variety of methods for scaffolding students' understandings and content learning. Vygotsky (1978) and Bruner (1978) suggested that students' language development is fostered through social interactions and opportunities to work with individuals who have more experience. The term *scaffolding* refers to the gradual release of the more experienced person's support until the student can accomplish a task independently. Within a classroom, scaffolding may involve grouping students for completing tasks, encouraging partners to read texts together, careful modeling and demonstration, and repetition of key points. It is important that teachers recognize when students may need additional support and assistance, when the support may be lessened, and when students are able to complete tasks independently.

For students with limited English proficiency, SI teachers can also scaffold support by adjusting their speech, paraphrasing, giving clear examples, providing analogies, and building upon students' responses. Teaching vocabulary, providing models of how to organize a written paper, and using graphic organizers to help structure complex information are all examples of how a teacher might provide scaffolding for students needing modification. You can see that what will be helpful to the ELL will most likely also be advantageous for the low-performing student.

Additional elements of effective SI include the following (Echevarria, Vogt, & Short, 2000):
- Content and language objectives are clearly defined, written (on the board or overhead), and presented orally.
- Appropriate grade-level content concepts—not "watered down" concepts or those for lower grades—are taught.
- Supplementary materials are used regularly (e.g., models, visuals).
- Activities are meaningful (not just silent seat-work), and they integrate content concepts.

- Content concepts are explicitly related to students' background knowledge and experiences.
- Key vocabulary is introduced, written, integrated into lessons, and reviewed frequently throughout the lessons.
- The teacher's speech is appropriate, and explanations of tasks are clear.
- A variety of techniques is used to clarify content (e.g., modeling, visuals, demonstrations, hands-on activities).
- A variety of grouping configurations (partners, small groups, whole class) occurs throughout the lessons.
- Techniques are used to elicit higher order thinking (e.g., questioning, strategy instruction, discussion, reciprocal teaching).
- Frequent student-student and student-teacher interactions take place.
- Reading, writing, listening, and speaking opportunities are frequent and integrated throughout lessons.
- Lessons are highly engaging and students are on task.
- Pacing of lessons is appropriate for students' language and skills proficiency.
- Assessments are authentic and ongoing throughout lessons (e.g., frequent checking for understanding).
- Key concepts and vocabulary are frequently referred to and reviewed.

Although all of these elements are considered to be components of effective teaching, they are of critical importance for ELLs and those who find content learning to be difficult. You can see how any and all of these can be infused into the many creative and innovative ideas presented in the other chapters of this book.

Making Content Text Accessible

Finding suitable texts for students needing modification is a continual challenge for content teachers. Grade-level textbooks generally contain the critical key content concepts necessary for students to meet standards; however, the books are often dense, difficult to read, sometimes uninteresting, and often, at least for ELLs, they contain few links to students' prior knowledge and background experiences. Clearly it is ineffective to just assign pages for homework and expect students to master the content. However, carefully written study guides with marginal notes that point out important information on particular pages, define key vocabulary, and summarize individual sections of text can be very helpful. These can be time-consuming to write, but once written they last the lifetime of the textbook. However, for some students, the study guides themselves are difficult to read and follow, and these students need even more structured support.

One way to provide this is to set aside a number of textbooks for students needing modification. With a highlighter pen, mark the most important information in the text chapters. This may include key vocabulary, key concepts, important people, dates, and topic sentences. Students with reading difficulties and ELLs can be held responsible for knowing all the highlighted information—all the critical concepts reflected in the content standards. Highlighted text does not preclude the need to *teach* the content, nor does it eliminate the need to teach key vocabulary. However, it does reduce the "reading load" of the text, therefore letting students focus primarily on what is important rather than bogging them down in extraneous information. Once again, the initial highlighting may be time-consuming, but once done, a parent volunteer or student aide (middle or high school) can highlight the remaining books to be used with the students needing modification. If some students feel uncomfortable using the highlighted text during class time, these can be checked out for at-home use.

Another way to increase textbook accessibility is to audiotape summaries of each chapter. Note that the entire chapter is not audiotaped—it could be, but there is much information in each chapter that is extraneous, though interesting. Therefore, providing students with taped summaries—probably more expanded than the ones provided in the textbook, will enable students with special needs to access the critical information. Time to audiotape may be a factor, but since the purpose here is access, the time is well spent.

Finally, it is always possible to rewrite textbook information at a much lower reading level; however, this has been done in the past with poor results. Reducing the reading level inevitably also requires that a great deal of content information be omitted. (Once my district responsibilities required that I rewrite the seventh-grade social studies curriculum so that students reading at the second- and third-grade levels could read it. Try to imagine information on ancient Sumeria written at the second-grade level—we got the reading level right but lost a great deal of information about Sumeria in the process!) This is also very time-consuming. It's better to try some of the other ideas suggested here first, including finding alternative texts on the same topic, such as magazines or information from the Internet. The main point is to resist the temptation to convey all the key concepts orally through lecture. These students, especially the ELLs, will never meet the content standards this way, and they also need practice with reading, writing, and talking about all the important key content concepts.

SQP2RS: Survey, Question, Predict, Read, Respond, Summarize

SQP2RS is an instructional framework for teaching content material that I based loosely upon the well-known SQ3R—Survey, Question, Read, Recite, Review (Ruddell, 1997; Vacca & Vacca, 1999). Rather than being a study skills technique for students to use while they're independently reading content text, SQP2RS represents an instructional framework for teaching content text material to all students, including those needing modifications. It reinforces the major comprehension strategies that highly proficient readers use (Dole, Brown, & Trathen, 1996; Dole, Duffy, Roehler, & Pearson, 1991; Keene & Zimmerman, 1997; Vogt & Verga, 1998). These strategies are essentially ways that effective readers think about text, and when we teach and reinforce them in all the content areas that involve reading, we are teaching students to "think like readers." We are also acknowledging that "just because students can't read doesn't mean they can't think." I would also add, "Just because students are acquiring English doesn't mean they can't think." When we teach and reinforce these thinking strategies through a structured format, students are better able to comprehend and retain content material.

The major comprehension strategies that proficient readers use in an interchangeable, integrated, and recurring manner include the following:
- Predicting and making inferences about subsequent events and outcomes
- Self-questioning to guide reading
- Monitoring and clarifying understanding by adapting strategies during reading
- Evaluating and determining what is described as author-based importance
- Summarizing and synthesizing important ideas and creating a coherent text

Note that these are not the only strategies used by effective readers, but these have been identified in the research literature (Dole et al., 1991) because (a) they distinguish between proficient and beginning or struggling readers (proficient readers use them and beginning or struggling readers don't), (b) proficient readers use them in nearly all kinds of text, (c) they can be taught, and (d) they transfer. That is, the more we teach, reinforce, and provide students with practice in using these strategies while they read, the more strategic and proficient they become (Vogt & Verga, 1998). All students, regardless of reading or language proficiency, can learn, practice, and use these strategies.

Steps of SQP2RS

SQP2RS is most effective when teaching students how to read expository text (e.g., chapters found in content textbooks) and informational text (e.g., articles found in newspapers, magazines, and on the Internet). The six steps of the process are described below:

1. *Survey.* The purpose of this step is to help students activate and utilize their background knowledge and experience about the topic and to "set the stage" for what's to come. Prior to beginning the reading of a chapter or an article, have students silently and independently survey the text. The first time you introduce the survey process, model it with a transparency made from the text material you'll be using. Incorporate a "think-aloud" (Bauman, Jones, & Seifert-Kessel, 1993) to model what you look for when you're trying to gain information quickly and succinctly, and talk through what you think is important to note. Allow students approximately 60–90 seconds to survey, depending on the age of the students. If the text is lengthy, have students survey only one section at a time. Keeping to the time limit is very important; you want the students to quickly assess what the text is about, not to begin reading.

2. *Question.* The purpose of this step is to engage students in formulating questions about the text. This is different from K-W-L (see chapter 9, 10, and 11). Here you ask students to generate questions they think will be answered by reading the text, rather than asking them what they want to know or are wondering about. These questions are directly related to the text they have just surveyed and should be ones they cannot answer. I usually say, "Write two or three questions that you can't answer now but that you think you'll find the answers to after reading this [article, chapter, section of chapter]." Model this step carefully the first time through the process. Work as a whole class and list questions on the board.

After you have used SQP2RS several times, you can have students generate questions with partners or groups (not independently, as discussion is important and beneficial). When the groups have each written several questions (they can look through the text for support), list them on the board, identifying with an asterisk any that have been generated by more than one group. These are deemed important because several groups have thought of them. You will find that at first the questions will be on a literal level; as students gain proficiency in self-questioning, their questions will begin to involve higher levels of thinking. The self-questioning step in the process should take no more than 5–7 minutes.

3. *Predict.* This step builds upon the questions that have been generated. Based upon them, ask students to predict two or three things they think they will learn as a result of reading this text. Use all the questions on the board as a guide, and narrow down to only the most important concepts. These predictions will guide the students' reading. Once again, it is important to model how to make predictions based on highlighted or boldface

headings in the text, the questions that have been generated, and even the questions that appear at the end of the chapter. Remember that the purpose here is to end up with two or three statements, such as "In this chapter, we will learn where gold was first discovered in California. We will learn who first discovered the gold. We will learn why the Gold Rush began." Obviously, with older students a compound sentence containing several predictions can be written. You may find that the predictions restate some of the questions; this is fine. Predicting and questioning are integrated thinking processes, so it is expected that there will be a relationship between them. The step should take about 3–5 minutes only.

4. *Read.* This step can be taken in any number of ways: independently, with partners or in groups, as a shared reading, or as a read-aloud by the teacher (see "Alternative Reading Options" below for other ideas). It is important to remember that if the text is long and difficult, it should be broken into smaller sections with the SQP2RS process repeated several times if necessary. Highlighted text may also benefit students needing modifications.

5. *Respond.* The purpose of this step is to review the questions that were previously generated to see if answers were found during the reading and to determine which predictions were confirmed or disconfirmed during the reading. It is important to discuss any questions that were not answered in the text and to contemplate which questions were answered and which were not, and why. I ask students the following: "Might we find answers to some of the questions in the next section of the text? In another chapter? Did the author take us in a different direction than we originally thought? Are there other questions that should be generated at this time for the next section of the text [or chapter]? Are there any questions we need to eliminate because it's clear the author is not going to be dealing with them? Are there any questions listed here that we could find answers to through our own research? Do you want to add any questions at this point?" This is intended to be a time of discussion, not of requiring students to write answers to the generated questions.

6. *Summarize.* At this point in the process, all students should be able to summarize the key content concepts introduced and explained in the text. Of course, the length and complexity of the summary depends on the students' abilities, language proficiencies, and grade level, but it is not unreasonable to expect a few sentences from everyone. I recommend that students collaborate on their summaries after they have written an initial draft independently. It may be helpful, if you have a group of students who need extensive modifications, to write key vocabulary on the board to help them incorporate these into their summaries. Once again, model the summarizing process so that you don't receive a "retelling" rather than a sum-

mary. Students might keep these brief summaries in one place, such as a journal or notebook, for later review and study. You can also collect the summaries if you wish.

As you were reading about SQP2RS, you may have noticed that the major comprehension strategies are all reinforced and practiced throughout the lesson. There is a great deal of scaffolding, thus providing success for students. You also may have thought, "If I do this every day, we'll only be on chapter 3 by March." Obviously you can't go through this process on a daily basis, but if you have students who need modifications or those who are just beginning to read complex content text (third grade and above), using SQP2RS periodically (once a week or so) may provide students' with the instruction, reinforcement, and support that they need. It also provides additional practice for students who are proficient readers but who tend to not read their text because they can "get by" without doing so.

For these students, also use SQP2RS, but select a very challenging text that will promote practice with the comprehension strategies. Often your best readers do not have to engage their thinking strategies because the texts are so easy for them to read. Challenge them occasionally to work through more difficult text by generating questions, predictions, and thoughtful summaries. Often these students need modifications, too, but for entirely different reasons than the students we have been discussing.

Alternative Reading Options

Frequently, during content area lessons where the entire class is reading the same text material, such as a textbook chapter, teachers find that one way to "get through" the text is by asking for student volunteers to read. Inevitably, one of the poorer readers enjoys this read-aloud time and volunteers eagerly. Most often, though, the best oral readers' hands fly up to take their turns, and the students who struggle to read just hope to make it through the period without having to embarrass themselves by reading aloud in front of their peers. If you remember back to when you were in elementary or middle school (or even high school, perhaps), you'll recall that the teacher had students read aloud "down the row," one student at a time. You may also recall that during this time you were frantically counting paragraphs in an attempt to have some time to "practice" before the teacher called on you to read. Did you ever count paragraphs incorrectly and practice the wrong one? I did, and then, all flustered, I had to make it through my paragraph "cold."

Or you may recall that the teacher "roamed," calling on unsuspecting students or asking for an occasional volunteer. If you were a good reader you were probably reading ahead in the chapter. If you were a poor reader, you were probably doing what other struggling readers have done in the past (it's been documented). You avoided eye contact with the teacher, you "forgot" your book that day, you seated yourself far away from the teacher, or (more seriously) you developed stomach problems, including ulcers, or other emotional reactions to the embarrassment of being a poor oral reader. I once heard Roach Van Allen, the "father" of the Language Experience Approach, state, "There's nothing so poor as some poor teacher listening to a poor group of poor readers read poorly." So, how do we get a group of students "through" complex text material?

First, we need to acknowledge that not every word of every chapter has to be read by every student. That doesn't mean that it's okay to skip the textbook entirely, because students do need to learn how to read textbooks, and they need to practice with actual textbook reading. It does mean that we have some flexibility in regard to how much and with what methods the text is read. Some sections or chapters may be skipped, and we can use a variety of other resources (e.g., the Internet, magazines, newspapers, videos) or creative exploratory activities and hands-on experiences to teach the key content concepts.

While reading the textbook or other content material, we can use a variety of methods to engage students in reading the text, depending on grade level and reading fluency. These are described below.

Student Oral Reading. If you want to have an oral reading of some chosen text, ask for student volunteers, and before they begin reading give time for the volunteer readers to practice their assigned "parts" (5 minutes for a paragraph works well). Try to use oral reading primarily for two purposes: assessment (privately at your desk) and performance (students have the opportunity to practice first). The "practice first" policy will result in much more fluent oral reading.

Teacher-Student Shared Reading. You begin reading orally, students can join in orally (a group reading), or they can read the next section of text silently or with partners. You can do this throughout lengthy text, skipping sections that don't contain key concepts or vocabulary that students must know.

Equal Portions. With partners, students divide up the reading orally. Because this is not a "public" event, students can usually read with a partner without "practice first." However, it is best to try to match students; have your most proficient readers partner with good readers, your good readers partner with average readers, and so on. If you partner your best readers with those who have difficulties, both students may experience frustration.

Page, Paragraph, or Pass. In small groups, students read aloud to each other. Each reader may choose to read a page, a paragraph, or to pass. This is especially effective in classes with reluctant readers, but use it only occasionally so that students don't "pass" too often.

Chime-in Reading. After students have read text once (or you've read it to them) you can practice oral fluency with this option. You or another capable reader begin by orally reading the selected text while walking around the room. As you walk, tap the shoulder or desk of individual students, who then "chime in" and continue reading aloud with you until the text section is completed and many students have joined the read-aloud.

Dyad Reading. Working in pairs, students take turns silently or orally reading sections of text. After reading a section, the first student summarizes what was read, with the other student assisting and clarifying, if necessary. For the next section, the roles are reversed continuing this way until the chapter (or article) is completed. If students need modeling, do so through role-playing.

Group Reading. A given selection is divided into parts and read orally by the assigned groups, characters' parts (in narrative), or some repeating refrain in literature or poetry.

Self-Assisted Reading. Students read silently and list or mark difficult words or sections of the text by writing on and placing a small sticky note on concepts or vocabulary not understood. After everyone finishes the reading, students work in groups to help each other solve the reading problems and clarify confusing points. Intervene and assist as needed.

Silent Reading With Support. Students sit with partners or in small groups. Each student reads the selection silently but can turn to the other(s), as needed to get help with words or sections of the text that are hard to understand.

Flexible Grouping Options

Students who need modifications benefit from collaborative or cooperative learning experiences with other students (Flood, Lapp, Flood, & Nagel, 1992). Note that nearly all the creative and innovative activities and approaches recommended in this book involve partners and small groups. Providing a variety of grouping options scaffolds students, teaches them to work with others, and promotes social interaction, which is so necessary for learning.

As you decide on the grouping configurations you wish to implement, it may be helpful to think of two different types of groups: instructional groups and interactive groups. The types of configurations that fall within each of these categories is described as follows.

Instructional Groups

Guided Reading. The teacher works with a small group of students, guiding their reading through text with questions and assistance; also DR-

TA (see chapter 14) with a small group or whole class.

Discussion Circles. Students work in small groups, with close teacher supervision, to answer preset questions, practice discussion techniques, and share a common piece of text (see Vogt, 1996).

Acceleration Groups. The teacher works with high-achieving students who need scaffolding and instruction with more challenging text.

Reteach or Review Groups. The teacher works with students who need additional assistance with or review of material already taught.

Interest or Research Groups. Students, with teacher support, pursue topics of mutual interest through research and reading.

Whole Class. The teacher teaches the entire class the same lesson.

Interactive Groups

Interactive groups tend to be more informal, and students usually work primarily with each other rather than with the teacher. The teacher's role with interactive groups is more of a facilitator.

Partners or Triads. "Turn to your partner and. . . ." Or the teacher selects partners to work together based on reading and language proficiency or some other criterion.

Small Groups. Often these are table groups in classsrooms where students usually sit with their desks arranged together in groups of four or five. They frequently work together, although these may not be the same as cooperative learning groups.

Cooperative Learning Groups. These groups are organized heterogeneously. Students are taught social skills, group dynamics, and content through structured collaborative activities and projects (see Johnson & Johnson, 1986).

Jigsaw Groups. Jigsaw (Aronson, 1978) is a cooperative learning group activity in which individuals from a "home" group join with other students to form new "expert" groups. Their responsibility is to learn or read content material in order to become an expert in a particular topic or section of text read. The expert students then return to their home cooperative learning groups and teach what they've learned to other group members. Obviously, it's important to monitor both the home and expert groups to make sure that information is being conveyed correctly. For students needing modifications, it may be helpful to partner students for the expert-group work.

It's not enough to just put students in groups and hope they cooperate. Rather, you need to teach and reinforce appropriate behavior and participation when students are working in groups. Whether students are in the primary grades or in high school, their group work needs teacher monitoring and supervision. It's important to brainstorm with them the kind of behavior that is appropriate during group work (e.g., listening to each other, no "put-downs," making sure everyone participates). It's also wise to have available a variety of "independent routines" (Page, 1999) that students can engage in when you are working with other groups or when students complete assignments. These include such things as written conversations (corresponding with a peer about the content topic, with a focus on explaining processes, vocabulary, key concepts, etc.); independent research activities (e.g., investigating unanswered questions posed during SQP2RS); RAFT writing (from the perspective of someone other than the most obvious; see chapter 11); explorations of the Internet to further enhance and expand textbook information (see chapter 10). If groups aren't working, it's a management problem and something that you must address; it's probably not the activity or the approach that's the problem. Carefully forming groups and then monitoring how well they're working together can solve many management issues.

Forming Groups

When forming groups in content classrooms, consider the following:
- The purpose of the groups
- The difficulty of the text that will be used
- The academic strengths of your students
- Students' linguistic strengths and needs (in both L1 and L2)
- Students' leadership abilities
- Students' choices (give them three) of whom they want to work with
- Students' attendance (distributing students with poor attendance among the groups)

Also ask yourself the following questions as you plan for instruction that involves various groups:
- How difficult is the text?
- How much background knowledge do the students have on this topic?
- How much scaffolding will students need?
- How much explicit instruction do I need to provide?
- How much group practice is needed?
- How much independence do I expect?
- Who might benefit from modifications in instruction?
- Who might need additional review and support after the lesson?

There is a great deal of evidence that flexibly grouping students for content instruction is beneficial for them both academically and socially. Carefully planning for activities that your students will complete in groups and then effectively managing those groups is well worth the time and effort.

Jumpstarting Content Concepts

As a reading specialist and special educator, I used to spend a great deal of time reteaching students what they had not succeeded with in their "regular" groups and classrooms. It seemed as if I was always playing "catch up" with the same students, the ones who needed the remediation. They had so much difficulty learning the content in the first place, and it didn't seem that the reteaching did much good. Therefore, I decided to try a different approach. I began to preteach these students, or provide them with a "jumpstart." The purpose was very focused, to prepare them for the prereading phase of the content lesson. For example, while studying earthquakes, my lesson plans included brainstorming with the entire class everything the students knew about the topic. I determined ahead of time which students would have little background information to contribute, which ones would know few vocabulary words related to earthquakes, and which ones would need longer processing time because of their level of English proficiency. Prior to the lesson, I worked with these students for about ten minutes, providing them with a Jumpstart that was basically an introduction to earthquakes so they could contribute with the class when the lesson began. After conducting a ministudy on Jumpstarting with fourth graders, I found that the students who received this extra support (a) were able to retain content information longer, (b) participated more frequently with higher quality participation, (c) were more eager, positive, and involved, and (d) were less likely to go off task or "drop out" of the activity. Since that time, teachers have found Jumpstarting to be an effective instructional approach with all ages of students and in all content areas.

In order for Jumpstart activities to be successful, they should do the following:

- Prepare students who have difficulties with learning content to participate in the prereading activity that the entire class will ultimately engage in.
- Precede the prereading activity, especially if the reading selection contains difficult or unfamiliar concepts or vocabulary or if it requires considerable background information.
- Enable struggling readers or ELLs to have extended learning time and repetition of key concepts.
- Reinforce key vocabulary, even if it is to be introduced and taught to the entire class at a later time.
- Lead to student discovery and be interactive (not just "teacher-telling").
- Be taught by the teacher, not a parent volunteer or aide, because you are the one who knows what the lesson objectives are.

Typical Jumpstart Activities

Although any type of brief background-building activity can work well as a Jumpstart, I have found the following to be especially effective:

- A picture or text walk—surveying the chapter, looking at the illustrations, graphs, charts, and the boldface headings.
- A structured preview: The teacher takes a more structured "walk" through a text, using topic sentences, headings and subheadings, end-of-chapter questions, and so on, to give a clear picture of what the chapter or article is about.
- Listing questions students have, especially if you're doing a K-W-L or SQP2RS.
- Listing vocabulary that students predict they might encounter in the text (e.g., earthquake words they have heard or know).
- Briefly introducing new key vocabulary and/or concepts.
- Predicting three or four things that students think they might learn.
- Beginning a graphic organizer that will be completed later with small groups or with the whole class. This "sets the stage," refreshing students' memory about how to do the organizer or introducing the process if it's unfamiliar.
- An oral reading of part of the text, to introduce the style or text structure.
- A background "chat" about the topic, asking what students know.

Even though these are the same types of activities that you might use with the entire class in order to activate their prior knowledge and build background, the students needing modifications require more time and a greater exposure in order to prepare them to be successful. Essentially, Jumpstarting is just a minilesson that is intended to provide a "front-loading" of information that will be needed as the lesson develops. The rest of the class can be kept engaged with a meaningful quickwrite, partner prediction, a silent reading of related text, or whatever you need to have them do so that you can work with the small group. Jumpstarting works, but as with many other types of other activities, use it selectively—when text material is difficult or you're starting to teach about a new, complex topic for which some students lack appropriate background information or experience.

Concluding Thoughts

There are few things in a teacher's career that are more disheartening than watching a conscientious student struggle for access to the content that other students appear to learn almost effortlessly. I began this chapter by describing George's frustration with learning, with school, and with the

Constitution. About 3 years after I had him as a middle school student (yes, he did pass the test), I saw him in class at his high school. Not surprisingly, he had been placed in all low-track academic classes and he no longer received special education support. I was at the school to observe George's student teacher, and I was sitting in the back of the classroom when he entered. I barely recognized him as the student I had known. At first George didn't see me, and as I watched him I was immediately struck by how disengaged, uninterested, and unmotivated he appeared. It was as if the "lights had gone out." The eager learner I had known seemed to have given up on school, and the image he projected was not just that of a sullen adolescent, but of a student who was merely showing up and doing his time.

Seeing George that day reinforced my belief that access to content and to learning is a student's right, and providing it is a teacher's major responsibility. Engaging *all* students in the types of creative and innovative activities described in this book is possible. Students needing modification can be successful content learners. Our job as teachers is to make that happen.

References

Adamson, H. D. (1990). ESL students' use of academic skills in content courses. *English for Specific Purposes, 9,* 67–87.

Allington, R. L. O., & Walmsley, S. A. (1995). *No quick fix: Rethinking literacy in America's elementary schools.* Newark, DE: International Reading Association.

Aronson, E. (1978). *The jigsaw classroom.* Thousand Oaks, CA: Sage.

Baumann, J., Jones, L., & Seifert-Kessel, N. (1993). Using thing-alouds to enhance children's comprehension monitoring abilities. *Reading Teacher, 47* (3), 184–193.

Bennici, F. J. & Strang, E. W. (1995). *An analysis of language minority and limited English proficent students from NELS 1988.* Washington, DC: U.S. Department of Education.

Bruner, J. (1978). The role of dialogue in language acquisition. In A. Sinclair, R. Javella, & W. Levelt (Eds.), *The child's conception of language* (pp. 241–256). New York: Springer-Verlag.

Chamot, A. U., & O'Malley, J. M. (1994). *The CALLA Handbook: Implementing the cognitive academic language learning approach.* Reading, MA: Addison-Wesley.

Cummins, J. (1994). Knowledge, power and identity in teaching English as a second language. In F. Genesse (Ed.), *Educating second language children: The whole child, the whole curriculum, the whole community* (pp. 33–58). Cambridge, England: Cambridge University Press.

Dole, J. A., Brown, K. J., & Trathen, W. (1996). The effects of strategy instruction on the performance of at-risk students. *Reading Research Quarterly, 31* (1), 62–88.

Dole, J., Duffy, G., Roehler, L., & Pearson, P. D. (1991). Moving from the old to the new: Research on reading comprehension instruction. *Review of Educational Research, 61* (2), 239–264.

Echevarria, J., & Graves, A. (1998). *Sheltered content instruction: Teaching English-language learners with diverse abilities.* Needham Heights, MA: Allyn & Bacon.

Echevarria, J., Vogt, M. E., & Short, D. (2000). *Making content comprehensible for English language learners: The SIOP model.* Needham Heights, MA: Allyn & Bacon.

Flood, J., Lapp, D., Flood, S., & Nagel, G. (1992). Am I allowed to group? Using flexible patterns for effective instruction. *Reading Teacher, 45,* 608–616.

Gunderson, L. (1991). *ESL literacy instruction: A guidebook to theory and practice.* Englewood Cliffs, NJ: Regents/Prentice-Hall.

Jimenez, R. T., Garcia, G. E., & Pearson, P. D. (1996). The reading strategies of bilingual Latina/o students who are successful English readers: Opportunities and obstacles. *Reading Research Quarterly, 31* (1), 90–112.

Johnson, D. W., & Johnson, R. T. (1986). *Learning together and alone* (2nd Ed.). Englewood Cliffs, NJ: Prentice-Hall.

Keene, E. O., & Zimmerman, S. (1997). *Mosaic of thought: Teaching comprehension in a reader's workshop.* Portsmouth, NH: Heinemann.

Moss, M., & Puma, M. (1995). *Prospects: The congressionally mandated study of educational growth and opportunity.* Washington, DC: U.S. Department of Education.

O'Malley, J. M., & Pierce, L. V. (1996). *Authentic assessment for English-language learners: Practical approaches for teachers.* Reading, MA: Addison-Wesley.

Page, S. E. (1999). *Effective management strategies for literacy-centered classrooms.* Unpublished workshop handout, Marion Community Schools, Marion, IN.

Peregoy, S. F., & Boyle, O. F. (1997). *Reading, writing, and learning in ESL: A resource book for K–12 teachers (2nd ed.).* New York: Longman.

Ruddell, M. R. (1997). *Teaching content reading and writing (2nd ed.).* Boston: Allyn & Bacon.

Short, D. (1991). *How to integrate language and content instruction: A training manual.* Washington, DC: Center for Applied Linguistics.

Short, D. (1994). Expanding middle school horizons: Integrating language, culture and social studies. *TESOL Quarterly, 28* (3), 581–608.

Short, D. (1999). Integrating language and content for effective sheltered instruction programs. In C. Faltis & P. Wolfe (Eds.), *So much to say: Adolescents, bilingualism, and ESL in the secondary school* (pp.105–137). New York: Teachers College Press.

Stanovich, K. E. (1986). Matthew effects in reading: Some consequences of individual differences in the acquisition of literacy. *Reading Research Quarterly, 21,* 360–407.

Tompkins, G. E. (1997). *Literacy for the 21st century: A balanced approach.* Upper Saddle River, NJ: Merrill/Prentice-Hall.

Vacca, R., & Vacca, J. A. (1999). *Content area reading: Literacy and learning across the curriculum* (6th ed.). New York: Addison Wesley Longman.

Vogt, M. E. (1989). *The congruence between preservice teachers' and inservice teachers' attitudes and practices toward high and low achievers.* Unpublished doctoral dissertation, University of California, Berkeley.

Vogt, M. E. (1996). Creating a response-centered curriculum with literature discussion groups. In L. Gambrell & J. Almasi (Eds.), *Lively discussions! Creating classroom cultures that foster discussion, interpretation and comprehension of text.* Newark, DE: International Reading Association.

Vogt, M. E., & Verga, M. (1998). Improving comprehension: Developing strategic readers. In C. Cox (Ed.), *Current research in practice.* Los Angeles: County Educational Consortium for the Improvement of Reading.

Vygotsky, L. (1978). *Mind and society: The development of higher psychological processes* (M. Cole, V. John-Steiner, S. Scribner, & E. Souberman, Eds. and Trans.). Cambridge, MA: Harvard University Press.

Waggoner, D. (1999). Who are secondary newcomer and linguistically different youth? In C. Faltis & P. Wolfe (Eds.), *So much to say: Adolescents, bilingualism, and ESL in the secondary school* (pp.13–41). New York: Teachers College Press.

Author Index

Subject Index

About the Editors

Maureen McLaughlin

Maureen McLaughlin is a Professor of Education at East Stroudsburg University of Pennsylvania. She earned her doctorate at Boston University in Reading and Language Development. Prior to her tenure in the Pennsylvania State System of Higher Education, Maureen spent fifteen years as a classroom teacher, reading specialist, and department chair in a public school system. she is the author, co-author, and editor of numerous publications including *Mathematics Performance Assessment: A Practical Guide to Implementation, Portfolios in Teacher Education*, and *Professional Portfolios: Applications in Education*.

In addition, Maureen is chair of the National Reading Conference's Ethics Committee and a volunteer in the International Reading Association's Reading and Writing for Critical Thinking Project. She is a frequent speaker at international, national, and state conferences and is an educational consultant to school districts and universities nationwide.

MaryEllen Vogt

MaryEllen Vogt is a Professor of Education and coordinator of reading. programs at California State University, Long Beach where she teaches graduate courses in reading. Prior to the university, she served for 15 years as a classroom teacher, special education teacher, reading specialist, and district resource teacher. She received her doctorate in Language and Literacy from the University of California, Berkeley. MaryEllen is past president of the California Reading Association and served on the Board of the International Reading Association. She has authored and co-authored articles, chapters, and books, including *Portfolios in Teacher Education* and *Making Content Comprehensible for English Language Learners: The SIOP Model.* In 1997, MaryEllen was inducted into the California Reading Hall of Fame, and in 1999, she received her university's Distinguished Faculty Teaching Award.

About the Contributors

Thomas W. Bean

Thomas W. Bean is a Professor of Reading/Literacy and Coordinator of the doctoral program in the Department of Curriculum and Instruction at the University of Nevada, Las Vegas. His numerous research articles and book reviews have been published in the *Journal of Educational Research, Reading Research Quarterly, Journal of Adolescent* and *Adult Literacy,* and other journals in literacy. He recently authored a chapter entitled: "Reading in the Content Areas: Social Constructivist Dimensions" in the Handbook of *Reading Research, Volume 3,* and is co-author of *Content Area Literacy: An Integrated Approach,* now in its sixth edition. He teaches graduate seminars in literacy research, literacy issues for a diverse society, and content area literacy. His most recent research has focused on reader response to multicultural literature in secondary English classrooms.

Barbara Call

Barbara Call is a fifth-grade teacher at Belvidere Elementary School in Belvidere, New Jersey. During the 13 years she has been teaching, she has taught first, second, third, and fifth grades. Barbara is a graduate of East Stroudsburg University, where she is currently pursuing a Masters Degree in Reading Education. She has traveled to Russia to participate in a teacher exchange program through the Hands Across the Water and is a Teacher Consultant for the New Jersey Geographic Alliance. Barbara has given numerous presentations regarding Russian culture and education, and presented a program concerning the use of poetry in the content area instruction at the International Reading Association Annual Convention in 1998. Barbara and her husband, Terry, live in the rural village of Hope, New Jersey.

Rita J. Corbett

Rita J. Corbett has been actively involved in mathematics education for 30 years. Her experiences include elementary and secondary classroom teaching, educational consulting, authoring and editing of math programs and support materials. She currently provides staff development, curriculum implementation and professional workshops to school districts through the RJC Consulting Company.

Rita's areas of expertise include Visualizing Mathematical Concepts, Questioning and Communication in Mathematics Education, as well as Technology Inclusion in Mathematics Education. Her graduate and undergraduate work were completed at the University of Nebraska.

Frederick J. Fedorko

Frederick Fedorko is a Professor of Education at East Stroudsburg University of Pennsylvania. He attended Edinboro State College where he received a B.S. degree in Elementary and Special Education. He went on to receive an M.Ed. for Reading Specialists at the University of Buffalo, and a Ph.D. in Curriculum and Instruction: Reading at the University of Akron. His teaching experience includes work in grades 1–9, work as a reading specialist, and work as a special education teacher. He currently teaches undergraduate and graduate reading courses.

Aileen Kennedy

Aileen Kennedy has taught at the elementary and intermediate grade levels, served as a building level reading specialist, and was a lead teacher in a school for learning disabled children. A speaker at state and national conferences, Aileen is currently an assistant professor of education at Villa Julie College in Stevenson, Maryland. She is also a consultant to school districts across the country and a doctoral candidate at the University of Maryland.

Donald J. Leu

Donald J. Leu is Professor and Director of Graduate Programs in Reading Education at Syracuse University. He completed his graduate work at Harvard University and the University of California, Berkley. He is a leading authority on the use of the Internet technologies in school classrooms to support the "new literacies" as we prepare children for their literacy and learning futures. His most recent work on this topic appears in *Reading Research Quarterly* and *The Handbook of Reading Research*. He is the co-author of *Effective Literacy Instruction* (Merrill/Prentice Hall) and manages the RTEACHER mailing list (listserv) for *The Reading Teacher*. His most recent book (with Deborah Diadiun Leu) is *Teaching with the Internet: Lessons from the Classroom*. (Christopher-Gordon). His home page, with links to this and other publications, is located at: http://web.syr.edu/~djleu/home/home.html.

Carl A. Lisandrelli

Carl A. Lisandrelli has been teaching social studies for 25 years at the middle school level. He also serves as Social Studies Department Coordinator and is a member of the District Supervision Committee. He is part of a five-teacher team. He has served as a member of several NEIU #19 school evaluation committees. He graduated from East Stroudsburg University. He is active in social studies organizations.

Elaine Slivinski Lisandrelli

Elaine Slivinski Lisandrelli has been teaching seventh-grade English at the middle school level since 1973. She earned both her graduate and undergraduate degree from Marywood University. She is also an adjunct professor at Marywood University. She has conducted numerous in-service courses for teachers and has presented workshops at several writing conferences. She has co-authored several educational texts. She has also written biographies of Maya Angelou, Bob Dole, Ida B. Wells-Barnett, and Jack London for Enslow Publishers and a biography of Ignacy Jan Paderewski for Morgan Reynolds Publishers. She is a member of NCTE, IRA, and SCBWI. She lives in Pennsylvania with her husband, Carl.

Jesse C. Moore

Jesse C. Moore is a Professor of Education and Chairperson of the Reading Department at East Stroudsburg University of Pennsylvania. He did his graduate work at Lehigh University and taught reading and English at both the junior and senior high school levels. For many years, Jesse has taught graduate and undergraduate courses and conducted inservice workshops that focus on content area reading. He serves on many statewide committees in Pennsylvania including the Reading Assessment Advisory Committee and the Academic Standards Task Force. Jesse is a Past President of the Keystone State Reading Association, and currently he is involved in a Professional Development School Project for future secondary school, content area teachers.

Donna Ogle

Donna Ogle is a professor in the Reading and Language Department of National-Louis University in Evanston, IL. Her major work has been in strategic reading and staff development for instructional change. The K-W-L strategy, which she developed for expository reading and learning, is widely used throughout the world. Donna is active in professional leadership, having served on the Board of Directors of both the National Reading Conference and the International Reading Association. She has published widely in journals, been on several videotapes and teleconferences, and is co-author of *Strategic teaching and learning: cognitive instruction in the content areas.* Currently she is a coordinator for the Reading and Writing for Critical Thinking Project providing staff development for teacher educators in Russia and other former Soviet countries, directs a Goals 2000 Project in five Chicago high schools, and serves as a senior consultant for the National Urban Alliance.

Elizabeth Paugh

Elizabeth Paugh is a teacher at the Stroudsburg Intermediate School in Stroudsburg, Pennsylvania. Betsy is a former research fellow and administrative assistant for the Center for Teaching and Learning at East Stroudsburg University, where she recently earned her M.Ed. in Reading. She presented at the International Reading Association's Annual Meeting in 1998 on the topic of poetry in the content areas.

Linda Poorman

Linda Poorman serves as a teacher on special assignment in the Colonial School District in New Castle County, Delaware. In this capacity she works with teachers and administration in grades K–12 on a wide variety of topics related to the implementation of standards-based instruction/assessment in Language Arts and Social Studies. In her most recent teaching assignment in middle school reading, Linda was elected teacher of the year by her faculty.

Linda has worked with students from pre-K through high school and is currently a facilitator for the Penn Literacy Network, a graduate level staff development program from the University of Pennsylvania. She also serves on the Delaware Office of Education's Middle Level Executive Committee for the development and implementation of statewide performance indicators in Language Arts.

Martha Rapp Ruddell

Martha Rapp Ruddell is a Professor of Education at Sonoma State University and Past-President of the National Reading Conference. She is the author of *Teaching Content Reading and Writing* (Allyn & Bacon, 2000) and co-editor of *Theoretical Models and Processes of Reading,* 4th edition (International Reading Association, 1994). Martha also represented the National Reading Conference and International Reading Association at International Literacy Day in Paris in 1999.

Brenda A. Shearer

Brenda Shearer is an Associate Professor of Reading Education at the University of Wisconsin-Oshkosh. Dr. Shearer has been a teacher in regular education, learning disabilities, and gifted education programs, as well as a K–12 Reading Specialist. She has more than 20 years of teaching experience in both urban and rural public school settings.

Brenda has made numerous presentations at the state, national, and international levels. Her articles and research have appeared in *The Reading Teacher, Journal of Educational Psychology,* and *National Reading Conference Yearbook.* She has assumed leadership positions in WSRA, IRA, and NRC, serves on the Review Board of *Reading Research Quarterly,* and was named Outstanding Faculty Member of 1996 at UW–River Falls. Dr. Shearer is currently serving as Chair of the National Reading Conference Field Council.

Cynthia Stevenson

Cynthia Stevenson currently acts as Professional Development Coordinator for Lakeville, MN area schools. Her 26-year educational career has included work as a classroom teacher in grades K, 1, 2, 4, and 6. She also worked as an educational consultant for Houghton Mifflin Publishing Company, in the areas of Language Arts and Mathematics and served as a Marketing and Product Development Specialist to create curriculum materials for elementary mathematics. Cynthia received a B.S. degree in Elementary Education from Moorhead, MN State University, and an M.Ed. in Educational Administration from the University of North Dakota.

Richard T. Vacca

Richard T. Vacca is a Professor of Education at Kent State University. He completed his doctoral studies at Syracuse University and has taught reading and English at the middle and high school levels. He served as a member of the Board of Directors of the International Reading Association and in 1996–97 completed a term as 42nd president of the IRA. Currently, he co-chairs IRA's Commission on Adolescent Literacy. He is co-author with JoAnne Vacca of *Content Area Reading* and *Reading and Learning to Read,* both published by Addison Wesley Longman. He has also authored *Whole Language in Middle and Secondary Classrooms* and *Case Studies in Whole Language.* In 1989, he was the College Reading Association's recipient of the A.B. Herr Award for Outstanding Contributions to Reading Education.

Amelia Vandever-Horwath

Amelia Vandever-Horwath is a sixth-grade teacher at East Hills Middle School in Bethlehem, Pennsylvania. She received her undergraduate degree from Cedar Crest College, where she majored in the fields of Sociology and Elementary Education. She earned a Master of Education degree in reading and a Master of Education degree in elementary education from East Stroudsburg University. She has spoken at the International Reading Association's Annual Convention on the topic of poetry in content area instruction. She resides in Bethlehem, Pennsylvania with her husband, George.

Mary Wright

Mary Wright is a Supervisor of Learning for the Colonial School District in New Castle, Delaware. In this role she is responsible for the administration of the district's Title I Program, Language Arts Curriculum and Staff Development for grades K–12; and the supervision of the district's staff development and instructional resource center. Mary received her doctorate in Educational Leadership in 1993 from Widener University.

During Mary's teaching career she has worked with students from grades K through graduate level in Reading, English, Journalism, and Elementary Education. She also teaches graduate level classes at the University of Delaware in the areas of Literacy Instruction and Teacher Preparation.